T0137214

Mobile Information Service for Networks

Changjun Jiang · Zhong Li

Mobile Information Service for Networks

Changjun Jiang
Department of Computer Science
and Technology
Tongji University
Shanghai, China

Zhong Li
College of Information Science
and Technology
Donghua University
Shanghai, China

ISBN 978-981-15-4571-9   ISBN 978-981-15-4569-6   (eBook)
https://doi.org/10.1007/978-981-15-4569-6

Jointly published with Science Press
The print edition is not for sale in China (Mainland). Customers from China (Mainland) please order the print book from: Science Press.

This Springer imprint is published by the registered company Springer Nature Singapore Pte Ltd.
The registered company address is: 152 Beach Road, #21-01/04 Gateway East, Singapore 189721, Singapore

Preface

The advanced methods of network mobile information services are the key points to support various information services. Human life is inseparable from these information services. Compared with the wired network environment, the current wireless mobile network environment is dynamic and uncertain. This brings many challenges from the data link layer to the application layer for the entire mobile information service methods and technical theories, such as the uncertainty problem brought about by neighbor discovery in networking, the instability problem in transmissions, the relationship mining between devices. Therefore, it is important to study the current supporting methods of network mobile information services and give related technologies for typical network mobile information service applications.

Mobile information service for networks can be defined as a platform-independent functional entity that provides various services based on the communication network platform. Mobile information service can be published on the network through various mobile devices. The services are represented in the form of various mobile applications.

This book mainly introduces the methods of mobile information service for networks. There are eight chapters in this book. First the book introduces the concept and the current development of mobile information service for networks. Then, the book introduces three main supporting technologies of mobile information service for networks. The technologies include the neighbor discovery technology in the data link layer, the routing and balanced association technology in the network layer, and the community structure detection technology in the application layer. Based on our mobile information service platform, this book introduces the development of related applications and the key technologies in the domains of intelligent transportation, smart tourism and mobile payment, such as trajectory analysis technology, location recommendation technology and mobile behavior authentication technology, which promote the development of mobile information service.

This book can be used as a reference for researchers in the field of computer science and technology, and also for researchers in the field of network mobile information service technology. The book includes lots of detailed and fundamental supporting technologies of mobile information service for networks. It shares many tips and insights into the development of related applications and the key technologies in the domains of intelligent transportation, smart tourism and mobile payment. It broadens the understanding of the real mobile information service platform in our project.

During the writing, we received many supports from Ph.D. students, postgraduate students of our research team. Thank you for providing relevant materials for this book.

Shanghai, China   Changjun Jiang
February 2020   Zhong Li

Contents

Chapter 1
Preliminary of Mobile Information Service for Networks

Abstract With the rapid development of network technology, mobile information service for networks is an important part of people's lives. This chapter first describes the concept of mobile information service for networks and the general network architecture. Then this chapter introduces the classification of the mobile information services for networks, and finally lists the roles of key technologies in mobile information service for networks according to a hierarchical structure. In this book, network neighbor discovery technology, efficient network routing, user association technology, and network community detection technology will be elaborated later. After introducing these main technologies, this book will introduce mobile information service platform for networks and related applications in intelligent transportation, smart tourism, and mobile payment. Mobile information service for networks involves many techniques and methods. This book is only a summary of authors' recent innovative work about smart city. We hope that with the development of the times, new technologies will emerge continuously.

1.1 Concept and Development of Mobile Information Service for Networks

The rapid development of wireless network technology promotes extensive use of mobile devices such as mobile phones, tablets, and ultrabooks. The mobile network provides a solid platform for mobile nodes interconnections and applications of related services. To deal with various scenarios of human activities, information service based on the wireless mobile network has become a research hotspot.

We define **Mobile Information Service for Networks** as a platform-independent functional entity that provides various services based on the communication network platform. Mobile information services can be published on the network through various mobile devices in the method of wireless access networks [1]. With the development of 5G and Internet of Things, the carriers of mobile services not only include handheld devices but also include physical devices related to individuals, such as vehicles [2–4].

© Springer Nature Singapore Pte Ltd. & Science Press 2020
C. Jiang and Z. Li, *Mobile Information Service for Networks*,
https://doi.org/10.1007/978-981-15-4569-6_1

According to preliminary data released by App Annie, an app analytics company, the number of APP downloads exceeded 204 billion in 2019, an increase of 6% compared to last year. The total expenditure on paid applications, in-app purchases, etc., is $120 billion. Mobile users spend an average of 3.7 hours on APP each day. The explosive development has made mobile information services penetrate into every corner of people's lives.

There are many disciplines involved in mobile information service for networks. This book conducts a layered introduction to analyze related theoretical methods, and introduces new application technologies. Since the current mobile information service for networks is different from traditional information services, the requirements of adaptability of network changes, efficiency, security, accuracy, energy and sociality all bring about great challenges to its further developments.

1.2 Network Communication Architecture

According to the types of applications and communication standards, mobile information service for networks can be deployed under a centralized, distributed, or hybrid network communication architecture.

(1) Centralized Architecture (e.g. cellular networks): A centralized server can exchange, share, and transmit data between content providers and mobile users. In this client/server structure, the user is a client and the server provides contents such as maps, and videos. Under the centralized architecture, data is passed through third-party applications or service providers. This architecture is widely used in the network communications nowadays. The centralized communication architecture can not only provide information services efficiently and conveniently, but also can control the network globally. However, there are also some problems such as single point failure, privacy leakage [5].

(2) Distributed Architecture (e.g. networks supporting Ad hoc communication modes): Mobile users can directly establish P2P transmission links by using technologies such as Wi-Fi and Bluetooth. Under this architecture, nodes use the "storage-carry-forward" protocol to keep real-time communications in the physical world. Services based on this type of architecture are some location-based services [6], such as E-SmallTalker [7], MobiClique [8], Who's Near Me. The distributed architecture can be used as an effective way to reduce the transmission pressure of centralized base stations. However, the distributed architecture cannot be applied in large-scale areas.

(3) Hybrid Architecture: The centralized architecture is usually used by service providers while the distributed architecture has been promoting by the academic communities. A hybrid architecture can perfectly combine the domains of industry and academy together. In a hybrid architecture, a distributed network usually assists a centralized network to realize various services.

1.3 Classification of Mobile Information Service for Networks

Referring to the 2019 APP classification list given by Internet Weekly & eNet Research Institute, the content of mobile information service for networks includes the following 14 types: (1) Social welfare; (2) Government functions, such as party affairs, police affairs, taxation, citizen cloud, and labour unions; (3) Audio and video entertainment, such as video, live broadcast, games, music, and radio; (4) News such as books, and comics; (5) E-commerce platform (domestic or overseas); (6) Travel and transport, such as maps, taxis, tour, ticketing, accommodation, guides, and car rental; (7) Health care, such as body-building and medical treatment; (8) Social; (9) Financial management, such as banking, securities, insurance, stocks, investment, and management; (10) Automobile industry, such as charging of new energy vehicles and vehicle after sales service platform; (11) Learning and education; (12) Enterprise, such as mailbox, enterprise cooperation, customer relationship management, and financial affairs; (13) Utility tools, such as input method, wallpaper, browser, network security protection, search engines, weather forecast, application market, calendar, and transmission backup; (14) Leisures, such as beauty makeup, meal ordering, house lease, home furnishings, community service, job hunting, and express logistics.

In addition, the main external impacting factors of mobile information service for networks are the mobile environment and the individual. Therefore, the mobile information service modes can be divided into instant services, location-based services and personalized services [9] based on the three factors: time, location and individual.

The instant service mode can provide users with required information and services according to users' instant needs in a mobile environment. The instant information includes vehicles' security warning in Chap. 6, news, financial market, instant communications, etc.

The location-based service mode provides users with required geographic information and other information services related to the geographical location. These services are based on the geographical locations of users in a mobile environment. The location-based services include vehicle trajectory analysis in Chap. 6, location recommendations in Chap. 7, weather forecast, chatting and making friends, etc.

The personalized service mode can provide targeted information services for the personalized needs of users. And it can also establish an information demand model for users by utilizing a mobile information service system based on the privacy and identifiability of mobile terminals. The personalized services include personal payment authentications in Chap. 8, personalized location recommendation, personalized search and subscription services.

1.4   Key Technologies of Mobile Information Service for Networks

In this book, we will introduce some key technologies of mobile information service for networks according to a hierarchical structure and application backgrounds. To begin with, we mainly introduce the major technologies of mobile information service for networks in three layers:

- Neighbor discovery technology in the data link layer.
- Efficient network routing and balanced association technology in the network layer.
- Network community detection technology in the application layer.

Then, we will introduce some extension technologies for three main applications involved in a smart city, i.e., intelligent transportation, smart tourism, and mobile payment. The content structure of this book is shown in Fig. 1.1.

The key technologies and methods of mobile information service for networks include the following aspects:

(1) Neighbor discovery technology. In the mobile information service, neighbor discovery is an important technology in the data link layer. It is a technology that can discover neighbor nodes and establish effective connections. This technology guarantees the first step of the network building. High efficiency, energy-saving, and scene adaptation are problems encountered by the current technology. Therefore, for social application scenarios and crowded scenarios, this book presents a role-based neighbor discovery method and a crowded scenario-based neighbor discovery method, respectively. More details will be provided in Chap. 2.

(2) Efficient network routing and balanced association technology. In the network layer, the efficiency of various information services, depends on fast data transmissions. Traditional routing protocols that depend on the network topology or

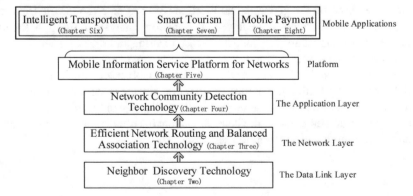

Fig. 1.1 Architecture of this book

simply depend on the encounter probability can no longer meet the requirements of efficient data transmissions. Therefore, for the multi-hop Ad hoc network, this book proposes a data forwarding algorithm LASS based on local activity and social similarity in slow mobile user network scenarios, and a cognitive routing protocol QCR in fast vehicle networking scenarios. Besides, for the centralized cellular network, the load balance of user associations is realized by utilizing spatio-temporal regularities of traffic flows based on reinforcement learning. More details will be provided in Chap. 3.

(3) Network community detection technology. In the application layer, the current mobile information service for networks is customized for individuals, therefore sociability is inherent in information services. Considering the different network communication architectures of mobile information services, this book explores new methods of community structure discovery and analyzes the relation between the underlying communication architecture and the top-level logical relationship network. In this part, we provide technical supports for recommendation algorithms, path planning and routing protocol design. More details will be provided in Chap. 4.

(4) Vehicle trajectory mining technology. After introducing the main technologies, this book details the current developments and latest technologies in the field of intelligent transportation. On the basis of previous work on the neighbor discovery technology in Chap. 2, this part focuses on analyzing the large data of vehicle trajectories in intelligent transportation. This part also solves the problem of accurate route estimation under sparse data and the problem of predicting vehicle behavior on the road based on coarse-grained GPS data. Vehicle trajectory mining technology can get rid of overdependence on hardware devices such as cameras, sensors and radar. Through analyzing historical data, drivers' driving habits can be extracted, and meanwhile, real-time warnings of driving behaviors can be realized by utilizing neighbor discovery wireless communication architectures. More details will be provided in Chap. 6.

(5) Personalized Location Recommendation Technology. This book details the current developments and latest technologies in the field of smart tourism. We mainly focus on location recommendation technology, because it is the basis of a series of issues in the application layer, such as tourism route selection, tourism product recommendation, traffic forecasting. To solve the problems of sparse check-in data and long tensor decomposition time in the location recommendation, this book presents a recommendation method which can accurately recommend locations and reduce computing time. This method is based on user social relationships in Chap. 4 and the similarities among users, time periods, and locations. In addition to the single-point location recommendation, a personalized location sequence recommendation is also provided in this book, which further enhances users' experiences of location services in smart tourism. More details will be provided in Chap. 7.

(6) Mobile payment authentication technology. This book details the current developments and latest technologies in the field of mobile payment. Based on our previous foundations in online transaction payments, this book focuses on

mobile terminals and analyzes the impact of user postures on gestures. This book presents a mobile authentication system architecture based on user gestures, and then introduces the model constructions and authentication methods of "login authentication" and "continuous authentication". More details will be provided in Chap. 8.

References

1. C. Jiang, H. Chen, C. Yan et al., Network information service platform and search service based on the platform. 201210445457.4, 2015-07-29
2. X. Tang, C. Jiang, Z. Ding et al., A Petri Net-based semantic web service automatic composition method. J. Softw. **18**(12), 2991–3000 (2007)
3. C. Yan, C. Jiang, Q. Li, The composition and analysis of web service based on Petri Net. Comput. Sci. (2), 100–103 (2007)
4. X. Fan, C. Jiang, X. Fang et al., Dynamic web service selection based on discrete particle swarm optimization. J. Comput. Res. Dev. **47**(1), 147–156 (2010)
5. M. Bakht, M. Trower, R.H. Kravets, Searchlight: won't you be my neighbor?, in *Proceedings of the ACM MobiCom.* (Istanbul, Turkey, 2012), pp. 185–196
6. J. Schiller, A. Voisard, *Location-Based Service.* (Netherlands, Elsevier, 2004)
7. A.C. Champion, Z. Yang, B. Zhang et al., E-SmallTalker: a distributed mobile system for social networking in physical proximity. IEEE Trans. Parallel Distrib. Syst. **24**(8), 1535–1545 (2013)
8. A.-K. Pietiläinen, E. Oliver, J. LeBrun, et al., MobiClique: middleware for mobile social networking, in *Proceedings of the ACM OSNs.* (Barcelona, Spain, 2009), pp. 49–54
9. Y. Mao, On the content and mode of mobile information service. Inf. Sci. **30**(2), 52–57 (2012)

Chapter 2
Technology of Neighbor Discovery for Networks

Abstract Neighbor discovery is one of the basic technologies of mobile information service for networks. It is the key to discover the surrounding nodes at the data link layer and organize the network effectively. Firstly, this chapter introduces the basic concept and the development of neighbor discovery in detail. According to popular social application scenarios, efficient neighbor discovery algorithms (Erupt and Centron) are introduced. In these algorithms, the Erupt algorithm divides the nodes into two categories according to their roles: the sponsor node and the participant node. Using a recession strategy, the sponsor consumes more energy in exchange for higher discovery efficiency. By creating a core group, the Centron algorithm solves the problem that communications between nodes will be affected by frequent collisions in the crowded region, which reduces the efficiency of discovery. The above algorithms are proved to be efficient in terms of energy, efficiency, and delay. Besides, these algorithms can provide inspirations for how to design better neighbor discovery algorithms in the future.

2.1 Introduction

Neighbor discovery refers to the process that the network node interacts with and discovers other nodes dynamically during the initialization [1, 2]. For example, some social applications [3–5], whose main application communication framework is centralized but its location-based sub-applications are distributed. Because the location of mobile nodes is uncertain, it is more challenging to build a distributed network architecture than a centralized one. Thus the node needs to adapt to dynamic changes of the network topology to discover neighbor nodes and establish an effective connection. Therefore, neighbor discovery algorithm serves as an important data link technology to accurately find neighbor in mobile information service for networks. Firstly, in this chapter, we simply review the mainstream methods of neighbor discovery. Then, aiming at daily social and crowded scenarios, this paper introduces a role based neighbor discovery method [6] and a crowded scenario based neighbor discovery method [7].

© Springer Nature Singapore Pte Ltd. & Science Press 2020
C. Jiang and Z. Li, *Mobile Information Service for Networks*,
https://doi.org/10.1007/978-981-15-4569-6_2

2.2   Related Work

The evolution of the neighbor discovery algorithm is mainly divided into three phases: synchronous, asynchronous, and derivative.

Most of the early neighbor discovery algorithms are embedded in the MAC protocol, such as S-MAC [8] and BMAC [9]. These algorithms mainly use the GPS of nodes or sending packets to synchronize the clock between two nodes. The work and sleep mechanisms between nodes are required to be consistent to achieve mutual discovery. However, these methods require redundant packets or power consumptions to maintain synchronization between nodes. Thus, These algorithms are difficult to implement in the mobile network for limited battery power supplies.

Later, McGlynn and Borbash separated the neighbor discovery algorithm from the MAC protocol for the first time and defined it as an independent protocol. They proposed an asynchronous neighbor discovery protocol called Birthday [10]. In Birthday, every node chooses whether it is working or not with a fixed probability in each timeslot. According to Birthday paradox, the node can discover each other through a random wake-up/sleep mechanism. Then, Vasudevan and others mapped the stochastic neighbor discovery to the classical stamp collector problem [11]. Through analizing of the efficiency of stochastic discovery strategy a Vasudevan et al. propsed more efficient strategy. However, a fatal drawback of the stochastic neighbor discovery strategy is that there is no upper bound for the time delay of discovery. That is, two nodes may never find each other.

In order to solve this problem, scholars have proposed a deterministic asynchronous neighbor discovery algorithm. The deterministic neighbor discovery algorithm is mainly divided into two types. One is the quorum-based algorithm [12, 13], and the other is the prime-based algorithm [14, 15]. The quorum-based algorithm divides time into a two-dimensional square matrix. Each node randomly chooses one row and one column as active slots. The discovery will occur when a pair of two nodes has at least two active slots overlapped. However, if two nodes are in different duty cycles, the time of two nodes cannot be divided into two square matrices of the same size. Then it is difficult for the quorum-based algorithm to achieve good discovery results. To solve this problem, Sangil Choi and others designed a protocol called BAND which used combinatorial theory. To a certain extent, BAND has improved the discovery delay bound and energy consumption of the quorum-based algorithm. The prime-based algorithm is mainly designed according to Chinese Remainder Theorem [16], among which Disco [17], U-connect [18] and Searchlight are the main representatives. In Disco, each node chooses a set of unequal prime numbers. When the sequence number of the timeslot is divisible by any of its prime numbers, the node turns into active state. U-connect proposes an inner product matrix of energy and delay so that each node only needs to select one prime number. This can improve discovery efficiency and ensure that the energy consumption of nodes is similar to Disco. Compared with the stochastic algorithm, Disco and U-connect have the upper bound of discovery delay, but the average delay doesn't perform as well as the stochastic algorithm. Searchlight makes some adjustments under symmetrical conditions. Searchlight mainly utilizes the rule that the offset between the working cycle is the same when they have the same duty cycle. In order to improve the average discovery efficiency, Searchlight designs a timeslot with two working states: anchor and probe. BlindDate is an improvement to Searchlight, the main purpose is to reduce the upper bound of the discovery delay.

However, it is difficult to improve the discovery efficiency in an asymmetric situation (nodes have different duty cycles) for the prime-based algorithm. Zhang and others [19] proposed an accelerated middleware based on demand change, called Acc. The main idea of Acc is to analyze the discovery relationship between direct and indirect neighbors of nodes on the basis of Disco. Acc adds some working timeslots in each cycle to achieve acceleration. Sun [20] proposed a unified framework called Hello to include all deterministic asynchronous neighbor discovery algorithms (e.g., Quorum, Disco, U-connect, and Searchlight). The Hello framework effectively reduces the discovery delay, but the energy consumption of the node is not taken into account.

The above neighbor discovery algorithm in asynchronous phases is mainly composed of stochastic algorithms and deterministic algorithms. After that, the neighbor discovery algorithm enters the derivative phase. In the derivative phase, the researchers mainly consider the influence of different factors on the discovery algorithm. Chen [21] focused on the effect of the neighbor discovery algorithm when the number of timeslots is not positive and the length of the timeslot is inconsistent. Then Chen proposed a non-integer neighbor discovery algorithm. Meng [22] combined this idea with the Searchlight algorithm to propose (A)Diff-Code neighbor discovery algorithm. (A)Diff-Code utilizes the encoding strategy algorithm based on non-integer to improve discovery efficiency when the number of timeslots is non-integer. Other researchers consider the efficiency of neighbor discovery in the case of multi-channel [23], multi-hop [24], multi-sending and receiving packets [25]. Combining four routing mechanisms in mobile ad hoc networks. In addition, some researchers have introduced neighbor discovery into multi-directional antenna environment [26, 27], multi-user environment [28], and cognitive network environment [29].

2.3   Role-Based Neighbor Discovery Algorithm

Recently, a lot of location-based social applications been developed to attract local individual users such as StreetPass and Vita. These applications require that nearby participants can be connected efficiently (low-latency and energy-efficient) in a limited time. The process of discovering and connecting such nodes is called neighbor discovery. Most of the existing neighbor discovery algorithms regard the nodes as the same roles. In fact, the role of nodes can be divided into active and passive in neighbor discovery. In this chapter, we mainly introduce a role-based neighbor discovery algorithm named Erupt. To achieve efficient neighbor discovery, Erupt distinguished active and passive roles and assign different discovery strategies to nodes with different role. Before introducing the role-based neighbor discovery, the wireless network model and assumptions are given.

2.3.1 Wireless Network Model and Assumptions

Node: We assume that N denotes the total number of nodes in the network. Each node has its unique ID(e.g. MAC address) so it can be distinguished from others. Each node is equipped with a radio transceiver that allows a node to transmit or receive messages asynchronously.

Neighbor: Two nodes become neighbor through neighbor discovery if and only if one node transmits message and the other one listens. When the transmission node has received the listening node's feedback, the two nodes become neighbor.

State: A node can be in one of three states: transmit, listening, or sleeping. A node in transmit state broadcasts a discovery message advertising itself to establish a connection with the surrounding nodes. A node which in listening state listens for discovery message. If such a message is heard, the node will feedback to the source address of the message through the listening channel. A node in sleeping state is neither broadcasting nor listening.

Role: In this section, two roles are defined for a node: the sponsor(SP) and the participant(PA). The sponsor node is either in transmit state or sleeping state. In contrast, the participant node is either in listening state or sleeping state and will not in transmit state.

Time: Time is divided into discrete timeslots. We let t denote the time cycle. The size of time cycle is determined by the duty cycle. The duty cycle is defined as the ratio of transmit or listen period to a complete cycle of a node. In addition, the working cycle can be used to define the sponsor node, which can be expressed as I. The expression of I is as follows:

$$I = t \cdot [(t/2)] \tag{2.1}$$

Note that t represents a time period.

Energy: Define energy consumption of a node is zero when a node is in sleeping state. When a node is in transmit state or listening state, we assume the energy consumption is the same in a timeslot, and we assume that it is 1.

2.3.2 Description of Erupt Algorithm

When some nodes start mobile social application, they will actively initiate neighbor detection. In other words, behind every neighbor discovery process, there is an initiative node called the sponsor. Therefore, mobile nodes in the network are divided into active and passive nodes. Passive nodes are called the participant. We find a common phenomenon that the sponsor will spend more energy to invite more devices to join the applications as soon as possible. When a sponsor does this, energy consumption in the network will show explosive growth. The ERUPT neighbor discovery algorithm is designed based on the above analysis, as is shown in Algorithm 2.1.

Algorithm 2.1 Erupt Algorithmic

---

1. if a node is in SP mode **then**
2. $k = 1$
3. **for** i from 1 to I **do**
4. when $i \% k \equiv 1$, the node is in working state
5. if $i \% \lfloor (t/2) \rfloor = 0$ **then**
6. $k = k + 1$
7. **end if**
8. **end for**
9. **else**
10. Randomly select number a, b from $\left(1, \lfloor (t/2) \rfloor \right)$ and $\left(\lceil (t/2) \rceil, t \right)$
11. **for** i from 1 to t **do**
12. **if** $i \% a = 0$ or $i \% b = 0$ **then**
13.   the node is in working state
14. **end if**
15. **end for**
16. **end if**

In Algorithm 2.1, when a node is in SP mode, we name it sponsor node. The sponsor node has a working cycle I, which is divided into all-out part and recession part. The sponsor node in the all-out part is always in transmit state, and the duration is a time cycle t.

The recession part is from the second time cycle to $\lfloor t / \lfloor t/2 \rfloor \rfloor$th. In recession part, a rule that the sponsor node broadcasts message when $t \equiv 1 (mod\,k)$ will be followed, where k is the serial number of current time cycle t of I. When a node is in PA mode, we name it participant node. It divides its time cycle into two parts. The former consists of $\lfloor (t/2) \rfloor$ timeslots, the latter consists of $\lceil (t/2) \rceil$ timeslots.

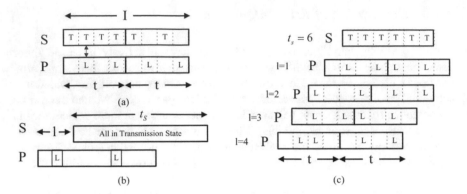

Fig. 2.1 The offset between the participant node and the sponsor node

Then the participant node randomly chooses one timeslot in listening state in each part and in sleeping state of the other timeslots.

2.3.3 Analysis of Two-Node Case

In this section, we will discuss the case where there are a sponsor node and a participant node in the network. In the two-node network, the discovery occurs when a node is in transmitting state and the other is in listening state. We define the two nodes S and P respectively. Node S is in the sponsor role, and node P is in the participant role. An example is shown in Fig. 2.1, the time cycle t of node S and P are set to 4. We let t_S denote the time cycle of node S and let t_P denote that of node P. I is the time difference between node S and P in the working cycle, which is composed of several time slots.

We analyze the ERUPT algorithm from two aspects. First, we investigate the average time it takes a sponsor to discover a neighbor. Here, such an average time is called the average latency. Second, we will show the duty cycle and energy consumption of the sponsor node and the participant node.

In Fig. 2.1a, node S is the sponsor node and node P is the participant node when time cycle $t = 4$. Figure 2.1b shows the offset between the time cycle of the participant node P to the sponsor node S while the sponsor node S starts its working cycle. Figure 2.1c shows the cases of different possible offsets, where $t_S = 6, t_P = 4$.

2.3.4 Average Latency

In this section, we discuss average neighbor discovery latency of the two-node case in ERUPT algorithm from two situations: $t_S \geq t_P$ and $t_S < t_P$.

Lemma 2.1 As shown in Fig. 2.1c, the offset l between the time cycle of the participant node P and the sponsor node S satisfies $l \in 0, 1, 2, \cdots, t_P - 1$.

We first discuss the case when $t_S \geqslant t_P$.

Lemma 2.2 When $t_S \geqslant t_P$, the discovery will occur in the all-out part of the sponsor node S in Fig. 2.1c.

Proof Based on the description of the sponsor node in the previous section, when node S starts its working cycle, it will broadcast messages in all timeslots in its all-out part. In Lemma 2.1, we know while node S begins to broadcast message l, which can be anyone in $\{0, 1, 2, \cdots, t_P - 1\}$. Whatever l is, t_S will contain one part of the participant node P (see Fig. 2.1c). Based on the description of the participant node, node P will randomly select a time slot in each part in listening state. So the sponsor node S will discover node P in its all-out part.

Theorem 2.1 When $t_S \geqslant t_P$, the average latency of node S discovering node P is almost $7t_P/24 + 1/2$.

Proof We assume the probability of $l \in \{0, 1, 2, \cdots, t_P - 1\}$ is the same. We introduce $k = \lceil t_P/2 \rceil$. When t_p is even, $t_P = 2k$. We calculate the expectation by dividing l into $0 \leq l < k$ and $k \leqslant l < 2k$ two cases, then put them together. We get the average latency is $\frac{7k^2+6k-1}{12k} \approx \frac{7t_P}{24} + \frac{1}{2}$. When t_P is odd, $t_P = 2k - 1$. Similar to the case $t_P = 2k$, we get the average latency is $\frac{7k^2-k-2}{12k-6} \approx \frac{7t_P}{24} + \frac{1}{2}$. So the average latency of node S discovering node P is almost $\frac{7t_P}{24} + \frac{1}{2}$.

In the case $t_S \leqslant t_P$, the sponsor node S may not discover the participant node P if t_P is large enough. So we will discuss the relationship between the discoverable probability and the choice of t_S in this case. First, we give an assumption to support our analysis. We assume $d_{SP} = t_P = t_S$, where d_{SP} denotes the difference of the time cycle between node S and node P. Then we let P_1 and P_2 denote the two parts in the time cycle of the participant node P. We have $P_1 = \lfloor t_P/2 \rfloor$, $P_2 = \lceil t_P/2 \rceil$ and $t_P = P_1 + P_2$. At last, we use p_{SP} to denote the discoverable probability and $p_{SP} = p_h + p_t$. Where p_h denotes the probability that the discovery occurs in the all-out part of the working cycle, and p_t denotes that in the recession part.

Theorem 2.2 The average value of p_h approaches $\frac{17}{24}$.

Proof We first discuss the case $1 \leqslant d_{SP} \leqslant P_1$. (i.e., $t_S < t_P \leqslant 2t_S$). There are four cases of l (Fig. 2.2a–d)). We calculate the expectation of l and use Pd_{SP} to denote it. Then we get the expectation of d_{SP} based on Pd_{SP}. So we have

$$p_h = \sum_{d_{SP}=1}^{P_1} Pd_{SP} = \sum_{d_{SP}=1}^{P_1} \left(1 - \frac{d_{SP}^3 - d_{SP}}{3P_1P_2(P_1+P_2)}\right) \approx \frac{23}{24} \tag{2.2}$$

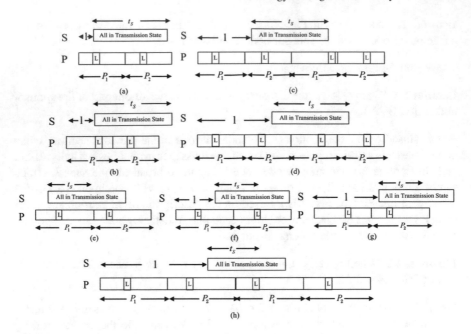

Fig. 2.2 Discovery probability of d_{SP} under different cases

Then we consider the case $P_1 + 1 \leqslant d_{SP} \leqslant P_1 + P_2 - 1$. It's equal to $t_P > 2t_S$. There are still four cases of l (Fig. 2.2e–h). We get the value of p_h under this case is

$$p_h = \sum_{d_{SP}=P_1+1}^{P_1+P_2-1} P_{d_{SP}} = \sum_{d_{SP}=P_1+1}^{P_1+P_2-1} \{1 + \frac{1}{3P_1 P_2 (P_1 + P_2)}[d_{SP}^3 - (3P_1 + 3P_2)d_{SP}^2$$

$$+ (3P_1^2 + 3P_2^2 - 1)d_{SP} - P_1^3 - P_2^3 + P_1 + P_2]\} \approx \frac{11}{24} \quad (2.3)$$

We combine Eqs. (2.2) and (2.3), and we get $p_h = \frac{17}{24}$.

Figure 2.2a–d shows four cases of l when $1 \leqslant d_{SP} \leqslant P_1$. Figure 2.2a shows the case $1 \leqslant l \leqslant d_{SP} - 1$ and the discovery probability is $1 - \frac{l}{P_1 P_2}(d_{SP} - l)$. Figure 2.2b shows the case $d_{SP} \leqslant l \leqslant P_1$ and the discovery probability is 1. Figure 2.2c shows the case $P_1 + 1 \leqslant l \leqslant d_{SP} + P_1 - 1$ and the discovery probability is $1 - \frac{l - P_1}{P_1 P_2}[d_{SP} - (l - P_1)]$. Figure 2.2d shows the case $d_{SP} + P_1 \leqslant l \leqslant P_1 + P_2$ and the discovery probability is 1. Figure 2.2e–h shows four cases of l when $P_1 + 1 \leqslant d_{SP} \leqslant P_1 + P_2 - 1$. Figure 2.2e shows the case $1 \leqslant l \leqslant P_1 - t_S$ and the discovery probability is $\frac{P_1 + P_2 - d_{SP}}{P_1}$. Figure 2.2f shows the case $P_1 - t_S + 1 \leqslant l \leqslant P_1$ and the discovery probability is $1 - \frac{l}{P_1 P_2}(d_{SP} - l)$ Fig. 2.2g shows the case $P_1 + 1 \leqslant l \leqslant d_{SP}$. Figure 2.2h shows the case $d_{SP} + 1 \leqslant l \leqslant P_1 + P_2$ and the probability is $1 - \frac{l - P_1}{P_1 P_2}[d_{SP} - (l - P_1)]$. Since p_t is hard to get the formula, we get it through experiments by using mathematical simulation tool. When $1 \leqslant d_{SP} \leqslant P_1$, $p_t \approx 0.0487$. When $P_1 + 1 \leqslant d_{SP} \leqslant P_1 + P_2 - 1$,

$p_t \approx 0.2555$. When $1 \leqslant d_{SP} \leqslant P_1 + P_2 - 1$, $p_t \approx 0.1440$. Obviously, even when the duty cycle of nodes is very low, sponsor nodes still have a certain probability to discover participant nodes.

2.3.5 Duty Cycle and Energy Consumption

Based on our assumption in Sect. 2.3.1, the energy consumption problem becomes the number of timeslots of a node in transmit state or listening state. We use E to denote the energy consumption and use DC to denote the duty cycle. In this section, we will discuss the energy consumption of the sponsor node S.

Theorem 2.3 The energy consumption in the working cycle of the sponsor node S is $E_S = \sum_{i=1}^{k} \lceil t_S / i \rceil$, and the duty cycle is $\dfrac{\sum_{i=1}^{\lfloor t_S/2 \rfloor} \lceil t_S/i \rceil}{t_S \cdot \lfloor t_S/2 \rfloor}$, where $k = \lfloor t_S/2 \rfloor$.

Proof Based on the description of Erupt algorithm, the node S will broadcast messages in all timeslots in the working cycle. In recession part, node S will broadcast messages $\lceil t_S/2 \rceil$ timeslots in the second time cycle, and $\lceil t_S/3 \rceil$ timeslots in the third and go on by the same analogy until the $\lceil t_S/2 \rceil$th time cycle ends. The energy consumption of all time cycles in the working cycle of the node S is

$$E_S = t_S + \left\lceil \frac{t_S}{2} \right\rceil + \cdots + \left\lceil \frac{t_S}{\lfloor t_S/2 \rfloor} \right\rceil = \sum_{i=1}^{\lfloor t_S/2 \rfloor} \lceil t_S/i \rceil \tag{2.4}$$

We can get the duty cycle of node S is, $DC_S = \dfrac{E_S}{I_S} = \dfrac{\sum_{i=1}^{\lfloor t_S/2 \rfloor} \lceil t_S/i \rceil}{t_S \cdot \lfloor t_S/2 \rfloor}$.

2.3.6 Analysis of the Multi-node Case

In this section, we will discuss the case where there are more than two nodes in the network. We assume the sponsor node is n_S, and the other $N - 1$ nodes are $n_1, n_2, \cdots, n_{N-1}$. We will analyze our algorithm from the simple case and the real case. In the simple case, each node has the same time cycle and the participant nodes have the same duty cycle. The real case means each node has its own time cycle. When two nodes or more than two nodes broadcast messages at the same time, a collision will occur. In this section, we do not consider this case that there are two or more nodes in sponsor mode in the network.

(1) The Simply Case

In this section, we will discuss the discovery latency of the Erupt in the simple case first. Discovery latency defines the number of the nodes that the sponsor node has discovered in certain timeslots. We let c denote the number of timeslots. We use t denote the time cycle and DL denote the discovery latency.

Theorem 2.4 In the simple case, the discovery latency has three cases.

When $1 \leqslant c \leqslant t_l - 1$,

$$\mathrm{DL}(c) = (N - 1) \cdot \left[\frac{2c}{t_f + t_l} - \frac{c^3 - c}{3t_f t_l (t_f + t_l)} \right] \qquad (2.5)$$

When $t_l \leqslant c \leqslant t - 1$,

$$\mathrm{DL}(c) = (N - 1) \cdot \left[\frac{-c^3 + c}{3t_f t_l (t_f + t_l)} + \frac{c^2}{t_f t_l} - \frac{(t_f + t_l)c}{t_f t_l} + \frac{t_f^2 + t_l^2 - t_f t_l - 1}{3t_f t_l} \right] \qquad (2.6)$$

When $c > t - 1$,

$$\mathrm{DC}(c) = N - 1 \qquad (2.7)$$

In Eqs. (2.5) and (2.6), $t_f = \lfloor t/2 \rfloor$ and $t_l = \lceil t/2 \rceil$.

Proof Based on Lemma 2.2, we know that all the participant nodes will be discovered in the all-out part of the working cycle of the sponsor node. When $c \leqslant t - 1$, we randomly choose n_r in $n_1, n_2, \cdots, n_{N-1}$. Then we focus on n_S and n_r. It's the same as the two-node case and the time cycle of n_S is c. The discovery probability between two nodes is shown in Eqs. (2.2) and (2.3). We replace P_1, P_2 and d_{SP} with t_f, t_l and $t - c$ in the Eqs. (2.2) and (2.3), where $t_f = \lfloor t/2 \rfloor$ and $t_l = \lceil t/2 \rceil$. Then we get the discovery latency showed in the Eqs. (2.5) and (2.6), where $1 \leqslant c \leqslant t_l - 1$ and $t_l \leqslant c \leqslant t - 1$ respectively. In addition, When $c \geqslant t$, obviously, DL(c)=$N - 1$.

(2) The Real Case

In daily life, each node has its own time cycle and duty cycle. Discovery latency depends on the choice of the time cycle of all nodes, especially the sponsor node. Based on Lemma 2.2, we find if $t_S \geqslant \max\{t_1, t_2, \cdots, t_{N-1}\}$, the participant nodes will be discovered in the all-out part of ns, where $t_S, t_1, t_2, \cdots, t_{N-1}$ denote the time cycle of $n_S, n_1, n_2, \cdots, n_{N-1}$ respectively. Then if we set the time cycle up to 100 timeslots, the sponsor node will discover all the participant nodes in above 2% duty cycle. It's hard to use a mathematical method to obtain the average discovery latency in this case. So we will demonstrate the advantages of our algorithm through simulation. We will not discuss details in this book, readers can refer to [6] for more imformation.

(3) Duty Cycle and Energy Consumption

Based on Theorem 2.3, the energy consumption in the sponsor node n_S is shown in Eq. (2.4). In the working cycle I_S, the participant node n_i at most has $\left\lceil \frac{ts \cdot \lfloor ts/2 \rfloor}{t_i} \right\rceil$ time cycles, where $i = 1, 2, \ldots, N - 1$. So the worst case of the energy consumption of all the participant nodes is $2 \cdot \sum_{i=1}^{N-1} \left\lceil \frac{ts \cdot \lfloor ts/2 \rfloor}{t_i} \right\rceil$. Put the energy consumption of the sponsor node and the participant node together, we get the energy consumption of the whole network is $E_{all} = \sum_{i=1}^{\lfloor ts/2 \rfloor} \left\lceil \frac{t}{i} \right\rceil + 2 \cdot \sum_{j=1}^{N-1} \left\lceil \frac{ts \cdot \lfloor ts/2 \rfloor}{t_j} \right\rceil$.

2.4 Neighbor Discovery Based on Crowded Scenes

In Section 2.3, we discussed the problem of different nodes playing different roles in neighbor discovery. However, the existing algorithms, including the Erupt mentioned in the previous section, all encounter the same problem: frequent collisions. The collisions occur in the neighbor discovery when a node is in the listening state, more than one nodes are broadcasting message simultaneously in the discovery range. Then the node cannot distinguish the sender due to receiving the conflicting packet, which in turn leads to failure of transmitting. Frequent collisions will obstruct the discovery efficiency, especially in places where nodes are dense. In this section, we propose a discovery protocol, named Centron, which is designed to improve the discovery efficiency in the crowded region. In the Centron algorithm, the mobile nodes are encouraged to construct non-overlapped core groups. In neighbor discovery, each group can be considered as a "big mobile node". The nodes in the core group negotiate with each other to reduce the collisions in the network.

2.4.1 Design of Centron Algorithm

The main purpose of the Centron algorithm is to improve the efficiency of neighbor discovery (reducing collisions) of mobile nodes in crowded region. In crowded region, we let the mobile nodes form small groups (named core group). The collision is reduced by the discovery strategy of the nodes in each group. This idea is inspired by atom construction. The nucleus in an atom is the core that attracts electrons to move around it. The main challenge is to leverage the necessary negotiations among the members in the core group to reduce collisions and improve the efficiency of discovery. Therefore, it is necessary to develop a suitable discovery strategy. We first give some assumptions about the crowded region. Then, we will describe the design of the Centron algorithm in detail.

2.4.2 Scene Model and Assumptions

Node: We let N denote the total numbers of the mobile nodes in the region. Each mobile node has its unique ID (e.g. MAC address) so it can be distinguished from others. Since the mobile nodes are crowded, lots of mobile nodes are located in a small area (e.g., stadium, auditoria and carriage). This results in highly overlapped of the discovery regions of the mobile nodes in the area. Hence, we assume that all the mobile nodes are in the discovery range of other nodes.

Mode: To simplify the working mode of node, two modes are provided for the mobile nodes: active and sleep. In the active mode, the mobile node can either broadcast discovery messages or listen to the channel. On the opposite, nodes in sleep mode will shut down their monitoring devices and are at rest. Hence, the discovery would occur when two mobile nodes are both in active mode.

Time: We separate time into discrete slots.

Channel: In this section, we assume that there are two channels with different frequencies in the network. In existing protocols, both channels are used for discovering neighbors. However, one channel is used for discovering neighbors while the other is for negotiation between core member nodes in Centron. In addition, the case of multiple channels will not be considered in this section and readers can perform the similar multi-channel expansion based on the two-channel situation.

Neighbor: When one mobile node accepts the discovery invitation by another node in the active mode, and it feeds back the reception message, they become neighbors.

Strategy: Each node has a discovery strategy, such as Birthday, Disco, U-connect and so on. In addition, we define the strategy cycle that stands for the time period that the protocol runs a complete deterministic strategy.

Collision: When a mobile node receives two or more packets concurrently, a collision will occur. Moreover, we assume that no partial packet recovery technology is applied in the collision.

2.4.3 Protocol Description

In this subsection, we describe the design of the Centron protocol. The process of the protocol consists of two parts: core formation and neighbor discovery.

Core Formation: When a single node discovers a mobile node again (in its neighbor list), it sends an invitation to construct a core group. If the mobile node has not already belonged to other core group and owns similar duty cycle, it will accept the invitation. Otherwise, it will refuse. When a core group is constructed, we name the mobile node launching the invitation creator and the other member, respectively. The

Time	1	2	3	4	5	6	7	8	9	10	11	12	13	14	15	16	17	18	19	20
Creator	S/d	S	D			D/d				D		S/d	D	S		D	d		D	
Member		d			D			d	S	S/D		d			D		d	S		S/D

Fig. 2.3 Example of core group node policy adjustment

creator enclosures its strategy in the invitation message, while the member will adjust its strategy to guarantee symmetry after it accepts the invitation. Besides, there are kinds of adjustment methods.

For example, if the core group's nodes are all using the Searchlight strategy, they can use different offsets of initial working time slot (each node has to adjust its own Searchlight cycle). If the nodes of the core group previously used the Disco, each node selects a different prime number. For convenience, we default that the creator and the members will divide up the total active timeslots. Figure 2.3 shows an example when the size of the core group is 2. In Fig. 2.3, the label S, D and d denote the state of active slot under the settings of Searchlight, Disco, and default respectively. The default strategy refers to the initial strategy used before the node became core group. The default strategy here is Searchlight. In Searchlight, it can be seen that the work cycle of the original creator node and member node is 10, and after adjustment, the cycle of both nodes is 20. Through effective cooperation, the two nodes are similar to a "big node" with the working cycle of 10. If both nodes use Disco, one node chooses a prime of 3 and the other node chooses a prime of 5. Then these two nodes can cooperate as a "big node" with Disco strategy and its primes are (3, 5).

Neighbor Discovery: After core formation, the core group act as a "big mobile node". The big node generates its own duty cycle and strategy. The new duty cycle depends on that of the core creator because the core creator embeds its own strategy in the invitation message. Besides, the creator and each member will have another negotiation to share their neighbor lists in a strategy period.

Figure 2.4 demonstrates the process of discovering neighbors and constructing the core group. The dotted line between the nodes denotes they are establishing core groups, and the solid line between the core group indicates that they are discovering each other. Figure 2.4a is the initial situation. Figure 2.4b shows the discovery status at a given moment after the initial state. Figure 2.4c gives the following possible discoveries after Fig. 2.4b, and we find 6 core groups are constructed.

However, there remains a problem. Intuitively, the negotiation still needs time and energy. Furthermore, the discovery message may have conflicts with the negotiation message if they are transmitted on the same channel. In this chapter, we consider the upper size of a core group is 3, since the negotiations among two or three nodes are convenient and consume little energy. The detailed analysis is shown in the next section. Moreover, we separate discovery and negotiation out by using two channels

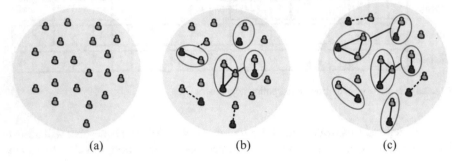

| (a) | (b) | (c) |

Fig. 2.4 The main process of Centron

to avoid unnecessary collisions. One channel is specialized in negotiation, and the other is for discovery. Besides, we assume that each negotiation lasts one timeslot.

2.4.4   Utility Analysis

In this section, we give an analysis of the discovery and the energy between our strategy Centron and the typical existing protocols (i.e., Birthday, Disco, U-connect, and Searchlight). Besides, the asymmetric situation will be taken into account.

(1)   Analysis of Discovery Probability

We introduce a variable named discovery probability to reflect the probability of a successful discovery during a selected timeslot in the region.

Existing Discovery Protocols Due to the different strategies, we extract the mutual feature from the existing discovery protocols to analyzing the discovery probability and then compare it with Centron. Table 2.1 gives the probability of classical strategies when a mobile node is in an active state. In the table, the probability column represents the probability that a mobile node is in active state during a given time slot. Note that P, P_1, P_2 are prime numbers, and t is a positive integer. These four parameters are determined by the duty cycle of the mobile node.

In the stochastic strategy, every mobile node has a certain chance to broadcast discovery advertisement. The Birthday protocol infers that when the probability

Table 2.1 Probability of active states in classical strategies

Type	Protocol	Probability
	Disco	$P_D = \frac{P_1+P_2-1}{P_1 P_2}$
Deterministic	U-connect	$P_U = \frac{P+1}{P^2}$
	Searchlight	$P_S = \frac{2}{t}$
Stochastic	Birthday	$P_B = \frac{1}{N}$

is $1/N$, the mobile nodes in the region have the highest discovery efficiency. For the deterministic protocols (e.g., Disco, U-connect, and Searchlight), though their strategies fix the sequences of the active time slots, the probabilities that a mobile node is in active mode at a randomly selected time slot are similar, determined by its duty cycle. Hence, all the deterministic protocols can be converted to a probability model by randomly selecting the starting timeslot. The starting time slot, that is, the node is in the first timeslot of the duty cycle. For a randomly selected time slot, p_a is used to indicate the probability that a mobile node is active. Conversely, the probability that a node is in the sleep is $1 - p_a$. In later chapters, superscripts (T) and (C) will be used to distinguish the existing strategy and the Centron strategy respectively.

Then, we infer the discovery probability in a randomly selected timeslot by the typical protocols. As illustrated in Sect. 2.4.2, the discovery occurs if and only if two mobile nodes are in the active mode. We obtain the discovery probability in Eq. (2.8).

$$P_S^{(T)} = \binom{N}{2} p_a^2 (1 - p_a)^{N-2} \tag{2.8}$$

When there are two channels, the condition improves that only if two nodes are active at the same channel. We revise the Eq. (2.8) as follows:

$$P_S^{(T)'} = \sum_{i=2}^{N} p_i \binom{N}{i} p_a^i (1 - p_a)^{N-i} \tag{2.9}$$

where p_i is the probability that occurs discovery when there are i nodes are active. p_i is illustrated in Eq. (2.10).

$$p_i = \begin{cases} 3/8 & i = 4 \\ \binom{i}{2} \Big/ 2^{i-1} & i \neq 4 \end{cases} \tag{2.10}$$

Centron Strategy We only consider the discovery probability at the discovery channel. The collisions have less impact on the negotiation at the negotiation channel than the impact on the discovery efficiency at the discovery channel. If a collision occurs in the core group construction, the creator can regard the target mobile node as refusing the invitation. If a collision occurs when neighbors exchange information, the negotiation message can be re-sent, because the sender and the receiver are neighbors.

We divide the whole discovery process of the Centron strategy into several time phases. In each phase, only a mobile node joins a core group. Since all the core groups are not allowed to overlap, we assume there are n_i nodes in the region for a time phase i. Through simple analysis, it is easy to know the discovery probability during a randomly selected timeslot in the phase i:

$$P_S^{(C)} = \binom{n_i}{2} p_a^2 (1 - p_a)^{n_i - 2} \tag{2.11}$$

Since our protocol uses two channels, we compare Eq. (2.9) with Eq. (2.11). Obviously, both two equations are associated with the number of mobile nodes N, n_i and active probability p_a. Hence, we introduce a function d with N, n_i, and p_a three parameters.

$$d(N, n_i, p_a) = P_S^{(C)} \big/ P_S^{(T)'} \tag{2.12}$$

This function can be used to quickly and intuitively evaluate the performance of the existing strategy and the Centron strategy.

(2) **Analysis of Energy Consumption**

Considering that most mobile devices are battery-powered, the energy consumption problem in the discovery is not negligible. Especially, each node in the Centron strategy has additional energy consumption in negotiation. It is essential to calculate the cost of the nodes in the Centron protocol and the typical protocols. Here, we evaluate the energy consumption by counting the number of active time slots for each mobile node. In this section, we demonstrate the energy consumption during ith time phase.

Due to the description in Sect. 2.4.3, the energy consumption of a mobile node, which belongs to a core group, consists of two parts: discovery and negotiation. By adjusting strategies among core groups, the energy consumption in discovery has reduced by half or by one-third compared with that of a single node. On the other hand, the energy consumption of negotiation includes two aspects: the energy consumption of core formation and neighbor sharing. Ideally, only one timeslot is necessary when a single node joins a core group, while the neighbor sharing needs one or two time slots for each strategy cycle.

We assume the ith time phase lasts T_i timeslots, and use notation τ to denote the length of a strategy cycle. In typical protocols, the energy consumption in the region is shown in the following equation:

$$E_i^{(T)} = \lfloor p_a \cdot T_i \cdot N \rfloor \tag{2.13}$$

where $\lfloor * \rfloor$ denotes the floor function.

In the Centron protocol, considering there exists m core groups, including two-node groups and three-node groups. Accordingly, the negotiation costs 1 timeslot and 3 timeslots for each type of group during a strategy cycle. Thus we can obtain the energy consumption as follows:

$$E_i^{(C)} = \lfloor p_a \cdot T_i \cdot n_i \rfloor + c_i \tag{2.14}$$

note that c_i denotes the cost of negotiation.

The value of c_i satisfies the following inequality:

$$\left\lfloor \frac{T_i}{\tau} \right\rfloor \cdot m' + 1 \leqslant c_i \leqslant \left\lceil \frac{T_i}{\tau} \right\rceil \cdot m' + 1 \tag{2.15}$$

where m' denotes the energy consumption of all core groups, which is equal to $2N - 2n_i - m$.

Equations (2.14) and (2.15) are based on the assumption that a big node has the same strategy cycle with a single node. In exceptional circumstances, the strategy cycle of core node group is longer, which means less negotiation cost.

We define a function e in Eq. (2.16) equals to the result that Eq. (2.13) minus Eq. (2.14). The parameters are the variable in Eqs. (2.13) and (2.14):

$$e\big(p_a, T_i, n_i, N, m'\big) = E_i^{(T)} - E_i^{(C)} \tag{2.16}$$

This function is similar to the previous function d. It can be used as a quick and intuitive indicator to compare the energy consumption performance of the existing strategy and the Centron strategy.

(3) Asymmetric Situation

The above analysis is based on the symmetric situation (nodes run the same duty cycle). However, the fact is that the mobile nodes in the region will apply their discovery strategies with different duty cycles due to their devices' various remaining energy. We let the random variable p_a denote the active probabilities of the mobile nodes in the region, and it obeys Uniform distribution with parameters l and u ($l < u$). Where l denotes the lower bound, u denotes the upper bound. The expectation of p_a, denoted as μ, is $\frac{u+l}{2}$.

$P_{ac}^{(T)}$ denotes the discovery probability under asymmetric situation by typical protocols. The discovery probability can be inferred from Eq. (2.9) (replace p_a with different probabilities p_a^*, * denotes different nodes):

$$P_{ac}^{(T)} = \sum_{i=2}^{N} p_i \sum_{1 \leqslant j_k \leqslant N}^{1 \leqslant k \leqslant i} \prod_{k=1}^{i} \frac{p_a^{(j_k)}}{1 - p_a^{(j_k)}} \prod_{1 \leqslant h \leqslant N} \big(1 - p_a^{(h)}\big) \tag{2.17}$$

and p_i is shown in Eq. (2.10).

By the same logic, we rewrite Eq. (2.11) to obtain the discovery probability of the Centron protocol under the asymmetric situation.

$$P_{ac}^{(C)} = \sum_{1 \leqslant j,k \leqslant n_i}^{j \neq k} \frac{p_a^{(j)} p_a^{(k)}}{\big(1 - p_a^{(k)}\big)\big(1 - p_a^{(j)}\big)} \prod_{1 \leqslant h \leqslant n_i} \big(1 - p_a^{(h)}\big) \tag{2.18}$$

Since p_a obey $u(l, u)$, we calculate the expectations in Eqs. (2.17) and (2.18) to compare the performance. Hence, we improve the Eq. (2.12) as follows:

$$d_a(N, n_i, p_a) = E\big[P_{ac}^{(T)}\big] \big/ E\big[P_{ac}^{(C)}\big] \tag{2.19}$$

Besides, we list the energy consumption under the asymmetric situation for the typical protocols and the Centron protocol in Eqs. (2.20) and (2.21),

$$E_{ai}^{(T)} = \sum_{1 \leqslant j \leqslant N} \big\lfloor p_a^{(j)} T_i \big\rfloor \tag{2.20}$$

$$E_{ai}^{(C)} = \sum_{1 \leqslant j \leqslant n_i} \big\lfloor p_a^{(j)} \cdot T_i \big\rfloor + c_{ai} \tag{2.21}$$

where $\sum_{1 \leqslant j \leqslant m} \gamma \big\lfloor \frac{T_i}{\tau_j} \big\rfloor + 1 \leqslant c_{ai} \leqslant \sum_{1 \leqslant j \leqslant m} \gamma \big\lceil \frac{T_i}{\tau_j} \big\rceil + 1$. Note that γ is a cost coefficient. When j is a two-node core group, $\gamma = 1$. Otherwise, $\gamma = 3$.

Similarly, we improve the Eq. (2.16) as follows:

$$e(p_a, T_i, n_i, N, m) = E_i^{(T)} - E_i^{(C)} \tag{2.22}$$

2.5   Application Discussion

Neighbor discovery can be applied to the environment of high-speed mobile nodes discovery. The check-in data obtained by neighbor discovery can effectively help the traffic management department in the analysis of vehicle flow and vehicle tracking application. In the vehicle behavior recognition and warning services in Chap. 6 of this book, neighbor discovery technology can help form a distributed network architecture between local vehicles. So, a vehicle can sense the surrounding environment and generate behavior vectors of surrounding vehicles. A single vehicle can perceive the behavior of surrounding vehicles in advance, which will greatly reduce service delay and avoid unnecessary network overhead.

References

1. S. Yang, Research on Neighbor Discovery Methods and Service Application of Mobile Networks. Doctor Degree Theses of Tongji University (2018)
2. L. You, Research on Group Neighbor Discovery Algorithms in Next-Generation Wireless Networks. Master Degree Theses of Nanjing University (2013)

3. Y. Wang, G. Cong, G. Song, et al., Community-based Greedy algorithm for mining top-K influential nodes in mobile social networks, in *Proceedings of ACM SIGKDD*, Washington, DC, USA, 2010, pp. 1039–1048
4. E. Park, S.I. Baek, J.Y. Ohm et al., Determinants of player acceptance of mobile social network games: an application of extended technology acceptance model. Telem. Inform. **31**(1), 3–15 (2014)
5. L. Zhu, LBSN-based personalized routes recommendation. Master Degree Theses of Harbin Institute of Technology (2014)
6. S. Yang, Z. Li, M. Stojmenovic, et al. ERUPT: a role-based neighbor discovery protocol for mobile social applications. Ad Hoc Sensor Wirel. Netw. 24(3/4), 265–281 (2015)
7. S. Yang, C. Wang, C. Jiang, Centron: cooperative neighbor discovery in mobile Ad-hoc networks. Comput. Netw. 136, 128–136 (2018)
8. W. Ye, J. S. Heidemann, D. Estrin, An energy-efficient MAC protocol for wireless sensor networks, in *Proceedings of IEEE INFOCOM*, New York, NY, USA, 2002, pp. 1567–1576
9. J. Polastre, J. L. Hill, D. E. Culler, Versatile low power media access for wireless sensor networks, in *Proceedings of ACM SenSys*, Baltimore, MD, USA, 2004, pp. 95–107
10. M. J. Mcglynn, S. A. Borbash, Birthday protocols for low energy deployment and flexible neighbor discovery in ad hoc wireless networks, in *Proceedings of ACM MobiHoc*, Long Beach, CA, USA, 2001, pp. 137–145
11. S. Vasudevan, M. Adler, D. Goeckel, et al., Efficient algorithms for neighbor discovery in wireless networks. IEEE ACM Trans. Netw. 21(1), 69–83 (2013)
12. J. Jiang, Y. Tseng, C. Hsu, et al., Quorum-based asynchronous power-saving protocols for IEEE 802.11 ad hoc networks. Mobile Netw. Appl. 10(1), 169–181 (2005)
13. S. Lai, B. Ravindran, H. Cho, Heterogeneous quorum based wake up scheduling in wireless sensor networks. IEEE Trans. Comput. 59(11), 1562–1575 (2010)
14. P. Dutta, D. E. Culler. Practical asynchronous neighbor discovery and rendezvous for mobile sensing applications, in *Proceedings of ACM SenSys*, Raleigh, NC, USA, 2008, pp. 71–84
15. A. Kandhalu, K. Lakshmanan, R. Rajkumar, U-connect: a low latency energy-efficient asynchronous neighbor discovery protocol, in *Proceedings of ACM IPSN*, Stockholm, Sweden, 2010, pp. 350–361
16. G.H. Hardy, E.M. Wright, *An Introduction to the Theory of Numbers* (Oxford University Press, New York, 1975)
17. M. Bakht, M. Trower, R.H. Kravets, Searchlight: won't you be my neighbor? in *Proceedings of ACM MobiCom*, Istanbul, Turkey, 2012, pp. 185–196
18. K. Wang, X. Mao, Y. Liu, BlindDate: a neighbor discovery protocol. IEEE Trans. Parallel Distrib. Syst. 26(4), 949–959 (2015)
19. D. Zhang, T. He, Y. Liu, et al., Acc : generic on-demand accelerations for neighbor discovery in mobile applications, in *Proceedings of ACM SenSys*, Toronto, Ontario, Canada, 2012, pp. 169–182
20. W. Sun, Z. Yang, K. Wang, et al., Hello: a generic flexible protocol for neighbor discovery, in *Proceedings of IEEE INFOCOM*, Toronto, ON, Canada, 2014, pp. 540–548
21. S. Chen, A. Russell, R. Jin, et al., Asynchronous neighbor discovery on duty-cycled mobile devices: integer and non-integer schedules, in *Proceedings of ACM MobiHoc*, Hangzhou, China, 2015, pp. 47–56
22. T. Meng, F. Wu, G. Chen, Code-based neighbor discovery protocols in mobile wireless networks. IEEE ACM Trans. Netw. 24(2), 806–819 (2016)
23. L. Chen, K. Bian, M. Zheng, Heterogeneous multi-channel neighbor discovery for mobile sensing applications: theoretical foundation and protocol design, in *Proceedings of ACM MobiHoc*, Philadelphia, Pennsylvania, USA, 2014, pp. 307–316
24. Y. Zeng, K.A. Mills, S. Gokhale et al., Robust neighbor discovery in multi-hop multi-channel heterogeneous wireless networks. J. Parallel Distrib. Comput. 92, 15–34 (2016)
25. A. Russell, S. Vasudevan, B. Wang et al., Neighbor discovery in wireless networks with multipacket reception. IEEE Trans. Parallel Distrib. Syst. 26(7), 1984–1998 (2015)

26. E. A. Felemban, R. Murawski, E. Ekici, et al., SAND: Sectored-Antenna Neighbor Discovery protocol for wireless networks, in *Proceedings of IEEE SECON* (Boston, MA, USA, 2010), pp. 1–9
27. H. Park, Y. Kim, T. Song et al., Multiband directional neighbor discovery in self-organized mmWave Ad Hoc networks. IEEE Trans. Veh. Technol. **64**(3), 1143–1155 (2015)
28. A. Zanella, A. Bazzi, B. Masini, Relay selection analysis for an opportunistic two-hop multi-user system in a Poisson field of nodes. IEEE Trans. Wireless Commun. **16**(2), 1281–1293 (2017)
29. A.A. Khan, M.H. Rehmani, Y. Saleem, Neighbor discovery in traditional wireless networks and cognitive radio networks. J. Netw. Comput. Appl. **52**, 173–190 (2015)

Chapter 3
High Efficient Routing and Balanced Association Technology of Mobile Networks

Abstract This chapter provides a detailed introduction of the important network layer technologies in network information services, i.e. efficient routing and user association technologies. For the multi-hop Ad hoc self-organized network, in the slow mobile user network scenario and the fast IoV scenario, the data forwarding algorithm LASS based on local activity and social similarity and the IoV cognitive routing protocol QCR based on traffic flows are given. In addition, for the centralized cellular network, by focusing on the spatial-temporal characteristics of the flows of people/vehicles, by means of reinforcement learning, user association load balancing is realized in a dynamic environment, which provides a high-quality service rate for mobile users. Routing and user association technologies are designed to achieve efficient data transfer in information services. They are network layer technologies at different network architecture levels. The content of this chapter provides the basis of "data highway" for the development of network mobile information services.

3.1 Introduction

In the current various mobile information services, efficient data transmission is an important guarantee and foundation of the information service network layer. It depends on the development of routing protocols and association technologies. And the technology has a lot to do with changes in the network architecture and network topology of the current information service. First, as far as the network architecture is concerned, in this book, we discuss two architectures that support network mobile information services in Sect. 1.2 of Chap. 1. One is a centralized cellular architecture, and the other is a more flexible distributed Ad hoc network architecture, i.e., data transmission occurs between mobile devices. For the cellular architecture, the choice of data transmission paths is not difficult. In fact, how to achieve balanced association of users in the area is the basis that affects the performance of network data transmission. As for distributed Ad hoc architecture, choosing a high-efficient and low-latency multi-hop transmission path is very important. Secondly, we divide the speed of network topology changing into three categories. The first one is the

© Springer Nature Singapore Pte Ltd. & Science Press 2020
C. Jiang and Z. Li, *Mobile Information Service for Networks*,
https://doi.org/10.1007/978-981-15-4569-6_3

slow mobile network topology change measured by the walking speed of people (1–10 km/h). The second one is the rapid mobile network topology change measured by the speed of the vehicles (20–150 km/h). The third is the hyper-high-speed mobile networks topology change measured by the speed of high-speed rails (more than 200 km/h). Therefore, the designs of routing protocols, which is aimed at mobile information services built on different network architectures and different network topology changes, are different.

The traditional routing protocols that depend on the topology or simply depend on the probability of encounter have been unable to meet the requirements of efficient data transmission in the era of information explosion. Firstly, in this chapter, we discusses the slow mobile user network scenario and the fast IoV scenario under the Ad hoc network architecture. In Sects. 3.3 and 3.4, the social information in the current information service and the intelligent means based on environmental awareness are used to give a new routing protocol design method for the network information transmission in these two scenarios. Secondly, as for the centralized cellular architecture, in Sect. 3.5 we break through the traditional assumption of steady flows and use reinforcement learning to achieve balanced loads of user association in the mobile environment. So that the rate of user association services in the base station transmission mode can be improved [1–6].

3.2   Related Work

(1)   Research on Multi-hop Routing Protocols in Mobile Networks

In terms of routing protocols, there are many multi-hop routing protocols under self-organizing network architecture. The main purpose of the routing protocols is to maximize the message delivery rate and minimize the average end-to-end transmission delay.

One of the major types of mobile network multi-hop routing protocols is based on the probability of encounter. For example, Epidemic [7] and Spray-and-Wait [8] are the two earliest data forwarding algorithms based on the probability of encounter. Thereafter, a lot of literatures used the nodes' encounter history information, spatial information, context information, etc. to predict the probability of encounters between nodes and their destination nodes in the future. These heuristic algorithms are designed to find those relay points that are most likely to meet the destination nodes. For example, Lindgren et al. proposed a routing algorithm called PROPHET [9], in which each node maintains an encounter history with other nodes. PROPHET is based on the time-weighted probability of nodes encounters. Wu [10] et al. used the Markov chain in the routing algorithm to predict the future encounter probability and considered the limitation of buffer capacity meanwhile.

Recently, researchers have found that social information has an important impact on data forwarding. And this is because social relationships can reflect people's preferences, which are very important for predicting the probability of nodes' encounters.

Therefore, several data forwarding algorithms based on social encounters have been proposed. For example, Daly et al. proposed SimBet [11] that exploits the nodes' betweenness and social similarity (measured by the number of common neighbors between two nodes); Hui et al. proposed BUBBLE RAP [12] for delay tolerant networks (DTN) that uses the global and local centrality of nodes in interest groups (or community structures) to improve data transmission performance; Gao et al. and Fan et al. studied data multicast and broadcast problems in DTN by defining the geo-centrality and geo-community of nodes in literature [13, 14] respectively; Nguyen et al. presented a routing algorithm that takes the number of common interest groups as social similarity in literature [15].

In addition, there is a large class of topology-based routing protocols, which are designed from the perspective of topologies or geographic locations between network nodes. There are some classic protocols including DSR, AODV, GPSR, DSDV, TORA, etc. [16, 17]. There are also some protocol design methods [18–22] based on road maps. However, these studies have problems with road dead ends, and there may be no mobile nodes on some expected data forwarding paths, which leads to the failure of these methods [23]. Although some of works in this field have improved on these issues, the cost of predicting paths in multi-hop Ad hoc networks is very large.

(2) **Research on Balanced Association Technology for Mobile Users**

Researches on user load association balancing in cellular networks have been made by using Markov decision process, game theory and other methods. For example, Andrews et al.'s research [24–28] focuses on load balancing of cellular networks, OFDM systems and massive MIMO systems; the problem studied by Cheng et al. [29, 30] is mainly to offload the traffic from the cellular network to the Wi-Fi association points. Besides, there are some network load balancing studies [31, 32] that consider social attributes and energy consumption.

In order to achieve load balancing, researchers usually convert the associated access problem into a convex optimization problem [33]. Then, the heuristic method [34], gradient projection and dual decomposition etc. are used to solve the optimization problem. After the associated access solution is obtained, the cell breathing technology [35, 36] can be used to dynamically adjust the base stations' transmit power according to the load state of the cellular coverage area. In the process, previous researches usually used Poisson Point Process (PPP) to model users in mobile networks. Using the PPP model does simplify the analysis and reduce the computational difficulty. But in many cases, especially for the dynamic flows (people flows/vehicle flows) in mobile networks, a uniform PPP model is unrealistic. The studies [37, 38] use the Markov decision process to study the associated access problems in discrete and random systems. However, complex environments are often unknown for users, so it is difficult to define a reasonable state transition model. There are also some works [39–41] that use game theory to solve network selection problems. But it needs to converge to Nash equilibrium, which is not easy.

3.3   Routing Protocol Based on Social Relationship in Mobile Networks

In this section, we first focus on the general slow mobile network scenario. As described in Sect. 3.2, there are many data forwarding algorithms based on encounters in mobile networks. Many of the literatures are generally based on the following not explicitly stated but important assumptions: two nodes with higher social similarity have higher probability of their encounter. Different algorithms use different social similarity measures, one common method of which is based on the number of common interests or groups of interests.

However, the social similarity indicator based on the number of common interest groups ignores the fact that members of the same interest group tend to have different levels of local activity. If a node of low local activity is used to transfer data, it will lead to inefficient packet delivery ratio and long time delay.

Figure 3.1a depicts the relay selection between Thomas and Stephen in message delivery. In Fig. 3.1b, different sizes of icons represent each node's different levels of local activity in its communities. In the overlapping area, one node has different local activity in each belonging communities respectively, depicted by overlapping icons of square and triangle or square and circle.

As depicted in Fig. 3.1a, assuming Laura, Thomas and Stephen are the members of rugby club in the university, i.e., they have a common interest; now, a message must be sent to Laura through Thomas or Stephen. Thomas has many interactions with other members in the rugby club, i.e., he is with high local activity. While, Stephen has another common interest with Laura, e.g., both are in the university chorus. Therefore, it is unclear how to determine which person should be chosen as a relay due to lack of measurement criteria. If we choose Stephen as the relay, the delivery ratio may be low because of his potential lower local activity than that of Thomas. Consequently, we need to choose a node having more common interests with the destination and having a higher local activity in the community as a relay

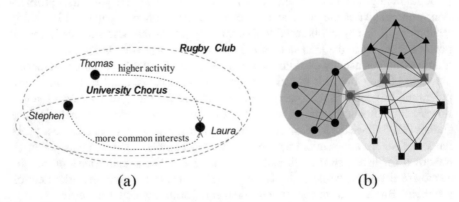

(a)   (b)

Fig. 3.1 Schematic diagram of the common interest groups

for this problem. In this section, multi-hop routing protocol based on local activity and social similarity in mobile networks, named LASS will be introduced and given below.

3.3.1 Local Activity

The local activity of node u in its interest group i is defined as the ratio of the probability of encounters between node u and all other nodes in the interest group i to the probability of encounters between any two nodes of the interest group i. The local activity of a node reflects statistical probability of encounters within the node's interest group. Specifically, the following definitions there:

Definition 3.1 Local Activity

Let $a_{u,i}^t$ denote the local activity of node u in a community with label i at time t. Then,

$$a_{u,i}^t = \frac{P_{u,i}^t}{Q_i^t} \tag{3.1}$$

where $P_{u,i}^t$ denotes the sum of the frequency of the encounters between node u and all other nodes in the interest group i before time t. The Q_i^t represents the sum of the frequency of encounters between any two nodes in the interest group i before time t.

Definition 3.2 Activity Vector

For each node u, the activity vector at time t is defined as

$$A_t(u) = \left(a_{u,1}^t, a_{u,2}^t, \cdots, a_{u,i}^t, \cdots, a_{u,K}^t\right) \tag{3.2}$$

where $a_{u,i}^t$ denotes the local activity value of node u in interest communities i at time t. The value of K represents the number of interest communities. An activity vector contains three types of information: time, the number of interest communities, and the local activity.

We give a metaphor to explain the meaning of the node local activity. Assuming there is a rugby club (community) in a university. Two students Stephen and Thomas are belonged to this club. If Thomas has many interactions with other members in the club, while Stephen has few interactions with members, we can say, Thomas has a high local activity and Stephen has a low local activity. If there exists more than one community which Stephen and Thomas are belonged to, Stephen and Thomas will have different local activity in each community. In data forwarding, local activity is important because if the message is given to a node having low local activity, it will bring about a low efficiency in terms of delivery ratio.

We find different nodes in the same community have different local activity values and the same node in different communities has different local activity values. Next, we take advantage of the node local activity to develop the social similarity between two nodes.

3.3.2 Social Similarity

After giving the definitions of node local activity and activity vector, we focus on the problem of node similarity. There are many kinds of social similarity measurements, such as Euclidean distance, Hamming distance, Cosine angular distance, Pearson correlation coefficient and Jaccard distance etc. These measurements are commonly used in information service networks, recommendation systems and Web search clustering analysis [42–45]. Every coin has two sides, and each measurement is the same under different conditions. More knowledge about similarity measure can be found in literature [46].

(1) **Euclidean Distance**

Euclidean distance is the most easily understood distance calculation method, derived from the distance formula between two points in Euclidean space. Euclidean distance between two n-dimensional vectors $A(x_{11}, x_{12}, \ldots, x_{1n})$ and $B(y_{11}, y_{12}, \ldots, y_{1n})$:

$$d = \sqrt{\sum_{k=1}^{n} (x_{1k} - y_{1k})^2} \tag{3.3}$$

(2) **Hamming Distance**

The Hamming distance between two equal-length strings s_1 and s_2 is defined as the minimum number of replacements required to change one of them to another. Its application field is generally information coding. In order to enhance fault tolerance, the minimum Hamming distance between codes should be as large as possible.

(3) **Cosine Angular Distance**

The cosine angular distance, also known as cosine similarity, is a measure of the difference between two individuals by using the cosine of the angle between two vectors in vector space. A vector is a directional line segment in a multidimensional space. If the directions of the two vectors are the same (i.e. the angle is close to zero), the two vectors are similar. To confirm whether the two vectors are in the same direction, it is necessary to calculate the angle of the vectors by using the cosine theorem. Cosine angular distance between two n-dimensional vectors $A(x_{11}, x_{12}, \ldots, x_{1n})$ and $B(y_{11}, y_{12}, \ldots, y_{1n})$:

$$\cos(\theta) = \frac{\sum\limits_{k=1}^{n} x_{1k} y_{1k}}{\sqrt{\sum\limits_{k=1}^{n} x_{1k}^2} \sqrt{\sum\limits_{k=1}^{n} y_{1k}^2}} \tag{3.4}$$

Compared with the Euclidean distance, the cosine angular distance pays more attention to the difference of the two vectors in the direction. Euclidean distance and cosine angular distance have different calculation methods and metric features, so they are suitable for different data analysis models. Euclidean distance can reflect the absolute difference of individual numerical characteristics, so it is more applied to the analysis that needs to reflect the difference from the data dimension. The cosine angular distance distinguishes the difference from the direction usually, but it is insensitive to absolute values.

(4) **Pearson Correlation Coefficient**

Pearson correlation coefficient is a method to measure the degree of correlation between random variables X and Y. The range of it is $[-1, 1]$. The larger the absolute value of the correlation coefficient, the higher the correlation between X and Y. When X is linearly related to Y, the correlation coefficient is 1 (positive linear correlation) or -1 (negative linear correlation). The Pearson correlation coefficient between two variables X and Y can be calculated by the following formula:

$$\rho_{X,Y} = \frac{N \sum XY - \sum X \sum Y}{\sqrt{N \sum X^2 - \left(\sum X\right)^2} \sqrt{N \sum Y^2 - \left(\sum Y\right)^2}} \tag{3.5}$$

(5) **Jaccard Distance**

Jaccard distance measures the difference between two sets by the ratio of different elements in the two sets to all elements. The Jaccard distance between two sets A and B:

$$J_d = \frac{|A \cup B| - |A \cap B|}{|A \cup B|} \tag{3.6}$$

In this section, two key aspects are mainly considered for the measure of similarity. One is local activity, and the other is the distribution of groups of interests to which the nodes belong. We hope that the local activity of the nodes is large and the distribution of the node-affiliated groups of interests is as consistent as possible with the distribution of the groups of interests to which the destination nodes belong. However, these above measurements cannot meet the expected requirements. For example, the Cosine angular distance and the Pearson correlation coefficient only pay attention to the distribution of the node-affiliated groups of interests; the Euclidean distance only pays attention to the size of the component values in the vectors, i.e., the size of the local activity; Jaccard distance only considers the number of affiliated groups of interests that are common to both nodes. Therefore, we need to carefully select the appropriate measure methods of similarity. Then, in combination with the two key aspects described above, the inner product method is selected here as the social similarity measure criteria in Definition 3.3 according to the input feature of social similarity, i.e., the activity vector, in Sect. 3.3.1.

Definition 3.3 Social Similarity

Given the activity vectors $A_t(u)$ of node u and $A_t(w)$ of node w, we define the social similarity between u and w at time t as $SS_t(u, w)$,

$$SS_t(u, w) = A_t(u) \cdot A_t(w) \tag{3.7}$$

where the symbol $\cdot$ denotes the inner product of vectors.

Local activity reflects the importance of nodes in the groups of interests. Guided by the destination node, the routing algorithm is designed to find a relay point with a great social similarity to the destination node. The relay point can ensure that the distribution of its affiliated groups of interests is similar to that of the destination node. And it has great local activity in the affiliated interest groups associated with the destination node. So, if a node has a larger inner product social similarity with the destination node, then the node has a greater chance of approaching the destination.

3.3.3   LASS Algorithm

The data forwarding rule of the algorithm LASS is to select a node with high social similarity to the destination node as a relay node. The higher social similarity indicates that the selected node and the destination node have more common interests and higher local activity in the groups of interests. This can guarantee the excellent performance of data forwarding.

Based on Definitions 3.1, 3.2 and 3.3, the description of LASS is presented in Algorithm 3.1. In order to make it clear, an example is also given to show the process of the data forwarding.

Algorithm 3.1 LASS: A Session from Node u **to** w **at Time** t

---

1. **for** each encountered node v_i do

2.   calculate $SS_t(u, w)$ and $SS_t(v_i, w)$

3.   **if** $SS_t(v_i, w) > SS_t(u, w)$ **then**

4.   add $SS_t(v_i, w)$ to the set $Temp^t$

5.   **end if**

6. **end for**

7. **if** $Temp^t \neq \varnothing$ **then**

8.   sort the values in set $Temp^t$ in descending order

9.   choose the largest $SS_t(v_i, w)$ from $Temp^t$

10.   node u transmits the message to node v_i

11. **else**

12.   node u maintains the message

13. **end if**

In Fig. 3.2, the data transfer session from node u to node w, the curved dashed line represents the transmission path obtained according to the LASS algorithm.

There is an example as shown in Fig. 3.2. At time t, node u transmits a message to destination node w in the mobile social network. Node u meets nodes v_1 and v_2. The activity vectors of node u, v_1, v_2 and w are

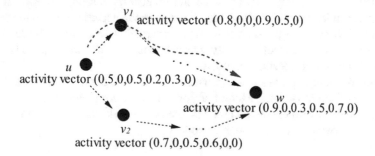

v_1 activity vector (0.8,0,0,0.9,0.5,0)

u activity vector (0.5,0,0.5,0.2,0.3,0)

w activity vector (0.9,0,0.3,0.5,0.7,0)

v_2 activity vector (0.7,0,0.5,0.6,0,0)

Fig. 3.2 Data transmission path diagram

$$A_t(u) = (0.5, 0, 0.5, 0.2, 0.3, 0);$$
$$A_t(v_1) = (0.8, 0, 0, 0.9, 0.5, 0);$$
$$A_t(v_2) = (0.7, 0, 0.5, 0.6, 0, 0);$$
$$A_t(w) = (0.9, 0, 0.3, 0.5, 0.7, 0)$$

According to Algorithm 3.1, we calculate the social similarity and gain $SS_t(u, w) = 0.91$, $SS_t(v_1, w) = 1.52$, $SS_t(v_2, w) = 1.08$. From above results, both nodes v_1 and v_2 can be used for next hop transmission. But $SS_t(v_1, w) > SS_t(v_2, w)$, so we finally choose node v_1 and transmit the message from u to v_1. After that, node v_1 keeps on doing the similar operations like above ways to complete the entire data transfer session.

3.3.4 Experiment and Evaluation

(1) Algorithm Comparison

In this section, we compare our LASS algorithm against some encounter-based strategies (Epidemic, PROPHET, Simbet, BUBBLE RAP and Nguyen's Routing). Particularly, the last three have social-aware properties further.

1. The Epidemic algorithm transmits the packet to all the encounter nodes until the packet reaches the destination.
2. The PROPHET algorithm estimates the probability of encounters between the two nodes in the future by time-weighting the encounter history, to select the node with the larger probability of encounters as the next hop relay.
3. The Simbet algorithm obtains the utility index of the nodes by calculating the intermediate centrality and similarity of the mobile nodes. The algorithm transmits the data packet to the encounter node whose utility index is higher than the current data packet holding node. The parameter settings of Simbet in this experiment: the similarity coefficient is set to 0.5 and the intermediate centrality coefficient is set to 0.5.
4. BUBBLE RAP algorithm proposes a hierarchical forwarding strategy. The node first transmits the packet along bubble of the node according to the global centrality. After the data packet arrives at the group of interests where the destination node is located, the local centrality is used to continue forwarding the data packet until it reaches the destination node.
5. Nguyen's Routing gives a data forwarding strategy based on the detection of groups of interests. If the encounter node shares more common interest groups with the destination node than the current packet holding node, then the packet will be forwarded to the encounter node .

(2)   **Datasets and Simulation Settings**

At present, many institutions or organizations provide or release some mobile information service network datasets, such as CRAWDAD, Haggle iMotes projects and Stanford SNAP Graph Library. In above collections, Infocom06 dataset, MIT Reality Mining dataset and Facebook dataset will be found. Based on them, some studies about relationship inference, behavior modeling and prediction, complex social studies and information dissemination are carried out. These datasets can be classified into two kinds, one kind is the social friendship information, and the other is the social proximity information. In our study, because we concern with the geographic encounter-based scenarios, the second kind of data (using Bluetooth discovery to gain proximity information) is appropriate for our experiments. To observe the impact of social on data forwarding, the MIT Reality Mining dataset is used here for this section of the experiment. In the MIT dataset, 97 users carry the Nokia 6600 mobile phone and are active on the MIT campus and its surrounding areas for 9 months. Our algorithm can also be applied to other datasets to validate its effectiveness. Of course, other datasets can also be used to validate the effectiveness of the LASS algorithm.

We choose the ONE simulator as our experimental tool [47]. It not only provides various mobile models including some complex mobility scenarios in daily life, but also can incorporate real world traces. In MIT trace files, one of the most important records is the contact between Bluetooth devices. It includes the start time, end time and communication peers of the encounter. These discrete contact events can be taken as the inputs of the ONE simulator. In order to model connecting and disconnecting, we reorder the start times and end times. Corresponding to communication peers, we set the start time as up and the end time as down. The form of the extracted trace data is like:

0	CONN	93	96	Up
0	CONN	93	14	Up
128	CONN	85	17	Up
129	CONN	94	29	Up
…				
1169	CONN	28	5	Down
1169	CONN	28	17	Down

For all simulations conducted in this work, each node generates 1000 packets during the simulation time. The packet size is distributed from 50 to 100 KB uniformly. Data transmission speed is 2 Mbps and the transmission range is in 10 m. The buffer size of each node is 5 MB. The source and destination pairs are chosen randomly among all nodes. Each emulation is repeated 20 times with different random seeds. Without losing precision, we set the update interval is 1. The interface of the underlying network is assigned to Bluetooth.

(3) **Metrics**

1. Delivery Ratio: the ratio of the number of successfully delivered messages to the total number of created messages.
2. Overhead Ratio: the proportion of the difference between the number of relayed messages and successfully delivered messages out of the successfully delivered messages.
3. Average Latency: the average messages delay for all the successful sessions.

(4) **General Comparison Experiment**

MIT Reality Mining Dataset is a long-term observation repository. Thus, some cumulative social phenomena (local activity, community structure etc.) require a period of time to reveal. Here, we make time to life (TTL) from 30 to 1 min. The experiment results are illustrated in Fig. 3.3a–f. Note that, we do experiments from date 2004-10-01 to date 2004-11-01. Because MIT is a long-term observation dataset, we choose a large TTL-1 month, instead of several days. A larger TTL (larger than 1 month) also can be done with more simulation time. But through our experiment analysis, the overall trend is similar with 1 month.

Figure 3.3a–c show the delivery ratio, overhead ratio and average latency of LASS, Epidemic and PROPHET algorithms respectively.

In terms of delivery ratio, shown in Fig. 3.3a, due to Epidemic's flooding-based copy strategy, Epidemic performs better than PROPHET during the initial phase. At time 3 days, the delivery ratio reaches the peak value, close to 50%. But after that, the delivery performance decreases because of network congestion resulting from large numbers of copies. Here, in order to avoid the serious decline of performance, we process Epidemic algorithm with copy-limits. Although the turning point still exists, its performance will not descend too much and will maintain relatively steady as time goes by. Similarly, the turning point also appears in PROPHET at 1 week because it needs redundant relays to adapt to the fluctuation of meeting probabilities. However, due to using the encounter history to predict the next hop, after the turning point, its delivery ratio shows better than Epidemic. By contrast, LASS goes up in steps and shows the best delivery performance among them, which outweighs Epidemic 32.63% and PROPHET 81.5%. At 1 month, it finally reaches 66.74% delivery ratio. Although LASS is also an unlimited copy algorithm like above two, its turning points will not emerge too early. This is because we use social similarity strategy to forward data. It means that the relay node has a high chance to meet the destination.

In terms of overhead ratio, illustrated in Fig. 3.3b, due to the nature of flooding, the disadvantage of Epidemic is obvious among the three algorithms. It exceeds 64.64% than PROPHET. However, thanks to its social similarity forwarding scheme, LASS performs best among them. To a great extent, through the whole TTL experiment period, the scheme controls the number of relaying copies with the overhead ratio only at 26.07% on average. In Fig. 3.3c, the delays of all the three algorithms arise with TTL increasing. However, due to Epidemic's large numbers of copies, it can achieve the lowest delay rapidly among three. PROPHET falls in between Epidemic and LASS. LASS is a little higher than PROPHET with 19.01%. This is because the

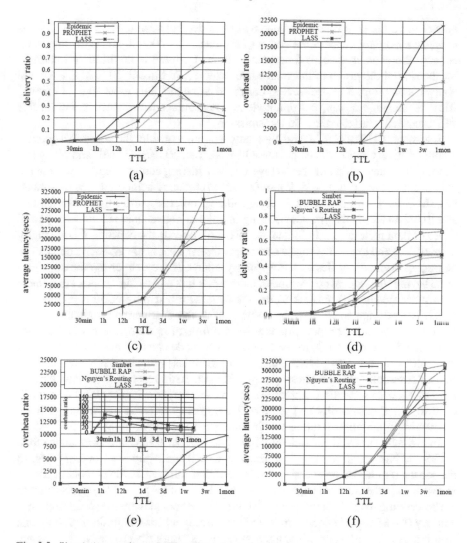

Fig. 3.3 Simulation results on MIT reality mining dataset

trade-off effect between the number of copies and the precise relay choosing strategy, i.e., when we aspire to find a good data forwarding scheme, the cost may be a little higher delay which is due to a relatively fewer copies.

Figure 3.3d–f show the delivery ratio, overhead ratio and average latency of our LASS, Simbet, BUBBLE RAP and Nguyen's Routing respectively.

In Fig. 3.3d, LASS performs best among four algorithms. Its delivery ratio is higher than Nguyen's Routing with 34.64%, BUBBLE RAP with 46.18% and Simbet with 120% on average. For Simbet, BUBBLE RAP and Nguyen's Routing, a common problem is that they do not consider contact frequency. If there exists a contact between two nodes at time t, an edge will be added between the two nodes. That is to say, they do not concern the contact frequency in a certain period of time, only concern the contact at some time point. Moreover, there is no different treatment for the side of the group of interests when detected. In Simbet, BUBBLE RAP and Nguyen's Routing, if the message is delivered to a node that has an edge (a contact) with the message holder, but this node has no contact with others in future, this delivering will lead to an invalid transmission.

If Simbet, BUBBLE RAP and Nguyen's Routing consider the contact frequency, a better delivery ratio will be possessed by Simbet, BUBBLE RAP and Nguyen's Routing than they had in the past. However, considering contact frequency is not the only decisive factor for LASS. Even if contact frequency is incorporated in Simbet, BUBBLE RAP and Nguyen's Routing, other problems restrict them. For Simbet and BUBBLE RAP, the problem is using the global betweenness in entire or partial phase of data forwarding. In Simbet and BUBBLE RAP, the concept of community is implicitly and explicitly considered respectively. That is to say, each node has its belonging community (ies), expect solitary nodes. If we deliver the message to a node having high global betweenness, although it indeed has high contact frequency with other nodes with respect to the entire network, it may be in a community which is irrelevant to or does not overlap with the destination community. As a relay, this node is not proper and increases the time of reaching the destination. For Nguyen's Routing, it tends to send messages to nodes having many interests with the destination. However, it may deliver them to nodes which have low local activity in their communities (or interests groups). It is the main reason for the low delivery ratio of Nguyen's Routing. Therefore, in this section, considering local activity in each weighted community and using social similarity to guide the routing path are the two important innovation factors in improving data forwarding.

In Fig. 3.3e, the overhead ratio of Simbet and BUBBLE RAP are much higher than LASS and Nguyen's Routing. The reason is LASS and Nguyen's Routing prefer to choose the similar interests nodes as relays, which can control the number of copies in sessions. In the enlarged legend, the overhead ratio of LASS and Nguyen's Routing are descending with TTL increasing. This is because both of them use social similarity strategy (LASS uses the inner product of forwarding utilities as similarity, Nguyen's Routing uses the number of common interests as similarity) to delivery message. As time goes by, the social phenomena becomes increasingly clearer, which makes the algorithms more and more suitable for the social network, i.e., just fewer copies can handle the data forwarding. On average, LASS keeps a low overhead ratio of 26.07%. It is better than Nguyen's Routing which is 44.72%. In Fig. 3.3f, the delays of four algorithms go up with TTL increasing. LASS and Nguyen's Routing are close to each other and slightly higher than BUBBLE RAP and Simbet. The gap is caused by few copies of LASS and Nguyen's Routing.

From above results and analysis, in terms of delivery ratio, we have LASS (66.74%) outweighs Epidemic 32.63%, Nguyen's Routing 34.64%, BUBBLE RAP 46.18%, PROPHET 81.5% and Simbet 120% on average. But in terms of overhead ratio, LASS is only with 26.07, outweighing Nguyen's Routing (with 44.72% overhead ratio on average) 41.7%. So LASS performs much better than Epidemic,

PROPHET, Simbet and BUBBLE RAP. All in all, LASS has proved its competitive ability, which can control delay in a reasonable range.

3.3.5 Privacy Preservation Discussion

In the social based routing algorithm, we need to pay attention to the problem of privacy preservation. On one hand, the social information can help improve routing efficiency. On the other hand, the leakage of social information is dangerous for users. Routing can be regarded as a network service. Therefore, sacrificing personal privacy to obtain a high-quality service experience coexists with each other in human activities.

In different applications and networking architectures, the requirements of privacy preservation are various. For example, the social relationship, the user behavior pattern, identification and some sensitive personal attributes can all become the objects of privacy preservation.

In previous studies, some applications use the popular C/S model, in which the centralized server collects and knows the global information. As an untrusted third-party, it may leak the information or deduce some sensitive personal information on the basis of the big data it owns. Some adversaries utilize the machine learning method or explore the identification correlation to get rules or models, and further derive the sensitive information. Then, the differentially private method [48, 49], privacy check based data releasing method [50], generating dummy data method [51], k-anonymous technology [52] and their varieties are often used to prevent the privacy leak.

Besides, some applications are based on P2P model, like searching a friend's approximate location, finding nearest friends. So, the aim of privacy preserving is to protect the adversary from profiling the users and exposing some sensitive information. Then, some multi-party based homomorphic encryption methods are developed [53–55]. Specially, with respect to the data forwarding, the conditional privacy preserving authentication technique [56] is used to protect the data packets from being captured and analyzed by the adversary; and the bilinear paring technique [57] is used to filter "junk" packets, like spam emails, when doing data forwarding in the network.

About privacy preservation, please refer to the relevant studies provided above.

3.4 Cognitive Routing Protocol for Internet of Vehicles

The previous section has introduced the design of an efficient multi-hop routing protocol in a general slow mobile network scenario. This section will describe another scenario where multi-hop routing protocol design in a fast mobile IoV network.

The feature of high speed results in the high dynamics of network topology, which is reflected in rapid channel changes and frequent handover [58]. This brings about a series of serious challenges on the routing performance of IoV (Internet of Vehicles). Moreover, most existing vehicular communication routing protocols are optimized for specific scenarios (e.g., highway driving, urban driving and platoon driving). However, the external states of a vehicle, such as traffic flows, road conditions and weather conditions, usually change rapidly [59]. The vehicle can only sense the states of surrounding vehicles locally without knowing the current state globally. It cannot cope with the network changes rapidly through applying a single routing protocol. Hence, there is a challenge that how to sense the traffic information in specific area and learn the regularities of dynamic changes in IoV for design of intelligent vehicle networking routing protocols.

In this section, here introduce a routing algorithm that based on Q-learning, called QCR (Q-learning Based Cognitive Routing). Through sensing the current state of the environment, QCR can learn the optimal strategy to achieve the good routing performance of IoV in dynamic networks based on different network scenarios.

3.4.1 Q-Learning Framework

Q-learning is a classic model-free reinforcement learning algorithm which can achieve fast convergence. It can solve the learning problems without environment models [60].

The learning problem is described by using the triple (S, A, r), where S represents all possible state spaces, A denotes all possible action, r represents the reward function. At each time step t, the agent assumed to observe an environment state s_t. It selects the action a_t from the action set A, then the state is converted from s_t to state s_t', finally the agent gets the immediate reward value r_t. Its simplest form, one-step Q-learning [61], is defined by

$$Q(s_t, a_t) \leftarrow Q(s_t, a_t) + \alpha \left[r_{t+1} + \gamma \max_a Q(s_{t+1}, a) - Q(s_t, a_t) \right] \qquad (3.8)$$

where $\gamma \in (0, 1)$ is a discount factor that balances between the immediate and future rewards. $\alpha \in (0, 1]$ is a learning rate. By selecting the action, the goal of Q-learning is to find the policy π to maximize rewards over time.

The value function $Q^\pi(s, a)$ maps each state-action pair (s, a). The optimal value function $Q^{\pi^*}(s, a)$ provides the maximal reward in every state. It is determined by solving the bellman equation [62]:

$$Q^{\pi^*}(s_t, a_t) = E\left[r(s_t, a_t) + \gamma \cdot \max_{a_{t+1}} Q^{\pi^*}(s_{t+1}, a_{t+1})\right] \qquad (3.9)$$

There is a key problem about exploration and exploitation in state-action space. The general approach is to use ε-greedy method. At each iteration i, the agent takes the optimal action $a_i = \arg\max_a Q^*(x_i, a)$ with probability $1 - \varepsilon$, otherwise it takes a random action. We show the Q-learning method in Algorithm 3.2.

Algorithm 3.2 Q-learning Algorithm

---

1. Initialize $Q(s_t, a_t)$;

2. For each episode;

3. **repeat:**

4.   Observe the current state $s = s_t$;

5.   Choose a_t from s_t using policy. (i.e. ε - greedy);

6.   Take action a_t;

7.   Receive immediate reward r_{t+1};

8.   Observe new state $s = s_{t+1}$;

9.   Update $Q(s, a)$ according to Equation (3.8);

10.   Update time $t = t + 1$ and current state $s = s_{t+1}$;

11. **until:** s is terminal;

3.4.2 An Overview of Q-Learning Based Cognitive Routing Algorithm

In this section, we design a routing algorithm that can sense the environment and learn optimal routing policies from the vehicular environment, called QCR. Table 3.1 offers a list of symbols used in this section.

Table 3.1 Notations of symbols

Symbol	Description
ρ	Vehicular density in certain area
v	Average vehicle speed (kmph)
S	State space
A	Action space
a_t	Take action at time slot t
r	Reward function
r_t	Single step reward received at time slot t
s_t	State at time slot t
π	Routing protocol selection policy
π^*	Optimal routing protocol selection policy
γ	Discount factor
α	Learning rate
i	Iteration times of update Q value
$Q(s_t, a_t)$	State-action pair value
$Q^{\pi^*}(s_t, a_t)$	Optimal state-action pair value
p	Packet deliver ratio
d	Average delay
ω	Weight in reward function
N	Possible state-action combinations

In QCR, base stations are used to collect vehicle status and deploy various routing protocols. The pseudo code for QCR is shown in Algorithm 3.2. The algorithm can obtain the optimal $Q(s, a)$. Q-learning table is initialized to 0. The vehicle firstly reports traffic information and network status to the base station. Then, the base station learns the optimal strategy according to the current scenario state, and selects a corresponding routing protocol. The action selection strategy uses ε-greedy method. If the value $Q(s, a)$ no longer changes after all states are explored, the algorithm eventually converges. After continuous learning, the algorithm can learn the optimal routing strategy for a given state.

Algorithm 3.3 Q-learning Based Cognitive Routing

---

1. For each pair $(s_t, a_t) \in N$, initialize $Q(s_t, a_t) = 0$;

2. For each episode;

3. **repeat:**

4.   Observe ρ, V;

5.   Evaluate s_t;

6.   Choose a_t using (ε-greedy);

7.   Take action a_t;

8.   Receive immediate reward r_{t+1};

9.   Observe new state $s = s_{t+1}$;

10.   Update $Q(s, a)$ according to Equation (3.8);

11.   Update time $t = t + 1$ and current state $s = s_{t+1}$;

12. **until:** $Q(s_t, a_t)$ coverage $\forall (s_t, a_t) \in N$;

---

(1) QCR State Space: We group the different average vehicle speeds and vehicle densities into different states. Let S denotes the state space. The searching table of Q-learning is only suitable for solving small-scale discrete space problems. In IoV environment, vehicle speed v and density ρ are continuous values, so we discrete the states for QCR. And we use $\{t, v, \rho\}$ to define the states. We give three classic scenarios according to the vehicle speed: "city" 0–40 kmph, "urban" 40–80 kmph and "highway" 80+ kmph. We also give three scenarios according the vehicle density: "sparse state" 0–50 vehicles per 2500 m², "normal state" 51–100 vehicles per 2500 m² and "congestion state" more than 100 vehicles per 2500 m². All the possible states are shown in Table 3.2.

(2) QCR Action Space: We define the set of action A of IoV. The action set includes various routing protocols such as VANET (Vehicular Ad-hoc Networks). This section uses GPSR (Greedy Perimeter Stateless Routing) and AODV (Ad-hoc On-Demand Distance Vector Routing). According to the Algorithm 3.3, for the current state s_t, the base station selects an action (i.e. a routing protocol for selecting and transmitting related action sets for vehicles in a designated area). In addition, the action set can be supplemented and updated in the future using the latest routing protocols.

Table 3.2 QCR states space

State	Average speed (kmph)	Vehicular density (the number of vehicles/2500 m^2)
0	0–40	0–50
1	41–80	0–50
2	80+	0–50
3	0–40	51–100
4	41–80	51–100
5	80+	51–100
6	0–40	100+
7	41–80	100+
8	80+	100+

(3) QCR Reward Function: We define QCR reward function by using routing performance metrics. Two key metrics should be considered for routing performance: packet delivery ratio and average end to end delay. They can reflect network reliability and network communication quality in IoV. We defined the reward function as follows:

$$r = w_1 p + w_2 d$$

where w_1 represents the weight of packet delivery ratio and w_2 represents the weight of average end to end delay. And $w_1, w_2 \in [0, 1]$. For safety applications, we can set w_2 relative higher than w_1, since applications require lower delay time. For non-safety applications, we can set w_1 higher.

3.4.3 Experiment and Evaluation

In this section, we evaluate QCR performance comparing with two classical routing protocols, i.e., AODV and GPSR. The simulation environment configuration and simulation results are given below.

(1) **Simulation Configuration**

We develop the simulation [63] model based on the simulator named Veins which is an open source framework for running vehicular network simulations. It is based on two well-established simulators: OMNeT++ [64], an event-based network simulator, and SUMO [65], a road traffic simulator.

In order to make the experiment more credible, we use the urban traffic flow trajectory data and road network of the Region of Sanfrancisco from the VANET project. The road network is set to 2500 m × 2500 m in Fig. 3.4.

Fig. 3.4 Example diagram of simulation area

In terms of the wireless configurations, we use IEEE 802.11p in the MAC layer. We use the shadowing propagation model to simulate the physical propagation in the physical layer and set communication range as 400 m. We randomly select the source-destination pairs in the simulation. Table 3.3 lists the simulation parameters.

(2) **Simulation Results**

The average speed and number of vehicles during the simulation are shown in Fig. 3.5. We compare QCR with two routing protocols AODV and GPSR, shown in Fig. 3.6.

Table 3.3 Experiment settings

Parameter	Values
Transmission range	400 m
Simulation time	360 s
Bitrate	18 Mbps
MAC protocol	IEEE 802.11 p
Data packet size	512 bytes
Playground size XYZ	2500 m * 2500 m * 50 m
Routing protocol	AODV, GPSR
Carrier frequency	2.4 GHz
Transmitter power	2 mW
Transport protocol	UDP
Propagation model	Nakagami
Discount factor	0
Learning rate	0.8
ε	0.2

Fig. 3.5 Scene state of the simulated vehicle

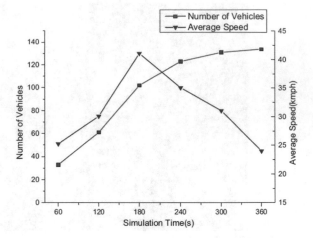

Fig. 3.6 Average packet delivery rate

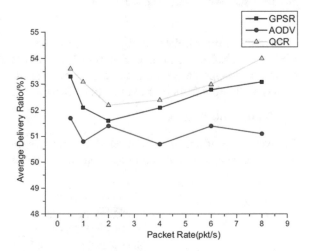

The results show QCR has the highest average delivery ratio than other protocols with varying the packet rate from 0 to 4 packets/second. Combining with Fig. 3.5, it can be seen that the algorithm in this section can cope with the changes of the IoV environment and obtain better data transmission effects during the whole simulation period.

3.5 Mobile User Association Method for Load Balancing Based on Reinforcement Learning

After discussing network routing issues in the previous Sects. 3.3 and 3.4, we will discuss another key issue of the network layer technology, i.e., the balanced association problem for mobile users. Here, there are two types of mobile users, one is users who hold mobile devices such as mobile phones, and the other is users who operate high-speed mobile tools (e.g. a vehicles).

At present, as 5G technology is about to be fully commercialized, more and more mobile users need to associate with heterogeneous base stations (different ties of transmitting powers, physical sizes and costs). In a city, there are great differences in mobile user association requirements. In the dense traffic area, the association requirements are more than that in the sparse traffic area. Under the traditional max-SINR scheme, a powerful/strong base station may attract more mobile users to associate with it. Even with a targeted deployment where the weak base stations are placed in the dense traffic areas, most users still receive the powerful downlink signal from the strong base stations. This will result in the strong ones having heavy loads while the weak ones having many idle resources. For mobile uses, even they associate with the strong base stations, the service rates are still very bad since the strong ones serve too many vehicles. So, a more balanced association scheme is needed for mobile users.

However, for the convenience of analyzing, many current methods assume that the flows of people/vehicle is steady and the channel quality is stable or has small fluctuations, which constitutes an approximately static scenario. However, in real world, the changes of the people/vehicle flows are not stable. The assumption results in the invalidation of association solution. Even if we apply them in the unknown dynamic environment, the lack of feedback signals from environment causes the gradient descent losing its direction. Besides, once the network scenario changes, the traditional association algorithms must rerun in the whole network with high costs. Fortunately, we find that there exist potential regularities of spatial-temporal distribution for mobile users. The goal of our study is to learn and utilize the spatial-temporal association experiences so as to directly obtain the association solution in the dynamic mobile users' environment.

To this end, we introduce the reinforcement learning method into this work. Reinforcement learning is learning what to do or how to map situations to actions so as to maximize a numerical reward signal. Different from the supervised and unsupervised learning, trial-error search and delayed reward are the two most important features of reinforcement learning. Through interacting with the unknown environment continuously, an agent should know in what states what actions should be taken so as to make a right decision. Drawing on the above ideas, we will introduce a user associated access method in mobile networks based on an online reinforcement learning approach, named ORLA.

3.5.1 Main Idea

In this Chapter, there are two challenging problems when designing ORLA.

(1) How to use the reinforcement learning model to define an association problem in the dynamic environment?
(2) How to utilize the spatial-temporal regularities to design ORLA in vehicular networks?

For the first challenge, we transform the association problem into an 'N-armed bandit problem'. We take advantage of a price-based idea to propose an initial reinforcement learning method. In the method, through feeding back from the current environment, we design a reward function that directs the change of price. The reward is defined as a deviation of all users' average service rates, which reflects the network load balance to some extent. Through learning, we can obtain the best association decision from the maximum long-term cumulative reward.

For the second challenge, we design a historical-based reinforcement learning method. After the initial reinforcement learning, each base station obtains its own historical association patterns (i.e. which users are associated with it). Since the users' movement has the spatial-temporal regularities, there may exist similarity between the historical associations and the current case. Thus the historical association patterns can be utilized as references. The detailed definition about association pattern is given in Sect. 3.5.3. When the network keeps up changing, the base station uses ε-greedy method to learn the association actions based on its historical association patterns. ORLA uses the Pearson distance and Kullback-Leibler distance to calculate the similarity between the current case and the historical recorded pattern. The similarity helps the base station to choose the appropriate action and accelerate learning. After that, based on the difference of association allocations between the current requirement and the historical decision, ORLA proposes a binary approaching method and a multi-spot diffusion method to obtain the association decision for the current network. Finally, when the historical-based reinforcement learning ends, each base station records the current association solution again for accumulation.

In this work, ORLA is executed on each base station in a distributed way. The learning and decision are put on the base station side. The user side does not need to do any sophisticated computation. After the initial reinforcement learning ends, we let the historical-based reinforcement learning always stay to cope with the dynamic changes. Each base station uses its historical experiences to give an association decision. Meanwhile, through a reward from the current environment, ORLA adjusts this decision to ensure it is a good solution. Then, ORLA avoids users trying blindly one by one in vehicular networks.

3.5.2 System Model and Assumptions

(1) System Model

In this section, the object discussed is a heterogeneous case with macrocells, picocells and femtocells coexisting in vehicular networks. The transmit powers of the three decrease in sequence.

We focus on downlink (DL) in the association scheme. We consider the single-BS association (i.e. one user is exactly associated with one base station).

Let B and V denote the sets of base stations and vehicles, respectively. During the connection period, we define the achievable rate as c_{ij}. Typically,

$$c_{ij} = \log_2\left(1 + \frac{P_j g_{ij}}{\sum\limits_{k \in B, k \neq j} P_k g_{ik} + \sigma^2}\right) \tag{3.10}$$

where P_j denotes the transmit power of base station j, σ^2 denotes the noise power level, and g_{ij} denotes the channel gain between vehicle i and base station j, which includes antenna gain, path loss and shadowing.

(2) The Measurement of Load Balancing

In this work, load balancing is a concept for describing the status of the whole network system, not for a single base station. Since each base station generally serves more than one mobile user, mobile users associated with the same base station need to share resources. Therefore, the key metric for performance is service rate, not SINR simply. The service rate experienced by a mobile user depends on the load of a base station (i.e. how the base station allocates its resources among its associated users). We set the start time as t_0 and the current time as t. If vehicle i is associated with base station j, we define the long term service rate as $R_{ij}(t)$, having

$$R_{ij}(t) = f_{ij}(t) \int_{t_0}^{t} x_{ij}(\tau) c_{ij}(\tau) d(\tau) \tag{3.11}$$

where τ is a time variable, satisfying $t_0 \leq \tau \leq t$. $f_{ij}(t)$ denotes the fraction of resources that the base station j serves user i, having $f_{ij}(t) = \frac{\sum_{\tau=t_0}^{\tau=t} x_{ij}(\tau)}{t-t_0}$. Let $x_{ij}(\tau)$ denote a scheduling indicator, $x_{ij}(\tau) \in \{0, 1\}$. If the base station j schedules the user i at time τ, we have $x_{ij}(\tau) = 1$, and vice versa.

When we measure the load balancing of a network, a good load balancing should satisfy the following two characteristics:

1. The overall service rate $\sum_{i \in V} \sum_{j \in B} R_{ij}$ is large.
2. The variance of users' service rates R_{ij} is small.

As for the above two characteristics, firstly, a network with good balancing means that the network congestion is not severe. So the overall service rates should be large. Secondly, the aim of mobile user association is to make most of the users can be associated with the base stations. Meanwhile, each associated mobile user should have a relative good service rate, with the rate fluctuating around the average level at least. Otherwise, a bad service rate below the average level greatly is meaningless for users.

Here, we need to point out that there are some other metrics of load balancing. For example, the utility function of delay can be used to measure the load balancing in Wi-Fi offloading problem. This metric is usually used to study the performance about offloading some services from base stations to Wi-Fi association points. In addition, the Jain's index of throughput can be used to measure the load balancing. This utility is similar to above two characteristics of service rate stated. Based on the application background and convenience for comparing with the similar schemes, we use the overall service rates and the variance of service rates as the metrics of load balancing in our following experiment.

(3) **Mobility and Resource Allocation**

Since we take into account time-varying channels and vehicle mobility, the proportional fair scheduling is adopted in this section. We have the allocation priority of vehicle i as,

$$AP_{ij}(t) = \frac{c_{ij}(t)}{R_{ij}(t-1)} \qquad (3.12)$$

According to Eq. (3.12), each mobile user calculates its priority at each time slot. The base station will schedule users based on the priority. We can see if the base station j continually schedules a user with good channel quality, the value of denominator increases. Then the priority decreases and the fraction of resources of the user to obtain also decreases.

Besides, for convenience, we set a threshold ϱ to update the achievable rate $c_{ij}(t)$. It means that if $|c_{ij}(t) - c_{ij}(t-1)| < \varrho$ (ϱ is a small positive number), we have $c_{ij}(t) = c_{ij}(t-1)$, otherwise, we update the achievable rate $c_{ij}(t)$.

3.5.3   Online Reinforcement Learning Association Method for Mobile Users

In this section, we discuss the design principle and give the detailed description of ORLA. The architecture of ORLA is shown in Fig. 3.7. In ORLA, we first design the initial reinforcement learning method to obtain the initial association results for mobile users in the dynamic environment. These association results are cumulated in each base station. After a period of learning, when the base station meets network changes again, the base station can use the historical association patterns to solve the

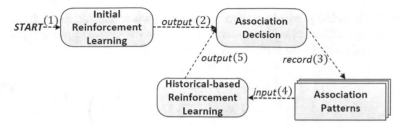

Fig. 3.7 The architecture of ORLA

new association results directly and adaptively (i.e. the historical-based reinforcement learning association method). Then the new obtained association results will be recorded again in each base station. In Fig. 3.7, we can see the association patterns, the historical-based reinforcement learning, and the association decision form a circle to adaptively handle the network changes.

1. Initial Reinforcement Learning

(1) Initialization:

Each base station knows its service supplies/resources K_j and its service demands D_j. The initial value of D_j is defined as the number of users that are in the communication range of base station j. Each user measures the SINR by using beacon signals and broadcasts its achievable rate c_{ij} to all base stations at each time slot.

Then, we define a price value for each base station as $\mu_j = D_j - K_j$. The price value can be either positive or negative. We also define a decision value between base station j and mobile user i as $d_{ij} = c_{ij} - \mu_j$. We can see if the base station j is over-loaded, its price μ_j is high. Then the decision value may be small.

Besides, through communicating with other base stations periodically, each base station can maintain an SINR matrix with the element c_{ij} and an association matrix with element $\{0, 1\}$. The value 1 means that there is an association between user i and base station j, and vice versa. If the achievable rates c_{ij} of some users are not received by the base stations, we set the corresponding values as 0 in the SINR matrix. The dimensions of the two matrices are both $|V| \times |B|$.

(2) The Initial Reinforcement Learning Method

Based on the above information, we design the initial reinforcement learning method for ORLA. It can be seen as a single-step reinforcement learning task. The theoretical model is an N-armed bandit problem. In ORLA, each base station acts as an independent learning agent.

- The environment is the current mobile networks.
- The action is defined as the base station trying to build associations with some users.
- The reward is defined as a reciprocal of the deviation of average service rate for all users (see Eq. (3.13)).

For a base station j, assume that we obtain the association results through learning, i.e., knowing which mobile users associated with base station j. The reward r_j defined for the association of base station j can be calculated as:

$$r_j = \frac{1}{\sum\limits_{i=1}^{|S_j|} \frac{1}{|S_j|} \cdot \left(R_{ij} - \left(\sum\limits_{k=1}^{|B|}\sum\limits_{i=1}^{|V|} R_{ik}\right)\Big/ |V|\right)^2} \tag{3.13}$$

where S_j denotes the set of vehicles associated with base station j. The values of S_j and R_{ij} can be obtained through the SINR matrix and the association matrix.

Before describing the learning method, we define a mathematical operator $Z \wr z$. It means that we calculate the value of function Z under the condition z.

At t-th iteration of initial reinforcement learning:

Step 1   Each base station calculates the decision value $d_{ij}(t) = c_{ij}(t) - \mu_j(t)$;
Step 2   Each base station sends the decision values to all users;
Step 3   Each user chooses the best decision value, i.e., $\text{argmax}_j d_{ij}(t)$, and tries to associate with the corresponding base station j. Then the set of actions $S_j(t)$ can be obtained. Note that in iterations, there may exist two or more set of actions that are totally equal, e.g., $S_j(t) = S_j(t + 1)$. In the following parts, we set an index l to differ the different set of actions, denoted as $S_j^l (l = 1, 2, \ldots)$;
Step 4   Based on Step 3, each base station can calculate its current reward $r_j(t)$ according to Eq. (3.13), i.e., the value $r_j(t) \wr S_j^l$;
Step 5   Calculate the long term average cumulative reward $Q_j(t)$ for the action set S_j^l, having

$$Q_j(t) \wr S_j^l = \frac{\left(Q_j(t-1) \wr S_j^l\right) \times \text{count}\left(S_j^l\right) + \left(r_j(t) \wr S_j^l\right)}{\text{count}\left(S_j^l\right) + 1} \tag{3.14}$$

where $\text{count}\left(S_j^l\right)$ represents a counter to calculate the cumulative number of choosing the action set S_j^l;

Step 6   Then we adjust the price value according to the three following points

- If the current reward $r_j(t) \wr S_j^l \geq \frac{\sum_{k \in B, k \neq j} r_k(t) \wr S_k(t)}{|B|-1}$, we maintain the price (i.e. $\mu_j = \mu_j(t)$);
- Else if $\left|\frac{\sum_{i=1}^{S_j(t)} R_{ij}(t)}{|S_j(t)|}\right| > \left|\frac{\sum_{k=1}^{B}\sum_{i=1}^{|V|} R_{ik}(t)}{|V|}\right|$, we decrease the price value with $\mu_j(t + 1) = (1 - \delta(t)) \cdot \mu_j(t)$;
- Else, we increase the price value with $\mu_j(t + 1) = (1 + \delta(t)) \cdot \mu_j(t)$, where $\delta(t) \in [0, 1)$ is a step size chosen in the experiment.

Step 7   If for all $S_j^l(l = 1, 2 \ldots)$, satisfying $\left| Q_j(t) \wr S_j^l - Q_j(t-1) \wr S_j^l \right| < \in (\in$ is a small positive number), the iteration ends. The base station obtains the final association results S_j^l based on $\text{argmax}_{S_j^l}\left(Q_j(t) \wr S_j^l \right)$. Else, we turn to Step 1 and iterate continually.

Step 8   According to the final association results S_j^l in Step 7, the base station performs the corresponding connection operation, and meanwhile, base station j records the association results in itself.

(3)   The Analysis of Initial Reinforcement Learning

In above initial reinforcement learning, there are two factors that motivate the iterations. One is the dynamic achievable rate $c_{ij}(t)$, the other is the price $\mu_j(t)$ resulting from the unbalanced associations. When the base station tries to build associations with some users, it will receive a reward corresponding to these actions. Although each base station makes decisions itself, we have the reward r_j containing the global average service rate to guarantee the effect of learning. Then if the reward is bad, the base station adjusts its price, i.e., we use reward r_j as a basis to adjust the price of a base station. Through multiple iterations, we learn the best cumulative reward of these actions according to Eq. (3.14). The optimal actions can be chosen based on the cumulative reward.

2.   **Association Pattern**

ORLA uses the initial reinforcement learning as a cold start. Due to network changes, each base station can cumulate a series of association patterns of its own after a period of time.

An association pattern of base station k is defined as under what kind of SINR condition and price value, which users are associated with the base station k. The association pattern can be described/recorded by using the three following elements.

- An SINR matrix. It is denoted by C_p^k with the element c_{ij}, of which k denotes the index of the base station, p denotes the sequence number of the pattern;
- An association matrix. It is denoted by A_p^k with the element $\{0, 1\}$, of which the value 0 or 1 means whether the user is associated with base station k or not;
- A price value. It has been defined in Initial Reinforcement Learning.

Those recorded patterns are the valuable experiences for our following historical-based reinforcement learning. When doing the historical-based reinforcement learning, new obtained association patterns are continually recorded in each base station.

3. **Historical-Based Reinforcement Learning**

Based on above pattern records, when the environment changes, base stations will face new association demands coming from users. Since the spatial-temporal regularities exist in mobile networks, we can use the historical association patterns to deal with the network changes. Here, each base station is also regarded as a reinforcement learning agent.

Then, we give the pseudo-codes of historical-based reinforcement learning in Algorithm 3.4.

- The environment is the current mobile networks;
- The action is defined as the base station choosing one of the historical association patterns;
- The reward is as same as the definition in Eq. (3.13).

In the historical-based reinforcement learning, we assume that on base station k, it has a set of pattern records P. So there are $|P|$ different kinds of actions. We initialize count(p) as the chosen times of the historical pattern p and $Q(p)$ as the cumulative reward of pattern record p(Lines 2–3). After that, for a current case p' with current SINR matrix $C_{p'}^k$ and current price $\mu_{p'}^k$ of the base station k, we calculate the similarity between the current case p' and each historical pattern p. If the maximal similarity is below a threshold λ (defined in experiments), we will turn to the phase of initial reinforcement learning (Lines 6–7). It means that the historical experiences have low utilities to solve the current association problem. Otherwise, we focus on choosing actions among the $|P|$ association patterns in the number of T iterations, $T > |P|$. The T iterations end until for all $p \in P$, we have $Q(p)$ converge, i.e., the value of $|Q_t(p) - Q_{t-1}(p)|$ is below a small positive number. Note that, since we consider the time varying channels, the new pattern p' may change after once iteration. This is the reason why we need to learn. The environment changes, the reward values in Lines 21–22 also change.

In Algorithm 3.4, there exists a trade-off problem between exploration and exploitation in the reinforcement learning. Exploration-only gives the chance to each action uniformly while exploitation-only gives the chance to the best rewarded action at present. Obviously, exploration-only can estimate the corresponding reward for each action with losing many chances to choose the optimal action. While, exploitation-only cannot estimate the expectation of the reward well for each action. If we want to maximize the final cumulative reward, we need to find a middle way between exploration and exploitation.

Algorithm 3.4 ORLA: Historical-based Reinforcement Learning

1. $r = 0$, P denotes the set of the historical association patterns;

2. **for** $(p = 1; p \leq |P|; p++)$ **do**

3. $\quad Q(p) = 0$, $\text{count}(p) = 0$;

4. **end for**

5. **for** $(t = 1; t \leq T; t++)$ **do**

6. $\quad$ **if** $(\max(\text{sim}(p', p)) < \lambda)$ **then**

7. $\quad\quad$ Turn to the phase of the initial reinforcement learning;

8. $\quad$ **else**

9. $\quad\quad$ **if** $(\text{rand}() < \varepsilon)$ **then**

10. $\quad\quad\quad$ **if** $(P \neq \varnothing)$ **then**

11. $\quad\quad\quad\quad$ Choosing pattern p with the condition $\text{argmax}_p(\text{sim}(p', p))$;

12. $\quad\quad\quad\quad$ $P = P \backslash \{p\}$;

13. $\quad\quad\quad$ **else**

14. $\quad\quad\quad\quad$ Choosing pattern p from the set P uniformly;

15. $\quad\quad\quad$ **end if**

16. $\quad\quad$ **else**

17. $\quad\quad\quad$ Choosing pattern p with the condition $\text{argmax}_p Q(p)$;

18. $\quad\quad$ **end if**

19. $\quad$ **end if**

20. $\quad$ Do $\text{sim}(p', p)$;

21. $\quad$ Calculating the reward r according to Eq. (3.13);

22. $\quad Q(p) = \dfrac{Q(p) \times \text{count}(p) + r}{\text{count}(p) + 1}$;

23. $\quad \text{count}(p) - \text{count}(p) + 1$;

24. **end for**

25. Making a final action decision, i.e., choosing the final pattern p with maximal $Q(p)$;

26. Do function $\text{allocation}(p', p)$;

27. Output the association matrix $A_{p'}^k$;

Here we use a ε-greedy method to choose the actions. It can balance the exploration and exploitation. When the random value is below the threshold ε, we first use the maximal similarity to choose the action (Lines 9–12). Then if all the patterns are traversed, we will choose the action uniformly which is equal probability from set P(Lines 13–15). When the random value is beyond the threshold ε, we choose the action with maximal cumulative reward (Lines 16–18). Through multiple iterations, the average reward $Q(p)$ of each action can be approached (Lines 20–23). In this method, the maximal similarity can guarantee the algorithm to find the possible optimal value quickly. Meanwhile, this method can traverse all historical patterns. Finally, we choose the association action with the best cumulative reward (Lines 25–26).

In Algorithm 3.4, there are two important components, Algorithm $\text{sim}(p', p)$ and Algorithm $\text{allocation}(p', p)$, shown in Algorithms 3.5 and 3.6. Algorithm $\text{sim}(p', p)$ is used to calculate the similarity between the historical pattern p and the current case p'. Algorithm $\text{allocation}(p', p)$ is used to allocate the possible association actions for vehicles in current case p' based on the historical association pattern p. We describe the two algorithms as follows.

(1) Similarity of Two Patterns

In this work, the similarity of two patterns is defined as the proximity degree of the distribution of service requirements c_{ij} under a certain distribution of prices. Therefore, in Algorithm $\text{sim}(p', p)$ (pseudo-codes in Algorithm 3.5), we first use the Pearson distance to calculate the distribution similarity of the service requirement c_{ij} between the historical pattern p and the current case p' for base station k (Lines 1–2). The Pearson distance is used to measure the correlation between two samples. It can be used in the situation with different orders of magnitudes or evaluation criteria. Since in our study, the current requirement c_{ij} in $C_{p'}^k$ and the historical c_{ij} in C_p^k may have different scales, the Pearson distance is suited to characterize the similarity between them. The range of value is $[-1, 1]$. The value 1 means the maximal positive correlation.

Then, we use the Kullback-Leibler distance to calculate the distribution similarity between the requirement ratio (Line 4) and the price ratio (Line 5) for the historical pattern p and the current case p' (Lines 3–6). The Kullback-Leibler distance is used to measure the similarity between two distributions. The range of value is $[0, 1]$. The value 0 means that the two distributions are the same.

Finally, we put different weights α and β on the Pearson distance and Kullback-Leibler distance, respectively. Usually we have $\alpha = \beta = 0.5$.

Algorithm 3.5 ORLA: Similarity of Two Patterns: $\text{sim}\,(p', p)$

---

14. **Input:** The current and historical SINR matrices $C_{p'}^k$ and C_p^k;

15. The current and historical prices $\mu_{p'}^k$ and μ_p^k;

16. **Output:** The similarity value;

1. Set $\text{vec}(k, p') = $ sort the k-th column of matrix $C_{p'}^k$;

17. Set $\text{vec}(k, p) = $ sort the k-th column of matrix C_p^k;

2. Calculate the Pearson distance $\text{PD}\big(\text{vec}(k, p'), \text{vec}(k, p)\big)$ between

   $\text{vec}(k, p')$ and $\text{vec}(k, p)$;

3. Set $\omega(k, p') = \sum_{j=k} c_{ij}, c_{ij} \in C_{p'}^k$,

18. Set $\omega(k, p) = \sum_{j=k} c_{ij}, c_{ij} \in C_p^k$;

4. Set $W(p', p) = \omega(k, p') / \omega(k, p)$;

5. Set $U(p', p) = \mu_{p'}^k / \mu_p^k$;

6. Calculate the Kullback-Leibler distance $\text{KL}(W(p', p) \| U(p', p))$;

7. Output the similarity value

19. $\alpha \cdot \text{PDvec}(k, p'), \text{vec}(k, p) - \beta \cdot \text{KL}(W(p', p) \| U(p', p))$;

---

(2) Association Allocation

In Algorithm 3.4, when the base station chooses a historical pattern p as its current action, ORLA uses allocation algorithm to make an association allocation for the current users based on the historical experience. The pseudocodes are described in Algorithm 3.6.

First, for a base station k, ORLA needs to solve how many users can be associated with it in the current case. Here, ORLA uses the proportional allocation method (Lines 1–5 in Algorithm 3.6). Let $\dim(\cdot)$ denote the dimension of a vector.

Second, ORLA needs to solve which vehicles can be associated with the base station k in the current case. It is classified into two situations (Lines 6–10 in Algorithm 3.6). Note that in Algorithms 3.7 and 3.8, some initialization/prior information has been provided in Algorithm 3.6 (Lines 1–4).

Algorithm 3.6 ORLA: Association Allocation: allocation (p' , p)

Input:

The current and historical SINR matrices $C_{p'}^k$ and C_p^k ;

The current and historical prices $\mu_{p'}^k$ and μ_p^k ;

The historical association matrix A_p^k ;

Output:

An association matrix $A_{p'}^k$ for SINR matrix $C_{p'}^k$;

1. Sort the elements c_{ij} in C_p^k with $j = k, c_{ij} \neq 0$ and put them into vector $X_{p,k}$;

2. Sort the elements c_{ij} in $C_{p'}^k$ with $j = k, c_{ij} \neq 0$ and put them into vector $X_{p',k}$;

3. Sort the elements c_{ij} in $X_{p,k}$ with the corresponding element in $A_p^k = 1$ and put them into vector $Y_{p,k}$;

4. Define a set $Y = \varnothing$ that is used to record the chosen association elements for the current case p' ;

5. Calculate the number of vehicles that requires to be associated as:

$$\text{NUM} = \frac{\mu_{p'}^k}{\mu_p^k} \times \frac{\dim\left(X_{p',k}\right)}{\dim\left(X_{p,k}\right)} \times \dim\left(Y_{p,k}\right);$$

/*let $\dim(\cdot)$ denote the dimension/length of a vector.*/

6. **if** $\left(\text{NUM} < \dim(Y_{p,k})\right)$ **then**

7.   Use binary approaching method to obtain association matrix $A_{p'}^k$, which is described in Algorithm 3.7;

8. **else**

9.   Use multi-spot diffusion method to obtain association matrix $A_{p'}^k$, which is described in Algorithm 3.8;

10. **end if**

11. Output the association matrix $A_{p'}^k$;

Situation 1: NUM $< \dim(Y_{P,k})$. It means that the number of users required to be associated in the current case p' is below the number of allocated users $\dim(Y_{P,k})$ in the historical pattern p. Here, we use a binary approaching method, described in Algorithm 3.7.

Algorithm 3.7 ORLA: Binary Approaching Method

---

1. Split the vector $X_{p,k}$ into two equal vectors $X_{p,k}^{up}$ and $X_{p,k}^{down}$;

    Split the vector $X_{p',k}$ into two equal vectors $X_{p',k}^{up}$ and $X_{p',k}^{down}$;

2. Count the common elements both in vectors $Y_{p,k}$ and $X_{p,k}^{up}$, denoted as

    N_{up} ;

    Count the common elements both in vector $Y_{p,k}$ and $X_{p,k}^{down}$, denoted as

    N_{down} ;

3. **if** (NUM $=1$) **then**

4.   Choose a non-zero value y random from $X_{p',k}$ except the elements in Set Y ;

5.   Set $Y = Y \cup \{y\}$;

6. **else if** ($\left|\dfrac{N_{up}-N_{down}}{\dim(X_{p,k})}\right| > \theta$ and $N_{up} > N_{down}$) **then**

7.   Choose a non-zero value y uniformly from vector $X_{p',k}^{up}$ except the elements in Set Y ;

8.   Set $Y = Y \cup \{y\}$, NUM $=$ NUM -1 ;

9.   Set $X_{p,k} = X_{p,k}^{up}$ and $X_{p',k} = X_{p',k}^{up}$;

10.   Do binary recursion continually;

11. **else if** ($\left|\dfrac{N_{up}-N_{down}}{\dim(X_{p,k})}\right| > \theta$ and $N_{up} < N_{down}$)**then**

12.   Do the similar operations as Steps 7-10 in the opposite vector;

13. **else if** ($\left|\dfrac{N_{up}-N_{down}}{\dim(X_{p,k})}\right| \leq \theta$) **then**

15.   Set $Y = Y \cup \{y, y'\}$,   NUM $=$ NUM $- 2$;

16.   Set $X_{p,k} = X_{p,k} : \left[1, \dfrac{l_p}{2}\right]$ and $X_{p',k} : \left[1, \dfrac{l_{p'}}{2}\right]$;

17.   Do the similar operations as Step 9-10;

18.   **end if**

19.   Set the corresponding values of set Y in matrix $A_{p'}^{k}$ as 1;

Situation 2: NUM $\geq$ dim$(Y_{P,k})$. It means that the number of users required to be associated in current case p' is beyond the number of allocated users dim$(Y_{P,k})$ in historical pattern p. Here, we use a multi-spot diffusion method, described in Algorithm 3.8.

Algorithm 3.8 ORLA: Multi-spot Diffusion Method

---

1.   Define a new set SPOT;

2.   Initialize an object rank that is used to label the rank location of an element in a vector;

3.   **for** (each element i in vector $Y_{p,k}$) **do**

4.   rank.i = the location of element i in vector $X_{p,k}$;

5.   Choose the corresponding element j with rank location

$$\text{rank}.j = \frac{\dim\left(X_{p',k}\right)}{\dim\left(X_{p,k}\right)} \times \text{rank}.i;$$

6.   Put the element j into the set SPOT;

7.   **end for**

8.   Set $q = \dfrac{\text{NUM}}{\dim\left(Y_{p,k}\right)}$;

9.   **for** (each element j in set SPOT) **do**

10.   Set the element j as a center spot in $X_{p',k}$ and choose number of q elements from $X_{p',k}$ with the nearest distance from the center spot j, including the spot itself.

11.   Put the number of q elements into the set Y;

12. **end for**

13. Set the corresponding values of set Y in matrix $A_{p'}^k$ as 1;

14. **if** ($\text{NUM} - q \cdot \dim(Y_{p,k}) \neq 0$) **then**

15. Turn to use the binary approaching method;

16. **end if**

---

(3) Analysis and Brief Summary

In Algorithms 3.7 and 3.8, the principle is to choose the users having the similar features to the historical association pattern.

When $\text{NUM} < \dim(Y_{p,k})$, we use the binary approaching method to scale down and find the appropriate elements. We utilize the binary method to partition the historical association vector continually and find the feature distribution of the associated users. Then, through dealing with the following four different cases (Line 3, 6, 11, 13 in Algorithm 3.7), we obtain the feature of historical association allocations. By using the same feature distribution, we can finally find the appropriate users for forthcoming associations.

When $\text{NUM} \geq \dim(Y_{p,k})$, we mainly utilize the multisport diffusion method to scale up and find the appropriate elements. First, we choose the equal number of elements from the current pattern p' with the same rank location in the historical pattern p (Lines 1–7). We call these elements as spots. Then, around these spot elements, we enlarge the search range and choose integral multiple elements (Lines 8–13). If having a remainder, we turn to the binary approaching method to complete the association allocation (Lines 14–16). Finally, we obtain the association matrix.

After the base station learns the association decision $A_{p'}^k$ by using the historical-based reinforcement learning, it informs users to associate with it. If the mobile user receives more than one associated signal, it will select the base station with the highest service rate for associated access.

3.5.4 Complexity Analysis

We analyze the complexity of ORLA from the following three aspects.

First, in initial reinforcement learning, we let each base station act as an independent agent. Although the association decision is made in a distributed manner, we still need some cooperative information to guide the iterations without losing the global aim of load balancing. The amount of cooperative information is order of $(I \cdot |B| \cdot |B - 1| + |B| \cdot |V|)$, where I is the total number of iterations. The information exchange includes the interactions among base stations (SINR matrix and association matrix) and the interactions between the base stations and users (c_{ij} broadcast).

First, in a big vehicular network, the network area is usually divided into many small areas based on road intersections. It is allowed that the load balancing is achieved only in small local areas. Thus the overhead of communication and computation can be controlled in local areas.

Second, in historical-based reinforcement learning, the action selection does not need to try blindly in many times since each action can be traversed by using similarity as its guidance. Besides, due to the spatial-temporal features of users' movement, there are many similar historical patterns. ORLA combines the similar ones and only maintains some representative association patterns. It guarantees the search space will not increase too large. Thus, the historical-based reinforcement learning can also converge well.

Third, since we push all the calculations on the base station side, not the user side, the computational capability can be guaranteed for some tasks like binary search and element sorting.

3.5.5 Experiment and Evaluation

In this section, we choose to use the vehicle movement data that can better reflect the capability of the method for experimental evaluation.

We use real-life GPS-based vehicle mobility traces to evaluate the efficiency of ORLA. Our dataset comes from QiangSheng taxi movement. The dataset contains traces about 117 taxis. The traces are collected from April 1st to April 30th in Shanghai, China, 2015. The taxi periodically sends reports back to the data collector via an onboard GPS-enabled device. The information in the dataset includes vehicle ID, latitude, longitude, timestamp, vehicle moving speed and other related information.

We capture an area to do experiments. The latitude of the captured area is between [31.15, 31.30]. The longitude is between [121.25, 121.45]. In this area, there are totally 76 vehicles and 20 base stations, including 5 macrocells, 5 picocells and 10 femtocells. The GPS locations of 20 base stations are provided in Fig. 3.8. The transmit powers of the three ties of base stations are 46 dBm, 35 dBm and 20 dBm, respectively. For the macros/picocells, we set the path loss $L(d_{ij}) = 34 + 40 \log d_{ij}$. For the femtocells, we set the path loss $L(d_{ij}) = 37 + 30 \log d_{ij}$, where d_{ij} denotes the distance between the vehicle i and base station j. The noise power σ^2 is -104 dBm. The bandwidth is 10 MHz. Besides, we set the similarity threshold λ as -0.25 in the experiment. With the experimental data, the validity and efficiency of ORLA in load balancing have been verified.

(1) **Loads among Different Base Stations**

Here compare ORLA with two association schemes, max-SINR and 3D (Distributed Dual Decomposition Optimization). The former is a traditional scheme, in which users choose the association base station with the maximal SINR. The latter is a popular method that transforms the user association to a utility maximization problem.

Fig. 3.8 The GPS locations
of 20 base stations

macrocells		femtocells	
Longitude	Latitude		
121.2878	31.22992	Longitude	Latitude
121.3751	31.23252	121.3517	31.18389
121.3394	31.27665	121.3522	31.17561
121.3113	31.17921	121.4135	31.18415
121.3594	31.24665	121.3093	31.20679
picocells		121.3874	31.20261
Longitude	Latitude	121.2867	31.29085
121.3989	31.27174	121.4359	31.18116
121.3237	31.28139	121.3474	31.22064
121.406	31.24337	121.3372	31.18457
121.2662	31.23806	121.409	31.21535
121.4051	31.19519		

Then, we compare loads among three different association methods. In Fig. 3.9,
we capture the association results when convergence ends. The max-SINR association results in unbalanced loads, in which the macrocells are over loaded, while
the picocells and femtocells only serve fewer users. In ORLA, the load is shifted to
the less congested femtocells, which suggests that our scheme ORLA alleviates the
asymmetric load problem. It shows the effectiveness of ORLA. The results of 3D
and ORLA are similar since the near-optimal results are both obtained by them.

Fig. 3.9 Number of
associations in three ties of
base stations

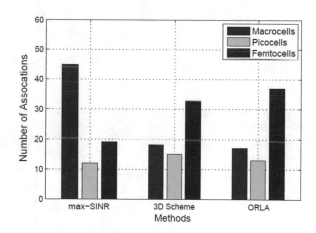

(2) **Service Rates and Convergence Time**

In Sect. 3.5.2, we give the metrics of load balancing, i.e., the overall service rates and the variance of users' service rates. The large overall service rates and small variance mean that the base stations are not congested and can provide enough resources to support the network services.

Figure 3.10 shows the cumulative distribution functions (CDFs) of the overall service rates for three different association schemes. First, we can see that the beginning point of ORLA is bigger than max-SINR and 3D scheme, and the tail of ORLA is also longer than them. Second, the CDF of ORLA improves at a low rate compared with max-SINR and 3D scheme. All above phenomena show that the bigger overall service rates occupy a high proportion in ORLA.

Figure 3.11 shows the distribution of service rates for 20 high activity vehicles. The variance values of service rates are 4.2359e-005, 3.0072e-005 and 2.3642e-005

Fig. 3.10 The CDFs of overall service rates for three comparison methods

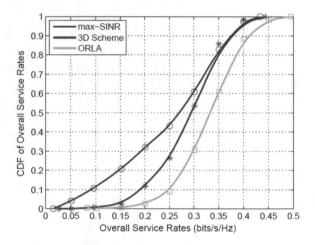

Fig. 3.11 The distribution of service rates

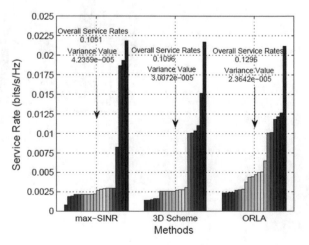

Fig. 3.12 The convergence
time of ORLA

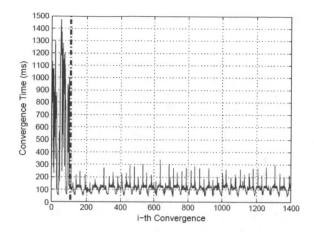

for max-SINR, 3D and ORLA, respectively. We obtain that ORLA has the largest
overall service rates with the smallest variance value. Therefore, combining Fig. 3.10
with Fig. 3.11, we can see that ORLA provides a more uniform user experience with
higher service rates for users. It also benefits the overall performance of the whole
network system.

Figure 3.12 shows the convergence time in 1400 successive convergence tests on
QiangSheng dataset. Each convergence contains multiple iterations. First, we can see
that the worst convergence time is still below 1500 ms. Second, there is an obvious
boundary in Fig. 3.12, marked by a dash line. The left side of the dash line represents
the t-th order convergence time of initial reinforcement learning, and the right side
represents the t-th order convergence time of historical-based reinforcement learning.
It means that, at the beginning, ORLA pays much more time to cope with the dynamic
users' movement (new arrivals and departures). After that, based on the historical
experiences, 75.9% convergence time is saved. All above phenomena verify the
effectiveness of ORLA.

3.6 Application Discussion

For mobile information services, efficient routing and balanced user association technology are the underlying basic technologies. Data transmission in various service
applications depends on efficient network routing. In addition, when a large number
of users access a certain application service, load balancing of traffic is important
for each user. In Chaps. 6–8, we describe and develop some transportation information service applications, route recommendation service applications, and payment
authentication service applications. In these applications, fast data packet exchange
and balanced traffic load are the cornerstones of ensuring high quality of service for
users.

References

1. C. Jiang, C. Yan, H. Chen, et al., A content-based winternet pipeline communication protocol routing algorithm: 201410489962.8, 2014-09-23
2. C. Jiang, D. Zhang, H. Chen, et al., A virtual vehicle routing method suitable for large-scale traffic flow simulation: 201110002566.4, 2011-01-07
3. C. Jiang, J. Cheng, C. Yan, A self-encoding network based network node filtering and its access routing construction method in IoV: 201510697871.8, 2015-10-23
4. Z. Li, C. Wang, S. Yang, et al., LASS: Local-activity and social-similarity based data forwarding in mobile social networks. IEEE Trans. Parallel Distrib. Syst. **26**(1), 174–184 (2015)
5. Z. Li, C. Wang, C. Jiang, User association for load balancing in vehicular networks: an online reinforcement learning approach. IEEE Trans. Intell. Transp. Syst. **18**(8), 2217–2228 (2017)
6. C. Wang, L. Zhang, Z. Li, et al., SDCoR: software defined cognitive routing for internet of vehicles. IEEE Internet Things J **5**(5), 3513–3520 (2018)
7. A. Vahdat, D. Becker, Epidemic routing for partially connected ad hoc networks. Report. (Duke University, 2000)
8. T. Spyropoulos, K. Psounis, C.S. Raghavendra, Spray and wait: An efficient routing scheme for intermittently connected mobile networks, in *Proceedings of the ACM SIGCOMM*. (Philadelphia, Pennsylvania, USA, 2005), pp. 252–259
9. A. Lindgren, A. Doria, O. Schelen, Probabilistic routing in intermittently connected networks. Mob. Comput. Commun. Rev. **7**(3), 19–20 (2003)
10. Y. Wu, Y. Zhu, B. Li, Infrastructure-assisted routing in vehicular networks, in *Proceeding of the IEEE INFOCOM*. (Orlando, FL, USA, 2012), pp. 1485–1493
11. E.M. Daly, M. Haahr, Social network analysis for routing in disconnected delay-tolerant MANETs. in *Proceedings of the ACM MANETs*. (Montreal, Quebec, Canada, 2007), pp. 32–40
12. P. Hui, J. Crowcroft, E. Yoneki, BUBBLE rap: social-based forwarding in delay-tolerant networks. IEEE Trans. Mob. Comput. **10**(11), 1576–1589 (2011)
13. W. Gao, Q. Li, B. Zhao, et al., Multicasting in delay tolerant networks: a social network perspective. in *Proceedings of the ACM MANETs*. (New Orleans, LA, USA, 2009), pp. 299–308
14. J. Fan, J. Chen, Y. Du, et al., Geocommunity-based broadcasting for data dissemination in mobile social networks. IEEE Trans. Parallel Distrib. Syst. **24**(4), 734–743 (2013)
15. N.P. Nguyen, T.N. Dinh, S. Tokala, et al, Overlapping communities in dynamic networks: their detection and mobile applications. in *Proceedings of the ACM MobiCom*. (Las Vegas, Nevada, USA, 2011), pp. 85–96
16. C. Perkins, E. Belding-Royer, S. Das. Ad hoc on-demand distance vector (AODV) routing. Report. (Network Working Group, 2003)
17. B.T. Sharef, R.A. Alsaqour, M. Ismail, Vehicular communication ad hoc routing protocols: a survey. J. Netw. Comput. Appl. **40**(1), 363–396 (2014)
18. M. Jerbi, S. Senouci, T. Rasheed, et al., Towards efficient geographic routing in urban vehicular networks. IEEE Trans. Veh. Technol. **58**(9), 5048–5059 (2009)
19. I. Leontiadis, C. Mascolo, GeOpps: geographical opportunistic routing for vehicular networks, in *Proceedings of the IEEE WoWMoM*. (Espoo, Finland, 2007), pp. 1–6
20. J. Nzouonta, N. Rajgure, G. Wang, et al., VANET routing on city roads using real-time vehicular vraffic information. IEEE Trans. Veh. Technol **58**(7), 3609–3626 (2009)
21. J. Jeong, S. Guo, Y. Gu, et al., TBD: trajectory-based data forwarding for light-traffic vehicular networks, in *Proceedings of the IEEE ICDCS*. (Montreal, QC, Canada, 2009), pp. 231–238
22. J. Jeong, S. Guo, Y. Gu, et al., TSF: trajectory-based statistical forwarding for infrastructure-to-vehicle data delivery in vehicular networks. in *Proceedings of the IEEE ICDCS*. (Genova, Italy, 2010), pp. 557–566
23. R.H. Khokhar, R.M. Noor, K.Z. Ghafoor, et al., Fuzzy-assisted social-based routing for urban vehicular environments. Eur. J. Wirel. Commun. Netw. **2011**(1), 178 (2011)
24. Z. Shen, J.G. Andrews, B.L. Evans, Adaptive resource allocation in multiuser OFDM systems with proportional rate constraints. IEEE Trans. Wirel. Commun. **4**(6), 2726–2737 (2005)

25. F. Boccardi, J.G. Andrews, H. Elshaer, et al, Why to decouple the uplink and downlink in cellular networks and how to do it. IEEE Commun. Mag. **54**(3), 110–117 (2016)
26. J.G. Andrews, S. Singh, Q. Ye, et al, An overview of load balancing in Hetnets: old myths and open problems. IEEE Wirel. Commun. **21**(2), 18–25 (2014)
27. Q. Ye, B. Rong, Y. Chen, et al., User association for load balancing in heterogeneous cellular networks. IEEE Trans. Wirel. Commun. **12**(6), 2706–2716 (2013)
28. H. Jo, Y. J. Sang, P. Xia, et al, Heterogeneous cellular networks with flexible cell association: a comprehensive downlink SINR analysis. IEEE Trans. Wirel. Commun. **11**(10), 3484–3495 (2012)
29. N. Cheng, N. Lu, N. Zhang, et al., Vehicular WiFi offloading. Veh. Commun. **1**(1), 13–21 (2014)
30. N. Cheng, N. Lu, N. Zhang, et al., Opportunistic WiFi offloading in vehicular environment: a game-theory approach. IEEE Trans. Intell. Transp. Syst. **17**(7), 1944–1955 (2016)
31. C. Yue, G. Xue, H. Zhu, et al.S3: Characterizing sociality for user-friendly steady load balancing in enterprise WLANs, in *Proceedings of the IEEE ICDCS*. (Philadelphia, PA, USA, 2013), pp. 491–499
32. H. Han, J. Yu, H. Zhu, et al., E3: energy-efficient engine for frame rate adaptation on smartphones. in *Proceedings of the ACM SenSys*. (Roma, Italy, 2013), pp. 1–9
33. H. Kim, G. De Veciana, X. Yang, et al., Distributed α-optimal user association and cell load balancing in wireless networks. IEEE/ACM Trans. Netw. **20**(1), 177–190 (2012)
34. S. Corroy, L. Falconetti, R. Mathar, Dynamic cell association for downlink sum rate maximization in multi-cell heterogeneous networks. in *Proceedings of the IEEE ICC*. (Ottawa, ON, Canada, 2012), pp. 2457–2461
35. Y. Bejerano, S. Han, Cell breathing techniques for load balancing in wireless LANs. IEEE Trans. Mob. Comput. **8**(6), 735–749 (2009)
36. S. Das, H. Viswanathan, G Rittenhouse, Dynamic load balancing through coordinated scheduling in packet data systems. in *Proceeding of the IEEE INFOCOM*. (San Francisco, CA, USA, 2003), pp. 786–796
37. S.E. Elayoubi, E. Altman, M. Haddad, et al., A hybrid decision approach for the association problem in heterogeneous networks, in *Proceedings of the IEEE INFOCOM*. (San Diego, CA, USA, 2010), pp. 401–405
38. E. Stevensnavarro, Y. Lin, V.W.S. Wong, An MDP-based vertical handoff decision algorithm for heterogeneous wireless networks. IEEE Trans. Vehi. Technol. **57**(2), 1243–1254 (2008)
39. D. Niyato, E. Hossain, Dynamics of network selection in heterogeneous wireless networks: an evolutionary game approach. IEEE Trans. Veh. Technol. **58**(4), 2008–2017 (2009)
40. S. Shakkottai, E. Altman, A. Kumar, Multihoming of users to access points in WLANs: a population game perspective. IEEE J. Sel. Areas Commun. **25**(6), 1207–1215 (2007)
41. E. Aryafar, A. Keshavarzhaddad, M. Wang, et al., RAT selection games in HetNets. in *Proceedings of the IEEE INFOCOM*. (Turin, Italy, 2013), pp. 998–1006
42. H.J. Ahn, A new similarity measure for collaborative filtering to alleviate the new user cold-starting problem. Inf. Sci. **178**(1), 37–51 (2008)
43. G. Guo, J. Zhang, N. Yorkesmith, A novel Bayesian similarity measure for recommender systems, in *Proceedings of the AAAI*. (Beijing, China, 2013), pp. 2619–2625
44. F. Papadopoulos, M. Kitsak, M.A. Serrano, et al., Popularity versus similarity in growing networks. Nature **489**(7417), 537–540 (2012)
45. J. Wu, Y. Wang, Social feature-based multi-path routing in delay tolerant networks. in *Proceedings of the IEEE INFOCOM*. (Orlando, FL, USA, 2012), pp. 1368–1376
46. H. Ma, I. King, M.R. Lyu, Effective missing data prediction for collaborative filtering, in *Proceedings of the ACM SIGIR*. (Amsterdam, The Netherlands, 2007), pp. 39–46
47. A. Keranen, J. Ott, T. Karkkainen, The ONE simulator for DTN protocol evaluation, in *Proceedings of the IEEE SIMUTools*, (Rome, Italy, 2009), p. 55
48. M. Fredrikson, E. Lantz, S. Jha, et al., Privacy in pharmacogenetics: an end-to-end case study of personalized warfarin dosing, in *Proceedings of the Usenix Security Symposium*. (San Diego, CA, 2014), pp. 17–32

49. N.E. Bordenabe, K. Chatzikokolakis, C. Palamidessi, Optimal geo-indistinguishable mechanisms for location privacy. in *Proceedings of the ACM CCS*. (Kyoto, Japan, 2014), pp. 251–262

50. M. Gotz, S. Nath, J. Gehrke, MaskIt: privately releasing user context streams for personalized mobile applications, in *Proceedings of the ACM SIGMOD*. (Pune, India, 2012), pp. 289–300

51. Y. Agarwal, M. Hall, ProtectMyPrivacy: detecting and mitigating privacy leaks on iOS devices using crowdsourcing. in *Proceedings of the ACM MobiSys*. (Taiwan, China, 2013), pp. 97–110

52. X. Liu, K. Liu, L. Guo, et al., A game-theoretic approach for achieving k-anonymity in location based services, in *Proceedings of the IEEE INFOCOM*. (Nassau, Bahamas, 2013), pp. 2985–2993

53. W. Dong, V. Dave, L. Qiu, et al., Secure friend discovery in mobile social networks, in *Proceedings of the IEEE INFOCOM*. (Lahaina, HI, USA, 2011), pp. 1647–1655

54. R. Zhang, Y. Zhang, J. Sun, et al., Fine-grained private matching for proximity-based mobile social networking. in *Proceedings of the IEEE INFOCOM*. (Munich, Germany, 2012), pp. 1969–1977

55. X. Li, T. Jung, Search me if you can: privacy-preserving location query service. in *Proceedings of the IEEE INFOCOM*. (Nassau, Bahamas, 2013), pp. 2760–2768

56. R. Lu, X. Lin, X. Shen, Spring: a social-based privacy preserving packet forwarding protocol for vehicular delay tolerant networks. in *Proceedings of the IEEE INFOCOM*. (San Diego, CA, USA, 2010). pp. 1–9

57. R. Lu, X. Lin, T. H. Luan, et al., PReFilter: an efficient privacy-preserving relay filtering scheme for delay tolerant networks. in *Proceedings of the IEEE INFOCOM*. (Munich, Germany, 2012), pp. 1395–1403

58. S. Alsultan, M. Aldoori, A. H. Albayatti, et al., A comprehensive survey on vehicular ad hoc network. J. Netw. Comput. Appl. **37**, 380–392 (2014)

59. Z. He, J. Cao, X. Liu, SDVN: enabling rapid network innovation for heterogeneous vehicular communication. IEEE Netw **30**(4), 10–15 (2016)

60. C. Jiang, J. Yu, C. Yan, et al., An improved traffic signal control method based on Q-learning, 201610135744.3, 2016-03-10

61. C. Watkins, P. Dayan, Technical note: Q-learning. Mach. Learn. **8**, 279–292 (1992)

62. R.S. Sutton, A.G. Barto, Introduction to Reinforcement Learning. (Cambridge, MIT Press, 1998)

63. C. Sommer, R. German, F. Dressler, Bidirectionally coupled network and road traffic simulation for improved IVC analysis. IEEE Trans. Mob. Comput. **10**(1), 3–15 (2011)

64. A. Varga, OMNeT++. (Berlin, Germany, Springer, 2010)

65. M. Behrisch, L. Bieker, J. Erdmann, et al., SUMO—simulation of urban mobility: an overview. in *Proceedings of the SIMUL*. (Barcelona, Spain, 2011), pp. 55–60

Chapter 4
Network Community Detection

Abstract This chapter introduces one of the important technologies of the application layer of network mobile information services, community structure discovery technology. As for the social attributes of mobile information services brought about by human activities, the community exploration methods for different scenarios are given from the perspective of the underlying communication network architecture. The focus of this chapter is to discover the relationship between the underlying communication architecture and the top-level community discovery to intuitively establish a community structure based on actual communication conditions. This has great benefits for discovering potential relationships and exploring unknown network structures.

4.1 Introduction

For the current thriving network mobile information services, the deep participation of people will make the mobile devices attached to the network users have social relationship attributes. Therefore, some unrelated physical entities (e.g. mobile phones, tablets, vehicles, etc.) have potential connections. These mobile devices and associations can be abstracted into a network structure consisting of vertices and edges that connect vertices. This topological link of the mobile device not only represents the physical link of the device, but also depicts the social relationships between nodes. This dynamic link not only reflects the free mobility of the device, but also reflects the complex social relationships between device holders. In such a network structure, an important technology which applies in network mobile information service application layer is network community discovery.

A community is a structure in which the nodes are very closely connected and the internal links are more than the external links [1, 2]. The concept originally came from the complex networks and then extended to the field of online and mobile social networks. Generally speaking, mobile social networks are mobile communication systems that contain user social relationships [3]. The network nodes are not limited to a person, but also include physical entities associated with the person, and its edge may be association relationships formed by the frequency of encounter, the degree of mutual trust, the degree of similarity of interest etc. Therefore, in the

© Springer Nature Singapore Pte Ltd. & Science Press 2020   71
C. Jiang and Z. Li, *Mobile Information Service for Networks*,
https://doi.org/10.1007/978-981-15-4569-6_4

current information world, many of the underlying mobile communication devices that are connected by the network mobile information service can be regarded as the generally mobile social networks after networking. In such a network, if people have a common interest or meet frequently with others, the physical devices held by these people or people can form a community. If the frequency of encounter is used to indicate the degree of contact between nodes, the community is defined as a group of nodes with a higher degree of association. However, the subjective nature of community definition is very strong, and there is currently no unified community definition. Most definitions are related to specific community detection algorithms or social applications, and community discovery is a method to discover communities in the network. Note that in the field of artificial intelligence such as machine learning, finding the tight structure between nodes is called "clustering" [4]. It is generally calculated using a vector of target features, focusing on finding a bunch of targets with similar properties. The concepts of community and clustering are not completely independent. In different contexts, the names are different.

It is possible for the community discovery in network mobile information services to clarify the relationship between network node associations and divide the structure of the network by discovering several communities. And it also supports recommendation algorithms, path planning, routing protocol design, etc. In this chapter, we explore the new method of community detection from the perspective of different network communication architectures faced by network mobile information services, and analyze the connections between the underlying communication architecture and the top-level logical relationship network to establish a bridge between them. This chapter firstly introduces some classic community detection algorithms. Then, for the distributed communication architecture, based on the frequency of user encounter, an adaptive weighted dynamic community detection algorithm is given to obtain the physical neighboring community. Then, for the hybrid communication architecture (distributed and centralized), here introduce a space- crossing community detection algorithm, so that the concept of physical neighboring community can be further expanded into a space-crossing community in geospatial space [5–7].

4.2   Related Work

Currently, many classic community detection algorithms have been applied to social networks, bioinformatics networks and commercial networks. Comprehensiveness literature [8, 9] can be used as primers in this field.

In the study of static community detection algorithms, Newman and Girvan made pioneering work. In literature [10], the community detection algorithm ranks according to the betweenness, and iteratively removes the edges to construct the final community structure and proposes the concept of MODULARITY Q to assess the quality of community detection results. Newman and Leicht et al. further extended the above work into weighted and directed community detection in literature [11, 12] respectively. Later, many optimization algorithms based on MODULARITY Q have been proposed [13–16]. In addition, Palla et al. proposed a K-CLIQUE milestone algorithm in the literature [17], which mainly solves the community overlap problem in community detection.

Along with the appearance of mobile networks, many dynamic community detection algorithms were proposed based on the remolded of the above static algorithms. For example, distributed community detection algorithm proposed by Hui et al. [18], AFOCS algorithm [19], FacetNet algorithm [20], iLCD algorithm [21].

For different network situations, these static or dynamic community detection algorithms may have some inefficiencies or inability to adapt to the network model when they are specific used. For example, the detection algorithms based on MODULARITY Q have resolution limit and extreme degeneracy problems [22]. The K-CLIQUE-based algorithm requires that the value of K be determined in advance. This value represents the size of the cluster structure CLIQUE, which limits the size of the community to some extent in advance. The FacetNet algorithm proposed in literature requires that the number of communities in the network be predicted in advance. This information cannot meet this requirement when the social network is actually used. The iLCD algorithm proposed in literature does not comprehensively consider the dynamic changes of the network, and only studies the dynamic increase of the edge in the network. Hui's distributed algorithm cannot handle community overlapping in dynamic environments. The AFOCS algorithm models the network as a binary graph. There is no weight on the edge to represent the frequency of node encounter or other social relationship attributes. In this way, the detected community is prone to a community composed of nodes with weak social relationships, which is a meaningless community. Therefore, we should consider the dynamics of the network, the physical meaning of the social relationship, the overlapping of the community structure, and the social characteristics of the space-crossing etc. to design a novel community detection algorithm.

4.3 Adaptive Weighted Dynamic Community Detection Algorithm

The above AFOCS is a newly detection algorithm that can handle dynamic and overlapped communities. However, it is only for unweighted graph and has some repeated operations on nodes and edges. Here, for the distributed communication architecture, this section presents an adaptive weighted dynamic community detection algorithm SAWD (Self-Adaptive Weighted Dynamic) based on the user encounter frequency.

First of all, SAWD gives the definitions of communication critical value and weighted density embryo to handle the weighted graph for helping achieve community detection. Using these two definitions can avoid making some low-weight edges form a meaningless community. Then, SAWD classifies the adding or removing nodes or edges into "out-pool" and "in-pool" cases to deal with the dynamic network changes using local information. SAWD has two steps:

(1) At first network snapshot, SAWD use a centralized community initialization algorithm to handle the mobile social network and get the initial weighted community structure;

(2) As time goes by, the structure of the network changes. SAWD will use dynamic tracking algorithms to deal with locally changing community structures.

4.3.1 Dynamic Weighted Graph

We model the mobile social network as a dynamic weighted graph which can be defined as a time sequence of network graph, denoted by $\mathcal{G} = \{G_0, G_1, \ldots, G_t, \ldots\}$, where $G_t = (V_t, E_t, W_t, F_t)$ represents a network snapshot recorded at time t, V_t denotes the set of nodes, $E_t = \{(u, v)|u, v \in V_t\}$ denotes the edge set, $W_t = \{w_{uv}^t \in [0, 1)|u, v \in V_t \text{ and } (u, v) \in E_t\}$ denotes the set of weights on edges at time t, and $F_t : E_t \to W_t$ is a mapping that assigns weights to edges. Both node set and edge set change over time. For a node u, let d_u^t and $N_t(u)$ denote the degree and the set of all its neighbors at time t respectively. Specially, here the following explanation for the definition of w_{uv}^t:

According to the physical movement of the node in the network, let $l_{uv}^t = 1$ represent an encounter between nodes u and v at time $t(0 \leq t < \infty)$. Then, use $\sum_{t=t_{now}-\Delta}^{t_{now}} l_{uv}^t$ to represent the sum of all encounters between nodes u and v from time $t_{now-\Delta}$ to t_{now}; let $\sum_{t=t_{now}-\Delta}^{t_{now}} l_*^t$ represent the sum of the number of encounters of all nodes from time $t_{now-\Delta}$ to t_{now}, and $0 < \Delta < t_{now-\Delta}$. Here define the probability of encounter between nodes u and v at the current time t_{now} as:

$$w_{uv}^{t_{now}} = \sum_{t=t_{now}-\Delta}^{t_{now}} l_{uv}^t \Bigg/ \sum_{t=t_{now}-\Delta}^{t_{now}} l_*^t \qquad (4.1)$$

In order to avoid the asymmetry of the device in detecting the encounter, we assume that $w_{uv}^{t_{now}} = w_{vu}^{t_{now}} = max\{w_{uv}^{t_{now}}, w_{vu}^{t_{now}}\}$. In the following, for the sake of simplicity, and not to confuse the meaning, the symbol t is used to represent the current time t_{now}.

In addition, we set the length of the sliding time window Δ to be a constant, which is an empirical value. According to the literature [23–28], this section uniformly sets the Δ of all algorithms to $6 * 3600$ s.

Table 4.1 Main notations

Notation	Meaning
$\mathcal{C}_t$	The community structure at time t
$N_t(u)$	The set of neighbor labels of node u at time t
$\text{Com}_t(u)$	The set of community labels of node u at time t
$\mathcal{C}_t(u)$	The set of all communities containing node u at time t
x_t	The average communication level at time t
$O_t(u,v)$	The weighted density embryo generated by (u,v) at time t
$\Phi(O_t(u,v))\frac{n!}{r!(n-r)!}$	The weighted density function
$\Gamma\left(C_i^t, C_j^t\right)$	Coupling coefficient
α	The threshold of combining criterion
$a_{u,i}^t$	The local activity value for node u in community i at time t
$\Lambda_t(u)$	The forwarding utility of node u at time t
$\text{SS}_t(u,w)$	The social similarity between node u and w at time t

4.3.2 Community Structure

Let $\mathcal{C}_t = \left\{C_1^t, C_2^t, \ldots, C_k^t\right\}$ denote the network community structure at time t, i.e., a collection of subsets of V_t, where the element $C_i^t \in \mathcal{C}_t$ and its induced subgraph form a community of G_t; k is an integer and represents the number of communities at each network snapshot. Particularly, allow $C_i^t \cap C_j^t \neq \emptyset$, i.e., the communities can overlap with each other. For a node u, let $\text{Com}_t(u)$ denote the set of labels of all communities containing u at time t, i.e., $\left\{C_i^t | i \in \text{Com}_t(u)\right\}$; let $\mathcal{C}_t(u)$ denote the set of all communities containing node u at time t. The community described in this section and the community detected by SAWD community detection algorithms can be called Physical neighborhood community. For the sake of simplicity, this section is collectively referred to as the community. Some notations are listed in Table 4.1.

4.3.3 Initializing Community Structure

In the initial period of community structure, at first, according to Weighted Criterion of Community (Definition 4.3), nodes are classified into different groups, i.e., raw communities. Then, on the basis of Combining Criterion of Communities (Definition

4.5), the highly overlapped raw communities will merge to form an initial weighted community structure.

Definition 4.1 Communication Critical Value

Define the median value of the set of weights $\{W_t\}$ as the communication critical value at time t, denoted by $\{x_t\}$. x_t is important because it can avoid some low weighted edges to form meaningless communities in social networks, i.e., those rarely meeting nodes can not form communities.

Given a communication critical value x_t, we can obtain a spanning subgraph of G_t by deleting edges whose weights are smaller than x_t; we call such spanning subgraph filtered graph, and denote it by $G_t(x_t)$.

Before defining the community, we give a notion called weighted density embryo.

Definition 4.2 Weighted Density Embryo

Given an edge (u, v) at time t, an induced subgraph of $G_t(x_t)$ whose all nodes belong to $N_t(u) \cap N_t(v)$ is called x_t-level weighted density embryo (WDE) generated by (u, v) at time t, denoted by $O_t(u, v; x_t)$.

For brevity, denote the node and edge sets of WDE $O_t(u, v; x_t)$, $O_t(u, v; x_t)$ as $O_t(u, v)$, $V_t(u, v)$ and $E_t(u, v)$, respectively, without confusion.

An example of weighted density embryo $O_t(u, v)$ is depicted in Fig. 4.1a.

In Fig. 4.1a, the grey subgraph shows a weighted density embryo $O_t(u, v)$. Correspondingly, $E_t(u, v)$ is the set of grey lines.

We define the weighted density of WDE $O_t(u, v)$ by

$$\Phi(O_t(u, v)) = \frac{|E_t(u, v)|}{\binom{|V_t(u, v)|}{2}} \tag{4.2}$$

Now, we can give a weighted criterion for judging whether a WDE is a community.

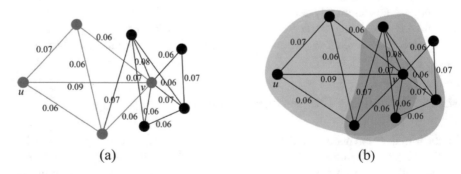

(a)   (b)

Fig. 4.1 Schematic diagram of WDE

Definition 4.3 Weighted Criterion of Community

A WDE $O_t(u, v)$ is a community iff the weighted density satisfies that $\Phi(O_t(u, v)) \geq \delta(O_t(u, v))$, where

$$\delta(O_t(u, v)) = \frac{\binom{|V_t(u, v)|}{2}^{\displaystyle 1 - \frac{1}{\binom{|V_t(u, v)|}{2}}}}{\binom{|V_t(u, v)|}{2}} \tag{4.3}$$

The threshold $\delta(O_t(u, v))$ is an increasing function, a relaxation version of the traditional density threshold, e.g., complete graph. According to Definition 4.3, some nodes and edges can be grouped into different raw communities, but there exist some substructures which are highly overlapped. Then, a combining criterion is necessary to help them merge into large ones. Before proposing the criterion, we give a notion called coupling coefficient.

Definition 4.4 Coupling Coefficient

For two weighted communities, say C_i^t and C_j^t, the coupling coefficient, denoted by $\Gamma\left(C_i^t, C_j^t\right)$, is defined as:

$$\Gamma\left(C_i^t, C_j^t\right) = \frac{\displaystyle\sum_{(u,v)\in C_i^t \cap C_j^t} w_{uv}^t}{\min\left\{\displaystyle\sum_{(u',v')\in C_i^t} w_{u'v'}^t, \displaystyle\sum_{(u'',v'')\in C_j^t} w_{u''v''}^t\right\}} + \frac{\displaystyle\sum_{u\in C_i^t \cap C_j^t} \sum_{v\in C_i^t \cap C_j^t} w_{uv}^t}{\min\left(\displaystyle\sum_{u'\in C_i^t} \sum_{v'\in C_i} w_{u'v'}^t, \displaystyle\sum_{u''\in C_j^t} \sum_{v''\in C_j^t} w_{u''v''}^t\right)} \tag{4.4}$$

The coupling coefficient is comprised of two parts, one is the intra edge weights ratio, and the other is the intra node weights ratio. Based on it, we have

Definition 4.5 Combining Criterion of Communities

Two communities C_i^t and C_j^t should be combined, if their coupling coefficient $\Gamma\left(C_i^t, C_j^t\right) \geq \alpha$, where α is a given threshold.

Note that the parameter α will be determined in the experiment, i.e., we will choose an optimal value of α that makes the community detection have a good effect. Figure 4.1b shows two weighted overlapping communities. The left shadow community is generated by the edge weighted 0.09 and the right shadow community arises from the edge weighted 0.08. Two communities overlap with each other.

The construction of initial communities is shown in Algorithm 4.1.

Algorithm 4.1 Constructing Initial Community Structure

Input: $G_0 = (V_0, E_0, W_0, F_0)$

Output: the set of initial communities C_{init}

1. $x_0 \leftarrow$ apply Definition 4.1 on G_0

2. $E' \leftarrow E_0$

3. **for** each $w_{uv}^t \in W_0$ **do**

4.   **if** $w_{uv}^t < x_0$ **then**

5. $E' \leftarrow E' \setminus (u, v)$

6.   **end if**

7. **end for**

8. sort the edge weight in a descending order from the largest weighted   edge $(u, v) \in E'$

9.   **if** $\mathrm{Com}_t(u) \cap \mathrm{Com}_t(v) = \emptyset$ **then**

10.   find $O_t(u, v)$ according to Definition 4.2

11.   **if** $\Phi, (O_t(u\ v)) \geqslant \delta, (O_t(u\ v))$ and $|V_t(u, v)| \geqslant 4$ **then**

12. $C_{raw} = C_{raw} \cup \{V_t(u, v)\}$

13.   **end if**

14.   **end if**

15. $C_{init} \leftarrow C_{raw}$

16. **end for**

17. **for** $C_i^t, C_j^t \in C_{raw}$ and $!Done$ **do**

18. **if** $\Gamma, (C_i^t\ C_j^t) \geqslant \alpha$

19. $C' \leftarrow$ combine C_i^t and C_j^t

20. $C_{init} = (C_{init} \setminus \{C_i^t, C_j^t\}) \cup \{C'\}$

21. $Done \leftarrow False$

22. **end if**

23. **end for**

4.3.4 Dynamic Tracking Method

After constructing the initial communities, with the time goes by, the edge weights will vary due to strength changes of social relationships, such as new person making friends with each other, user joining in or withdrawing from the entire social network or local communities. So, we need to cope with the dynamic changes. Here, we regard a network as a "pool". Reflected in the weighted graph, the changes can be classified into two types:

(1) The number of nodes changes and the weight of edges also changes, called "out-pool" changes;
(2) The number of nodes does not change but the weight of edges changes, called "in-pool" changes.

  As soon as finding the social changes, the dynamic tracking method can deal with all the changes of nodes and edges simultaneously. The "out-pool" case includes adding foreign nodes to the current social network and removing nodes from the network. The "in-pool" case includes adding edges and removing edges operations. The detailed procedures are presented in Algorithms 4.3–4.6. Some explanations about the tracking method are described as follows:

(1) Through checking the sets V_t and E_t, we can find the insertion or deletion actions of nodes or edges. Especially with varying edge weights, the adding and removing edges are found by Algorithm 4.2.
(2) For simplicity, we assume that every node has a community label set $\text{Com}_t(u)$, including solitary nodes. In final experiment results, if we find the number of nodes in a community is only one, we will discard it.
(3) We distinguish two types of nodes, one is the foreign node with its $\text{Com}_t(u) = \emptyset$ and its $N_t(u) = \emptyset$, i.e., it is not in the current network pool. The other is the solitary node with its $\text{Com}_t(u) \neq \emptyset$ and its $N_t(u) = \emptyset$, i.e., it is in the current network pool. Let CS^t denote the set of solitary nodes at time t.

Algorithm 4.2 Finding Changed Edges

Input: the community structures G_{t-1} and G_t

Output: the set of ΔE_t

17. $x_{t-1} \leftarrow$ apply Definition 4.1 on G_{t-1}

18. $E'_{t-1} \leftarrow E_{t-1}$

19.   **for each** $w_{uv}^t \in W_{t-1}$ **do**

20.   **if** $w_{uv}^t < x_{t-1}$ **then**

21. $E'_{t-1} \leftarrow E'_{t-1} \setminus (u,v)$

22.   **end if**

23.   **end for**

24. $x_t \leftarrow$ apply Definition 4.1 on G_t

25. $E'_t \leftarrow E_t$

26.   **for each** $w_{uv}^t \in W_t$ **do**

27.   **if** $w_{uv}^t < x_t$ **then**

28. $E'_t \leftarrow E'_t \setminus (u,v)$

29.   **end if**

30.   **end for**

31.   compare E'_{t-1} and E'_t

32.   get the set of changed edges ΔE_t

Next, the dynamic tracking algorithm in this section will be divided into the following two cases: the "out pool" case and the "in pool" case.

"Out-Pool" Case: The "out-pool" case contains tracking foreign nodes algorithm and tracking missing nodes algorithm.

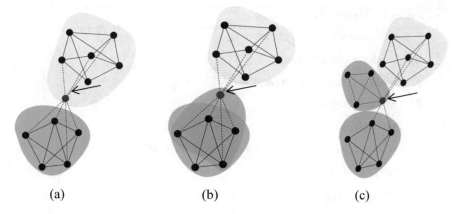

  (a)   (b)   (c)

Fig. 4.2 Tracking foreign nodes

In Fig. 4.2: The red node is a foreign node with adding edges depicted by dotted lines. In Fig. 4.2a, the foreign node joins its adjacent community. In Fig. 4.2b, the foreign node forms new communities with neighbors. In Fig. 4.2c, the foreign node unites the solitary nodes to form a new community.

Here analyze Algorithm 4.3 about adding foreign nodes case. There are two possibilities, one is the node added without edges, and the other is added with edges. If node u satisfies the former case, we simply join u to the current community structure. If node u is the latter case, it becomes a little complicated and needs three possible operations:

(1) Because u is added with edges, it may join to its adjacent communities, i.e., step 11–15;
(2) Uniting its neighbors, the foreign node u may form new communities, i.e., step 17–19;
(3) Considering the set of solitary nodes, node u may shape new communities, i.e., step 23–26.

Algorithm 4.3 Tracking Foreign Nodes

Input: the current community structure C_t

Output: the updated structure C_{t+1}

1. **if** node u is added without edges, **then**
2. $CS^t = CS^t \cup \{u\}$
3. **else** u with edges
4. $x_t \leftarrow$ apply Definition 4.1 on the community graph of C_t
5.   **for each** $w_{uv}^t \in W_t$ **do**
6.   **if** $w_{uv}^t < x_t$ **then**
7. $E_t \leftarrow E_t \setminus (u,v)$
8.   **end if**
9.   **end for**
10.   update the set of $N_t(u)$
11. $C_1^t, C_2^t, \ldots, C_k^t \leftarrow$ adjacent communities of u
12.   **for** $i = 1$ to k **do**
13. $O_t(u,v) \leftarrow$ the generated subgraph of $G_t(x_t)$ based on $C_i^t \cup \{u\}$
14.   **if** $\Phi(O_t(u,v)) \geqslant \delta(O_t(u,v))$ and $|V_t(u,v)| \geqslant 4$ **then**
15. $C_i^t \leftarrow C_i^t \cup \{u\}$
16.   **else**
17. $O_t(u,v) \leftarrow$ the induced subgraph of $G_t(x_t)$ based on $C_i^t \cap N_t(u)$
18.   **if** $\Phi(O_t(u\ v)) \geqslant \delta(O_t(u\ v))$ and $|V_t(u,v)| \geqslant 4$ **then**
19.   define $V_t(u,v)$ of $O_t(u,v)$ as a new community C'
20.   **end if**
21.   **end if**
22.   **end for**
23.   **for** $v \in CS^t$ and $\text{Com}_t(u) \cap \text{Com}_t(v) = \varnothing$ **do**
24. $O_t(u,v) \leftarrow$ the generated subgraph of $G_t(x_t)$ based on $N_t(u) \cap N_t(v)$
25.   **if** $\Phi(O_t(u\ v)) \geqslant \delta(O_t(u\ v))$ and $|V_t(u,v)| \geqslant 4$ **then**

26.   define $V_t(u,v)$ of $O_t(u,v)$ as a new community C'

27.   **end if**

28.   **end for**

29. **end if**

30. merge overlapping communities on $C_1^t, C_2^t, \ldots, C_k^t$ and C'

31. update C_t to C_{t+1}

Secondly, Fig. 4.3 shows the relevant diagram of the algorithm for Tracking Missing Node. The red node represents the missing node with removing edges depicted by dotted lines. In Fig. 4.3a, the remaining structure can maintain the original shape. In Fig. 4.3b, the remains form two new communities.

Analyze the Algorithm 4.4 about tracking missing nodes. There are several possibilities for operation:

1. If node u is a solitary node or $d_u = 1$, we simply remove the node from the current community structure.
2. Otherwise, there are two operations:

    (1) One is the remaining structure can maintain the original community, i.e., step 10–13;
    (2) The other is the remains may form new communities, i.e., step 15–17.

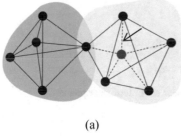
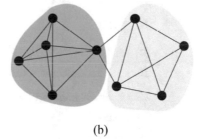

           (a)   (b)

Fig. 4.3 Tracking missing nodes

Algorithm 4.4 Tracking Missing Nodes

Input: the current community structure C_t

Output: the updated structure C_{t+1}

1. **if** u is a solitary node or $d_u^t = 1$ **then**

2. $C_t \leftarrow C_t \setminus C_t(u)$

3. **else**

4. $x_t \leftarrow$ apply Definition 4.1 on the community graph of C_t

5.   **for** each $w_{uv}^t \in W_t$ **do**

6.   **if** $w_{uv}^t < x_t$ **then**

7. $E_t \leftarrow E_t \setminus (u, v)$

8.   **end if**

9.   **end for**

10. **for** each subset C_i^t in $C_t(u)$ or $C_t(v)$ **do**

11. $O_t(u, v) \leftarrow$ the generated subgraph of the filter graph $G_t(x_t)$ based   on the remaining nodes in one subset C_i^t of $C_t(u)$

12.   **if** $\Phi(O_t(u, v)) \geqslant \delta(O_t(u, v))$ and $|V_t(u, v)| \geqslant 4$ **then**

13. $C_i^t \leftarrow V_t(u \; v)$

14.   **else**

15.   sort the weight of $E_t(u, v)$ in a descending order

16.   from the largest weighted edge $(u, v) \in E_t(u, v)$

17.   do Algorithm 4.1 step 10-15 to gain new communities sequence C'

18.   **end if**

19. **end for**

20. **end if**

21. merge overlapping communities

22. update C_t to C_{t+1}

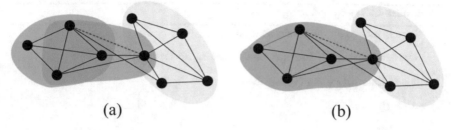

Fig. 4.4   Tracking adding edges

"In-Pool" Case: The "in-pool" case contains tracking adding edges algorithm and tracking removing edges algorithm.

Firstly, Fig. 4.4 shows the relevant diagram of adding edges algorithm. The red dotted line represents an adding edge. In Fig. 4.4a, the new edge shapes a new community. In Fig. 4.4b, for an adding edge, one of its endpoints joins the community of the opposite side.

Here discuss Algorithm 4.5 about adding edges case. There are two possibilities, one is two endpoints of the adding edge are in the same community, the other is in the different communities. In the former case, community structure does not change, because adding edges increases the weighted density of communities. In the latter case, we further divide it into two operations:

(1) If the adding edges come from nodes in the current network, we decide whether the edge (u, v) can form a new community, i.e., step 4–8. Besides, we still need to judge whether the node u or v will join the community of the opposite side, i.e., step 10–15.
(2) If the adding edges come from the new foreign nodes, we only need to process the edge (u, v), i.e., judging whether to shape a new community or not, described in step 19–21. Some operations about two endpoints have been done in Algorithm 4.3.

Algorithm 4.5 Tracking Adding Edges

Input: the current community structure C_t

Output: the set of initial community C_{init} the updated structure C_{t+1}

1.   **if** $Com_t(u) \cap Com_t(v) \neq \varnothing$ **then**

2. $C_{t+1} \leftarrow C_t$

3.   **else**

4.   **if** $Com_t(u) \neq \varnothing$ and $Com_t(v) \neq \varnothing$ **then**

5.   **if** $Com_t(u) \cap Com_t(v) = \varnothing$ **then**

6. $O_t(u,v) \leftarrow$ the induced subgraph of $G_t(x_t)$ based on $N_t(u) \cap N_t(v)$

7.   **if** $\Phi(O_t(u\ v)) \geqslant \delta(O_t(u\ v))$ and $|V_t(u,v)| \geqslant 4$ **then**

8.   define $V_t(u,v)$ of $O_t(u,v)$ as a new community C'

9.   **else**

10.   **for** each subset C_i^t in $C_t(u)$ or $C_t(v)$ **do**

11. $O_t(u,v) \leftarrow$ the induced subgraph of $G_t(x_t)$ based on one   subset C_i^t

      of $C_t(u) \cup \{v\}$ or $C_t(v) \cup \{u\}$

12.   **if** $\Phi(O_t(u\ v)) \geqslant \delta(O_t(u\ v))$ and $|V_t(u,v)| \geqslant 4$ **then**

13. $C_i^t \leftarrow C_i^t \cup \{v\}$ or $C_i^t \leftarrow C_i^t \cup \{u\}$

14.   **end if**

15.   **end for**

16.   **end if**

17.   **end if**

18.   **end if**

19.   **if** $(Com_t(u) = \varnothing$ and $Com_t(v) \neq \varnothing)$ or $(Com_t(v) = \varnothing$ and $Com_t(u) \neq \varnothing)$

20.   only do Algorithm 4.5 step 5-8

21.   **end if**

22. **end if**

23. merge overlapping communities

24. update C_t to C_{t+1}

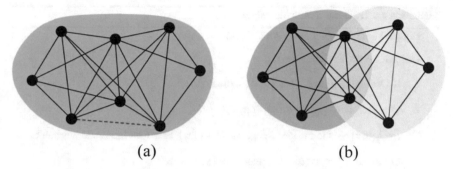

(a)   (b)

Fig. 4.5 Tracking removing edges

Secondly, Fig. 4.5 shows the relevant diagram of tracking removing edges. The red dotted line represents a removing edge. In Fig. 4.5a, the remaining structure can still maintain. In Fig. 4.5b, the remaining structure forms two new communities.

Here analyze Algorithm 4.6 about tracking removing edges case. There are also two possibilities, one is two endpoints of the removing edge are in the same community, the other is in the different communities. In the former case, the community structure does not change. In the latter case, we only need to concern the case that the removing edges come from the existing networks. If the removing edges come from the missing nodes, the corresponding operations have been done in Algorithm 4.4. Therefore, in Algorithm 4.6, there are two possible operations:

(1) We judge whether the remaining structure can still maintain or not, i.e., step 2–5;
(2) Otherwise, the remains can form some new communities, i.e., step 7–9.

Algorithm 4.6 Tracking Removing Edges

Input: the current community structure C_t

Output: the updated structure C_{t+1}

1. **if** $\text{Com}_t(u) \neq \varnothing$ and $\text{Com}_t(v) \neq \varnothing$ **then**

2.   **for** each subset C_i^t in $C_t(u)$ or in $C_t(v)$ **do**

3. $O_t(u,v) \leftarrow$ the induced subgraph of $G_t(x_t)$ based on the remaining nodes in one subset C_i^t of $C_t(u)$ after removing (u,v)

4.   **if** $\Phi\{O_t(u\ v)\} \geqslant \delta\{O_t(u\ v)\}$ and $|V_t(u,v)| \geqslant 4$ **then**

5. $C_i^t \leftarrow V_t(u,v)$

6.   **else**

7.   sort the weight in $E_t(u,v)$ in a descending order from the largest weighted edge $(u,v) \in E_t(u,v)$

8.   do Algorithm 4.1 step 10-15 to gain new communities sequence C'

9.   **end if**

10.   **end for**

11. **end if**

12. merge overlapping communities

13. update C_t to C_{t+1}

4.3.5 The Complexity of Community Detection Method SAWD

Lemma 1 *The time complexity of Algorithm 4.1 is* $O(M + M \log M + N^2)$.

Proof Assuming there are N nodes and M edges in a social weighted graph. First, time complexity of getting the median of the set of weights W_t is $O(M)$. Next, because there are M edges which require to compare with the median, the time complexity of comparison is $O(M)$. Then, for Step 6, time complexity of sorting the weighted edges is $O(M\log M)$. Finally, from Step 7 to Step 12, we have to find the intersection of $N_t(u)$ and $N_t(v)$. Because $|N_t(u)| + |N_t(v)| = d^t(u) + d^t(v)$, the time complexity for each weighted edge is $\sum_{u \in V_t} d^t(u) = 2M$. From Step 13 to Step 17, suppose there are N_0 raw communities in C_{raw} at Step 12, according to Lemma 11.8 in literature [29], when the number of nodes in the intersection of any two communities is upper bounded by a constant, the number of raw communities N_0 is $O(N)$, so the time complexity of combining is $O(N^2)$. Therefore, the total time complexity of Algorithm 4.1 is $O(M + M \log M + N^2)$.

Lemma 2 *The time complexity of Algorithm 4.2 is $O(M)$.*

Proof First, time complexity of getting the median of the set of weights is $O(M)$. Next, because there are M edges which require to compare with the median, the time complexity of comparisons is $O(M)$. Finally, the time complexity of getting the difference set of the two edge sets at time slot $t-1$ and t is $O(M)$. Therefore, the total time complexity of Algorithm 4.2 is $O(M)$.

For Algorithms 4.3–4.6, because they locally deal with the network changes (including judging a new community and combining the overlapped communities), the time complexity of them is upper bounded by Algorithm 4.1.

4.3.6 The Goodness of Fit for SAWD Detection Method

The goodness of fit for the community detection is measured by NMI score $N(X|Y)$ (Normalized Mutual Information) between the proposed detection method results X and the ground truth/the benchmark results Y. NMI score $N(X|Y)$ is an entropy method in information theory. The higher the NMI score is, the more similar the two community partitions are. Usually, if the experimental dataset has the ground truth result itself, ground truth will be chosen as the comparison object; if the experimental dataset has not the ground truth itself, the benchmark result will be used as the comparison object. We choose benchmark-LFR [30] to validate the goodness of fit for our SAWD detection method.

(1) **Parameter Choosing for Combining Threshold**

Our detection algorithm SAWD does not need any prior user-input information about communities, e.g., the number of communities. The only parameter required to be fixed is the combining threshold value α. An optimal value α of is associated with the goodness of fit for our SAWD detection method. By the following benchmark experiments, we determine an appropriate value for α to guarantee a good detection effect. Once gained, it will be used in the step of constructing initial static community and does not need to change its value in future dynamic operations. Moreover, it is only concerned with the detection method, not with the real mobile social networks.

(2) Network Generation for NMI Experiments

We choose LFR undirected and weighted benchmark to generate a synthetic social network. That is to say it can produce undirected weighted graphs with possible overlapping communities and satisfies the power-law degree distribution. Here are some of the parameters set as follows: exponent for the weight distribution $\beta = 1.5$ and the number of memberships for the overlapping nodes $om = 2$. We freeze the number of nodes $N = 1000$, topology mixing parameters $\mu_t = 0.1$ or $\mu_t = 0.5$ and the number of overlapping nodes $on = 100$ or $on = 300$. Then, we vary the weighted mixing parameter μ_w from 0–0.6 to find the best value of α. In particular, the weighted hybrid parameter μ_w represents the ratio of the strength of the node to its external nodes and the total strength of the node in the network. The larger μ_w is, the smaller the strength of the node in its community. The smaller strength will increase the difficulty of community detection.

(3) Evaluation Metric

We use NMI overlapping version in literature [31] as an evaluation metric. It is one of the most important entropy measures in information theory. $N(X|Y)$ can be interpreted as the average relative lack of information to infer random variable X given Y, $N(X|Y) \in [0, 1]$. The higher the NMI score is, the more similar the two community partitions are. If $(X|Y)$ equals 1, it means the two kinds of community partitions are exactly coincident. Therefore, we make our detection algorithm SAWD as X, the LFR benchmark as Y.

(4) Experiment Results and Analysis

From large numbers of tests, we obtain the combining threshold α ranging from 0–1.8. We select the representative values 0.4–1.4 to analyze an appropriate value for α. Because in this scope, the NMI score shows better than in other scopes.

In the following, four network scenarios are obtained by setting parameters, so that the optimal α value is observed. At first, set the topology mixing parameters μ_t. The small value of μ_t means a clear mixing topology and a dense community inner structure. Secondly, set the number parameter of overlapping nodes. The small on represents that the separation between communities is relatively large. The four network scenarios are set as follows: (a) $\mu_t = 0.1$ and $on = 100$; (b) $\mu_t = 0.1$ and $on = 300$; (c) $\mu_t = 0.5$ 且 $on = 100$; (d) $\mu_t = 0.5$ 且 $on = 300$. In these four scenarios, α varied from 0.4 to 1.4 at 0.1 interval. The final appropriate value of α (i.e. $\alpha = 0.6$) was obtained. When $\alpha = 0.6$, the NMI score is the biggest among all the NMI score. NMI achieves 0.86 approximately on average when $\alpha = 0.6$. It means that the quality of the detected communities is good to close to the benchmark LFR.

4.3.7 Problem Discussion

(1) Choice about the Communication Critical Value

With continual adding and removing actions, the communication critical value x_t is generated by calculating the median value of the weight set W_t at each snapshot. This method can tackle both uniform and power-law distribution. However, it may have some more precise mathematical methods than ours to deal with the problem, which can be studied in the future.

(2) Algorithm Deployment

The premise of deployment implementation is to know what information a node can get and how to obtain it. A node has perfect knowledge of its neighbors and some local approximation knowledge captured by its neighbors. Some required information is transferred through node to node.

SAWD community detection is performed in a centralized manner, and community initialization is performed only once globally. However, the latter dynamic tracking algorithm is a partial execution, eliminating the complexity of global repeated replacement. The base station periodically pushes the community detection result to all nodes to complete the global control work.

4.4 Space-Crossing Community Detection

In Sect. 4.3 above, we studied the physical neighborhoods and explored the physical proximity of users. However, it is more common in social networks that two users of a friend relationship with far geographical distance communicate frequently through public infrastructure, such as base station (BS) and access point (AP). Then the previous community structure is not enough to deal with this situation [8].

Traditionally, a community is defined as a group of tightknit nodes with more internal than external links. In social networks, such links can be clearly established between friends based on social relationships, and the distance between friends can be long or short geographically. But on communication-based social graphs, these links are often obtained based on the encounter of direct connected physical devices. For example, one link represents the Bluetooth or WIFI connection of the mobile phones or portable tablets. Faced to the situation, this section expands the traditional community concept. Let's take the infrastructure AP as an example to discuss the following. Considering some long-distance nodes without direct links among them could also communicate frequently through APs. Thus, the definition of community changes in nature. The links within the community are no longer the former direct communication links, but should also include some long-distance links with strong communication capabilities. Then, we give a new definition of community in this hybrid communication architecture with access points called space-crossing community. The space-crossing community reflects the aspects of the AP support and the social community attribute simultaneously. This section will introduce the detection method for space-crossing communities in detail. At first, a lightweight merge criterion CA is given, which determines the initial space-crossing communities according to the AP network load. Secondly, a local merge criterion CB is also given to adapt to the subsequent dynamic community detection needs.

4.4.1 Descriptive Definition of Space-Crossing Community

In a hybrid underlying network, each mobile user and static AP can be viewed as an independent participant. First, in view of the frequent interaction (physical proximity) among the mobile user-mobile user and the mobile user-APs, the user and the AP nodes will form a partial dense group according to the interaction frequency, which we call the physical neighboring community, i.e. the community detected by the SAWD algorithm in Chap. 4.

Then, some remote nodes located in different physical neighboring communities containing APs can communicate through the AP connection. We merge these physical neighboring communities that use AP nodes for convenient communication to form a group that spans geospatial space and call it a space-crossing community.

Whether it is a physical neighboring community or a space-crossing community, it represents a structure with relatively outstanding communication capabilities. We allow space-crossing communities can overlap with each other.

4.4.2 Space-Crossing Community Detection Algorithm

In the dynamic and hybrid underlying networking environment, we detect the space-crossing communities in two basic ways. First, according to our dynamic graph, we use the SAWD method in Sect. 4.3 to obtain some physical proximity communities at each time slot. Second, using combination criterion CA (at time slot t_1) or combination criterion CB (in all subsequent time slots), we get final space-crossing communities at each time slot. Then, we have two sequences. One is a dynamic time sequence of physical proximity communities, denoted by $\{\mathcal{PP}_0, \mathcal{PP}_1, \cdots, \mathcal{PP}_t, \cdots\}$. Let $ComPP_t(i)$ represent the i-th physical proximity community at time t in $\mathcal{PP}_t$. The other is a dynamic time sequence of space-crossing communities, denoted by $\{\mathcal{SC}_0, \mathcal{SC}_1, \cdots, \mathcal{SC}_t, \cdots\}$. Let $ComSC_t(i)$ represent the i-th space-crossing community at time t in $\mathcal{SC}_t$.

At the initial network snapshot, based on network graph G_1 (the nodes in G_1 contain APs and mobile users) defined in Sect. 4.3.1, the community initialization algorithm of SAWD is applied to obtain the initial set of physical proximity communities $\mathcal{PP}_1$.

We give a combination criterion CA to obtain the initial set of space-crossing communities $\mathcal{SC}_1$. Combination criterion CA is described as following steps:

1. System dispatches the sequence numbers (natural number) to each AP. Each AP maintains a mark (undone) which means the belonging community did not apply yet the CA combination operation at current time slot.
2. Suppose that, for simplicity, according to ascending the sequence number (from small to large sequence number), several APs are randomly grouped into different connected components in which APs are connected one by one (a chain).
3. A certain AP r will first check in its left order AP r'(i.e., the sequence number of r' is smaller than r):

    (1)   if the AP r' has a link with AP r;
    (2)   the mark of combination criterion CA of AP r' is undone;
    (3)   they are not in the same physical proximity communities.

4. If the above three conditions are satisfied, combine the physical proximity communities containing r and r' into a new space-crossing community; and set the mark of combination criterion CA of AP r and r' as done.
5. Otherwise, the same operations (3) and (4) will be done for the AP r' in its right order (the sequence number of r' is larger than r). Therefore, assuming there are R APs in a certain connected component of APs, the number of space-crossing communities will be at most $\frac{R}{2}$. Pseudo-codes of combination criterion CA in simulation are shown in Algorithm 4.7.

Algorithm 4.7 Combination Criterion CA

Input: The physical proximity community structure $\mathcal{PP}_1$ at time slot t_1.

Output: The space-crossing community structure $\mathcal{SC}_1$ at time slot t_1.

1.   int OCA [the number of APs]

2.   **for**$(k = 0; k < |OCA|; k + +)$ **do**

3.   set $OCA[K] = 0$

         /* 0 denotes the $k + 1$-th AP have not done CA combination */

4.   **end for**

5. $\mathcal{SC}_1 \leftarrow \mathcal{PP}_1$;

6.   for an AP r

7.   **if** (the r-th and the $r - 1$-th APs are not in the same physical proximity communities && the $r - 1$-th AP has a communication link with the r-th AP && $OCA[r - 2] \neq 1$) **then**

8.   let LA denote the set of the labels of physical proximity communities containing the r-th AP;

9.   Let LB denote the set of the labels of physical proximity communities containing the $r - 1$-th AP;

10.   **for** $(i = 0; i < |LA|; i + +)$ **do**

11.   **for** $(j = 0; i < |LB|; j + +)$ **do**

12.   C $\leftarrow$combine $ComPP_1(LA[i])$ and $ComPP_1(LB[j])$

13. $\mathcal{SC}_1 \leftarrow \{\mathcal{SC}_1 \backslash \{ComPP_1(LA[i])\} \cup \{ComPP_1(LB[j])\}\} \cup \{C\}$

14.   **end for**

15.   **end for**

16. $OCA[r - 1] = 1; OCA[r - 2] = 1$

17. **else**

18.   **if**(the r-th and $r + 1$-th APs are not in the same physical proximity communities && the $r - 1$-th AP has a communication link with the r-th AP && $OCA[r] \neq 1$) **then**

19.   The same operations (Step 8 - Step 13) are done for r-th AP and $r + 1$-th AP ;

20. $OCA[r - 1] = 1; OCA[r] = 1$;

21.   **end if**

22. **end if**

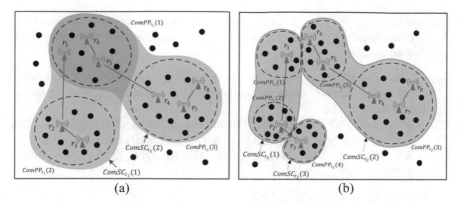

Fig. 4.6 Schematic diagram of space-crossing community detection algorithm

Figure 4.6 shows a schematic diagram of the space-crossing community detection algorithm. The solid line in the figure represents the wired link between APs; the virtual circle out of the physical neighboring community; the shadow covers the space-crossing communities. Figure 4.6a gives an intuitive illustration of the combination criterion CA in time slot t_1. Suppose that, after finished the community initialization algorithm of SAWD, we have three physical proximity communities $ComPP_t(1) \sim ComPP_t(3)$, which contain mobile users and APs. There are three connected components of APs ($r_1 - r_2 - r_3, r_4 - r_5 - r_6, r_7 - r_8$). According to the combination criterion CA, in the first connected component, the space-crossing communities $ComSC_t(1)$ can be formed by $r_1 - r_2$; in the second connected component, the space-crossing communities $ComSC_t(2)$ can be formed by $r_4 - r_5$. Since r_7 and r_8 are already in the same physical proximity community, there is no need to apply the combination criterion CA.

For subsequent time slot $t (2 \leq t < \infty)$, based on $\mathcal{PP}_{t-1}$, the dynamic tracking algorithm of SAWD is applied to obtain the set of physical proximity communities $\mathcal{PP}_t$. In the algorithm SAWD, dynamic network changes are classified into four simple actions: adding new nodes, adding edges, removing nodes and removing edges. For each kind of changes, Algorithms 4.3–4.6 in this chapter give corresponding methods to adaptively find the updated physical proximity communities.

Based on above $\mathcal{PP}_t(2 \leq t < \infty)$, we apply combination criterion CB to obtain the set of space-crossing communities $\mathcal{SC}_t(2 \leq t < \infty)$. Combination criterion CB is described as follows.

(1) At time slot $t(2 \leq t < \infty)$, each AP maintains an initial mark (undone), meaning that the community did not yet apply the CB combination operation at the current time slot.

(2) When a certain AP r whose mark of combination criterion CA is done finds that the size of its belonging physical proximity communities changes.

(3) A certain AP r will first check in its left order AP r'(i.e., the sequence number of r' is smaller than r):

① if the AP r' has a link with AP r;
② the mark of combination criterion CB of AP r' is undone;
③ they are not in the same physical proximity communities.

(4) If the above three conditions are satisfied, combine (update) the physical proximity communities containing r and r' into a new space-crossing community; and set the mark of combination criterion CB of AP r and r' as done.

(5) Otherwise, the same operations (3) and (4) will be done for the AP r' in its right order (the sequence number of r' is larger than r).

The combination criterion CB adaptively and locally combines (updates) the changed physical proximity communities into new space-crossing communities as network evolves. Pseudo-codes of combination criterion CB in simulation are shown in Algorithm 4.8.

Algorithm 4.8 Combination Criterion CB

Input: The physical proximity community structure $\mathcal{PP}_t(2 \leq t < \infty)$

Output: The space-crossing community structure $\mathcal{SC}_t(2 \leq t < \infty)$

1. $\mathcal{SC}_t \leftarrow \mathcal{PP}_t$
2. int OCB[the number of APs];
3. **for** $(k = 0; k < |OCB|; k + +)$ **do**
4.   set $OCB[K] = 0;$

    /* 0 denotes the $k + 1$-th AP have not done CB combination */

5. **end for**
6. **if** (the size of physical proximity community containing r-th AP changes in $\mathcal{PP}_t$ && $OCA[r - 1] = 1$) **then**
7.   **if** (the r-th AP and $r - 1$-th AP has a communication link && they are not in the same physical proximity communities && $OCB[r - 2] \neq 1$) **then**
8.   combine the physical proximity communities containing r-th AP and the physical proximity communities containing $r - 1$-th AP to form new space-crossing communities;
9.   set $OCB[r - 1] = 1$ and $OCB[r - 2] = 1;$
10.   **else**
11.   **if** (the r-th AP and $r + 1$-th AP are not in the same physical proximity communities && the $r + 1$-th AP has a communication link with the r-th AP && $OCB[r] \neq 1$) **then**
12.   the same operations (Step 8-13) are done for r-th AP and $r + 1$-th AP;
13. $OCB[r] = 1$ and $OCB[r - 1] = 1;$
14.   **end if**
15.   **end if**
16. **end if**
17. update $\mathcal{SC}_t;$

Figure 4.6b illustrates the combination criterion CB at time slot t_2. Based on Fig. 4.6a, we suppose that four kinds of network changes (adding new nodes, adding edges, removing nodes and removing edges) have taken place. After finished the dynamic tracking algorithm of SAWD, we have a new physical proximity community structure containing $ComPP_t(1) \sim ComPP_t(5)$. We find that the physical proximity communities where APs r_1, r_2, r_3, r_5, r_6 belong to have changed. Therefore, using combination criterion CB, in Fig. 4.6b, due to r_1 and r_2 , $ComPP_t(1)$ and $ComPP_t(2)$ are locally combined to form a new space-crossing community

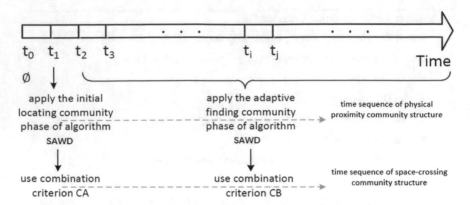

Fig. 4.7 Different methods applied at different time phases

$ComSC_t(1)$; due to r_5, $ComPP_t(3)$ and $ComPP_t(5)$ are also locally combined to form a new space-crossing community $ComSC_t(2)$.

Figure 4.7 shows the call order of different algorithms and combination criteria at different time phases in space-crossing community detection. Two dash arrows show the results of two basic ways. It can be summarized as follows.

(1) At time slot t_0 (initial time slot), the graph is null.
(2) At time slot t_1, according to the cumulative contacts among devices between time slot t_0 and time slot t_1, we obtain graph G_1. Based on the social graph G_1, by using initial community phase of algorithm SAWD, we obtain $\mathcal{PP}_1$.
(3) Based on $\mathcal{PP}_1$, we use combination criterion CA to obtain $\mathcal{SC}_1$.
(4) Then, at time slot t_2, since the social graph changes, by using dynamic tracking algorithm of SAWD, based on $\mathcal{PP}_1$, we obtain $\mathcal{PP}_2$.
(5) Based on $\mathcal{PP}_2$, we use combination criterion CB to obtain $\mathcal{SC}_2$.
(6) For time slot t_3 to infinity, we repeatedly do step (4) and step (5) to get $\{\mathcal{PP}_{3'}\mathcal{PP}_{4'}\}$ and $\{\mathcal{SC}_{3'}\mathcal{SC}_{4'}\ldots\}$ in space-crossing community detection.

The combination criteria CA and CB are relatively simple and practicable criterions for merging community structures. The idea of coupled combination mainly guarantees that the APs will not bear much overhead for the combination workload. In real application, based on AP communication load, a more complex and alternative combination criterion can be introduced in Sect. 4.4.3.

4.4.3 Discussion of Combination Criterion

In real application, each AP has records of the number of sessions that happened through the AP itself and the source-destination pairs of the sessions. Here, we give an alternative method of the combination criterion, called load clique expanding.

1. The rules that should be kept in load clique expanding method are

   (1) Let the APs joining the physical proximity community combination benefit largest (i.e., clique maximization) and balance the workload.
   (2) Let physical proximity communities in which their members often communicate with each other through the containing APs combine into space-crossing communities.

2. The load clique expanding method is described in the following steps.

   (1) For each AP connected component, put the existing APs in a certain AP connected component into a temporary set TS;
   (2) Randomly select one AP in set TS, and put it into put it into a clique set KS;
   (3) Choose another AP r_{new} in set TS having wire or wireless links with all existing APs in clique set KS in the network;
   (4) Calculate the AP Load and Link Load;

   Assuming that, at time t, in the existing clique set KS, there are r APs in r different physical proximity communities with the number of members $m_1, m_2, \ldots, m_r$ respectively. In clique set KS, the AP LOAD of AP r_i is defined as $c(i, t) \cdot \binom{m_i}{2}$. The LINK LOAD between AP r_i and AP r_j is defined as $d(i, j, t) \cdot m_i \cdot m_j$. Coefficient $c(i, t)$ denotes the average session happening ratio through r_i in its belonging physical proximity community before time t. Coefficient $d(i, j, t)$ denotes the average session happening ratio between AP r_i and r_j before time t and the source destination pairs are in AP r_i 's and r_j 's belonging physical proximity communities.

   (5) For each AP r_i in clique set KS, if $d(i, new, t) \cdot m_i \cdot m_{new}$ is beyond $max\left\{c(i, t) \cdot \binom{m_i}{2}, c(new, t) \cdot \binom{m_{new}}{2}\right\}$, then put the new AP r_{new} into the clique set KS.
   (6) Repeat step 3.–5., until the clique set KS will not change. Then, a clique set of APs forms.

   After using the load clique expanding method, at each time slot, we can obtain several cliques of APs in the network. According to these cliques, we combine the physical proximity communities that contain the APs in the same clique to form new space-crossing communities.

4.5 Application Discussion

Community detection helps to clarify the relationship between network nodes. It establishes a mapping between the underlying communication architecture and the logical relationship of nodes. On one hand, community detection can feed back to the social based routing algorithm in Chap. 3. The discovered node relationship can directly associate with the underlying physical communication and speed up the efficiency of the routing. On the other hand, community detection technology can help improve the route recommendation service in Chap. 7 in this book. In the route recommendation service, the relationship between users, physical location, and time needs to be clarified. This relationship mining can be enhanced through the community detection technology.

References

1. M. Girvan, M.E.J. Newman, Community structure in social and biological networks. Proc. Natl. Acad. Sci. **99**(12), 7821–7826 (2002)
2. M.A. Porter, J. Onnela, P.J. Mucha, Communities in networks. Not. AMS **56**(9), 1082–1097 (2009)
3. N. Kayastha, D. Niyato, P. Wang et al., Applications, architectures, and protocol design issues for mobile social networks: a survey. Proc. IEEE **99**(12), 2130–2158 (2011)
4. J. Changjun, C. Hongzhong, Y. Chungang et al., *A Adaptive Clustering Method and System Based on Aggregation Coefficient*. 201410512802.0 (2014)
5. L. Zhong, *Research on Data Forwarding Protocol Design and Performance Analysis of Mobile Social Networks*. Tongji University Doctoral thesis (2015)
6. Z. Li, C. Wang, S. Yang et al., LASS: local-activity and social-similarity based data forwarding in mobile social networks. IEEE Trans. Parallel Distrib. Syst. **26**(1), 174–184 (2015)
7. Z. Li, C. Wang, S. Yang et al., Space-crossing: community-based data forwarding in mobile social networks under the hybrid communication architecture. IEEE Trans. Wirel. Commun. **14**(9), 4720–4727 (2015)
8. S. Fortunato, Community detection in graphs. Phys. Rep. **486**(3), 75–174 (2010)
9. A. Lancichinetti, S. Fortunato, Community detection algorithms: a comparative analysis. Phys. Rev. E **80**(5), 056117 (2009)
10. M.E.J. Newman, M. Girvan, Finding and evaluating community structure in networks. Phys. Rev. E **69**(2), 026113 (2004)
11. M.E.J. Newman, Analysis of weighted networks. Phys. Rev. E **70**(5), 056131 (2004)
12. E. Leicht, M.E.J. Newman, Community structure in directed networks. Phys. Rev. Lett. **100**(11), 118703 (2008)
13. A. Clauset, M.E.J. Newman, C. Moore, Finding community structure in very large networks. Phys. Rev. E **70**(6), 066111 (2004)
14. R. Guimera, L.A.N. Amaral, Functional cartography of complex metabolic networks. Nature **433**(7028), 895–900 (2005)
15. V.D. Blondel, J. Guillaume, R. Lambiotte et al., Fast unfolding of communities in large networks. J. Stat. Mech.: Theory Exp. **2008**(10), 10008 (2008)
16. M. Rosvall, C.T. Bergstrom, Maps of random walks on complex networks reveal community structure. Proc. Natl. Acad. Sci. **105**(4), 1118–1123 (2008)
17. G. Palla, I. Derenyi, I.J. Farkas et al., Uncovering the overlapping community structure of complex networks in nature and society. Nature **435**(7043), 814–818 (2005)
18. P. Hui, E. Yoneki, S.Y. Chan et al., *Distributed Community Detection in Delay Tolerant Networks* (Kyoto, Japan, Proc. ACM MobiArch, 2007), p. 7
19. N.P. Nguyen, T.N. Dinh, S. Tokala et al., *Overlapping Communities in Dynamic Networks: Their Detection and Mobile Applications* (Las Vegas, Nevada, USA, Proc. ACM MobiCom, 2011), pp. 85–96
20. Y. Lin, Y. Chi, S. Zhu et al., Analyzing communities and their evolutions in dynamic social networks. ACM Trans. Knowl. Discov. Data **3**(2), 8 (2009)

21. R. Cazabet, F. Amblard, C. Hanachi, *Detection of Overlapping Communities in Dynamical Social Networks* (Minneapolis, MN, USA, Proc. IEEE SocialCom, 2010), pp. 309–314
22. A. Khadivi, A.A. Rad, M. Hasler, Network community-detection enhancement by proper weighting. Phys. Rev. E **83**(4), 046104 (2011)
23. P. Hui, J. Crowcroft, E. Yoneki, Bubble Rap: social-based forwarding in delay-tolerant networks. IEEE Trans. Mobile Comput. **10**(11), 1576–1589 (2011)
24. W. Gao, Q. Li, B. Zhao et al., *Multicasting in Delay Tolerant Networks: a Social Network Perspective* (New Orleans, LA, USA, Proc. ACM MobiHoc, 2009), pp. 299–308
25. J. Fan, J. Chen, Y. Du et al., Geocommunity-based broadcasting for data dissemination in mobile social networks. IEEE Trans. Parallel Distrib. Syst. **24**(4), 734–743 (2013)
26. J. Wu, M. Xiao, L. Huang, *Homing Spread: Community Home-Based Multi-copy Routing in Mobile Social Networks* (Turin, Italy, Proc. IEEE INFOCOM, 2013), pp. 2319–2327
27. N. Cheng, N. Lu, N. Zhang et al., Vehicular WiFi offloading. Veh. Commun. **1**(1), 13–21 (2014)
28. H. Zhu, M. Dong, S. Chang et al., *ZOOM: Scaling the Mobility for Fast Opportunistic Forwarding in Vehicular Networks* (Turin, Italy, Proc. IEEE INFOCOM, 2013), pp. 2832–2840
29. M.T. Thai, P.M. Pardalos, Handbook of Optimization in Complex Networks (Springer, German, 2012)
30. A. Lancichinetti, S. Fortunato, Benchmarks for testing community detection algorithms on directed and weighted graphs with overlapping communities. Phys. Rev. E **80**(1), 016118 (2009)
31. A. Lancichinetti, S. Fortunato, J. Kertesz, Detecting the overlapping and hierarchical community structure in complex networks. New J. Phys. **11**(3), 033015 (2009)

Chapter 5
Platform of Mobile Information Service for Networks

Abstract This chapter mainly introduces the architecture of the mobile information service platform for networks. The detailed business process description is given for the optimization subsystem of resource scheduling, online monitoring subsystem of network transaction, and the traffic online analysis and service subsystem. In the sixth, seventh and eighth chapters, based on the platform, the latest work of mobile information service for networks will be introduced in three aspects: intelligent transportation, smart tourism, and mobile payment.

5.1 System Design

According to service demands, the platform of mobile information service for networks is divided into five layers: data resource layer, basic platform layer, key technology support layer, business management and application technology layer, service interface and information publication layer, as shown in Fig. 5.1.

The data resource layer mainly provides the corresponding database to the system, such as transportation information database, video database, social information database, transaction traffic database, gesture perception database, software behavior database. If the data source is a heterogeneous distributed system, a local cache of remote databases should be constructed at the data resource layer [1].

The basic platform layer mainly includes data acquisition and preprocessing platform, data storage and access platform. The data acquisition and preprocessing platform implements the acquisition of multi-source data and analyzes the data's quality, quantity, type, semantics preliminarily. Then the preprocessing platform strips out the noise and incorrect data, classifying and extracting useful data to form a virtual data plane. The data storage and access platform realize the interface function such as data storage, access (including access to heterogeneous databases), transmission.

The key technology support layer provides technologies that support the specific application above from the data link layer to the application layer. These technologies mainly include neighbor discovery, efficient routing, balanced access, resource scheduling optimization, network community discovery.

© Springer Nature Singapore Pte Ltd. & Science Press 2020
C. Jiang and Z. Li, *Mobile Information Service for Networks*,
https://doi.org/10.1007/978-981-15-4569-6_5

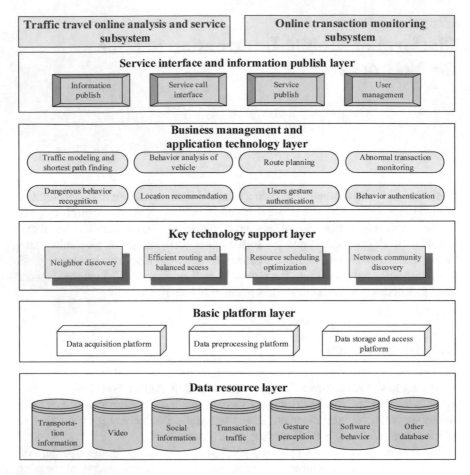

Fig. 5.1 Overall architecture of the system

The business management and application technology layer mainly involves technologies in applications such as intelligent transportation, smart tourism, and mobile payment. The main technologies include traffic modeling and shortest path finding, behavior analysis of vehicle, dangerous behavior recognition of vehicle, location recommendation, route planning, gesture authentication of users, abnormal transaction monitoring, and behavior authentication.

The service interface and the information publication layer mainly includes service call interfaces of Web Services and its publication, user authentication, user management. This layer mainly integrates the on-demand service and provides a unified service calling interface. Figures 5.2 and 5.3 respectively show the business process of mobile information service platform for networks and its supporting platform—Sugon cloud.

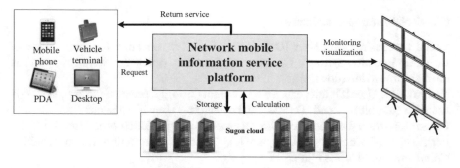

Fig. 5.2 The business process of the system

Fig. 5.3 Sugon cloud platform

5.2 Design of Data Format

In data resource layer, large amount of data are stored in various databases. In this section, we select some mainly used data to introduce the design of data format.

(1) Transportation Information Database

Taxi GPS Data: Vehicle ID (integer), Location (double), Speed (double), Passenger State (integer), Driving Direction (double), Timestamp (double), Brake State (boolean), Whether in Highway (boolean)

Bus GPS Data: Vehicle ID (integer), Location (double), Speed (double), Driving Direction (double), Timestamp (double), Line Code (ASCII), Mileage (double), Station Number (integer)

(2)   Social Information Database:

Social Check-in Data: User ID (integer), Check-in Location (double), Name of Check-in Location (string), Category of Location (integer), Name of Location (string),Timestamp (double)
Weibo Data: User ID (integer), Weibo Content (string),Comment (string), Check-in Location (double), Friend ID (integer), Forwarding User ID (integer)
Communication between Mobile Devices through Bluetooth: User ID (integer), Time of Connection Up (double), Time of Connection Down (double), Communication User ID (integer)

(3)   Transaction Traffic Database

Traffic Data: Page Views (integer), Number of Visitors (integer), Login Time (double), Online Time (double)
Transaction Data: Transaction Amout/Price (double), Number of Transactions (integer), User ID (integer), Name of Product (string), Place (integer), Transaction Time (double)

(4)   Gesture Perception Database

Collected Data through Touch Screen: Timestamp (double), XY coordinates (double), Pressure (double), Touch Area (double)
Collected Data through Orientation Sensor: XYZ coordinates of orientation (double)
Collected Data through Acceleration Sensor: XYZ coordinates of acceleration (double)

(5)   Software Behavior Database

Software Behavior Data: User ID (integer), Platform Code of Third-party Payment (double), Platform Code of E-commerce (double), Interface of Behavior Petri Net Model (string).

5.3   Subsystem of Resource Scheduling Optimization

The Internet is increasingly promoting the personalization of users. However, the user's autonomy is limited in the traditional task scheduling structure. The service quality is used as the only metric in traditional task scheduling, lacking the user's personalization.

Therefore, in order to make full use of resources attached to different domains and establish a resource-sharing model for the service industry, the concept of "virtual supermarket" is proposed [2, 3]. It's a unified, standard and shared resource management model based on virtualization technology. This model can effectively manage complex data and related equipment, improving resource utilization and establishing a comprehensive data security system. The model is divided into 4 layers: local resource management, global resource service, local resource service, and user management. As shown in Fig. 5.4, the local resource directory is formed through the registration of local resources. Then the global resource directory is formed through aggregation of local resource directories. After resource requests and collaboration, the global resource directory service is mapped to a local logical resource service. Finally, the task can invoke the local logical resources by autonomous task scheduling.

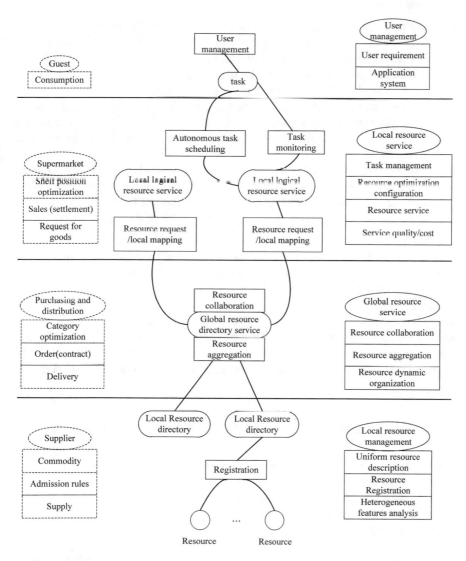

Fig. 5.4 Model of the virtual supermarket

"Virtual supermarket" focuses on the organization and management of cross-domain resources. The cross-domain resource has characteristics of heterogeneity, distribution, autonomy and huge quantity. So in the "virtual supermarket", cross-domain resources are selectively transparent to users, that is, they are not completely transparent. Users will have great autonomy since this model take the personalized needs of users into account.

The resource allocation system based on "virtual supermarket" includes the following parts.

(1) The user request broker module can receive the autonomous resource request of users. According to the requested resource type, the module generates a universally unique identifier (UUID) and task request. The task request will be written into the task pool of its corresponding type.
(2) The task pool is used to store the user's task request.
(3) The task pool monitor is used to listen to the task pool, obtain the task request, and perform the action of corresponding resources. Then, the result will be sent to the user request broker module and returned to the user by the user request broker module.
(4) The resource is located in the resource layer. Resource types include computing resources, data, application, and storage. The user layer is composed of the user's autonomous resource request. The user request broker module handles concurrent autonomous requests by writing the task pool in a mutually exclusive way.

The task pool stores the task requests in a queue and generates queue files. When task request volume is greater than the service processing capability, the user request broker module will write the request into the queue. Task requests in the queue are suspended until they are woken up and called. The task pool monitor listens for the changes in the queue of the task pool. When there is a suspended request in the queue and the corresponding resource is idle, the request in the queue will be sequentially awakened and the resource service will be invoked. The corresponding result will be exported to the user request broker module. The specific process is shown in Fig. 5.5.

5.4   Online Monitoring Subsystem of Network Transaction

This section presents the design of the online monitoring subsystem of network transaction in mobile information service platform. To monitor transactions in real-time [4], this subsystem mainly focuses on behavior data of end-user and key software, transaction data of platform. The subsystem mainly includes data acquisition, processing, and presentation, its visualization architecture is shown in Fig. 5.6 [5, 6].

The behavior monitoring and data visualization system can be deployed on the server of Windows or Linux. The supporting technology in the second layer adopts some mature frameworks, such as the software development model MVC (model

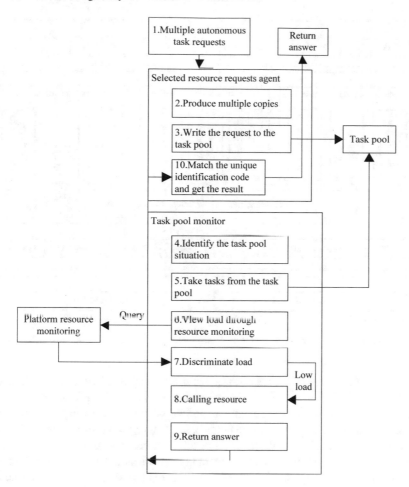

Fig. 5.5 Flowchart of resource allocation

view controller), which supports the multi-terminal access to monitoring interface in the way of Web Service. The overall system is based on Java. Specifically, the MVC framework adopts SpringMVC which can be well support for Restful, iBatis is used in the data persistence layer, Velocity is adopted in the view layer. We use the visual tool HighCharts based on Javascript, so the terminal device that supports the internet and Javascript can access this monitoring visualization system. The entire system can be deployed on the Apache server which is available on Windows and Linux [7].

Above the supporting technology layer, there are four middlewares: the real-time data calling service, the data cleaning module, the data processing module, and the data permission module. The monitoring subsystem puts high importance in the real-time nature of the data, so the purpose of providing real-time data calling services from the bottom layer to the upper layer is to provide the real-time data. Since

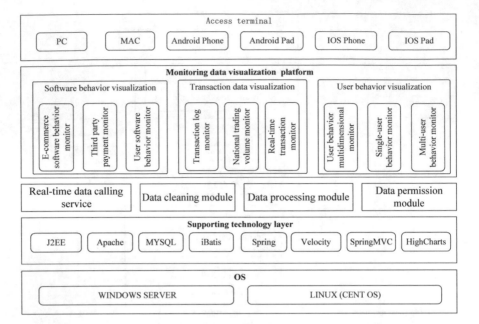

Fig. 5.6 System architecture of behavior monitoring and data visualization in network transaction

the source of the data is not necessarily from the local database and may be from the third party. The service in this part should be accessible to both external and internal data sources. The data cleaning module performs necessary preprocessing in irregular data, such as some partial fields being empty, conversion between discrete and continuous data. The main function of the data processing module is to further process the data for presentation at the upper layer, such as data classification and data format filling. The data permission module ensures the security of the transaction data by controlling the granularity of data.

Above the middleware layer, there is a visualization platform for the monitoring data. The visualization platform consists of three parts, each part consisting of three sub-parts. The first part is the visualization of software behavior. It mainly monitors e-commerce, third-party payment, and behavior of software. They are presented in three sub-parts. The presentation shows the logs of software behavior by scrolling lists. The same abnormal transaction can be highlighted in a multi-platform perspective to help people analyze abnormal transactions. The second part is the visualization of transaction data, which is used to present transaction data. The data is obtained from the monitored external e-commerce platform through real-time data services. The visualization of transaction data includes the following 3 sub-parts. (1) The transaction log monitor displays transaction logs of key business processes in a scrolling manner and is related to the log of software behavior. (2) The national trading volume monitor shows national trading volume by heat maps of country and histograms of provinces. (3) Real-time transaction monitor provides real-time transaction data invoked by external services, including real-time transactions volume and turnover. The data is shown in line chart and you can also choose to present two hours, the previous day, and the same period of transaction data. The last part is the visualization of user behavior, which is the visualization of the monitoring data of users' behavior. The part includes the following 3 sub-parts. (1) The multidimensional monitor of user behavior includes the gesture and posture of the user, the distribution of the user's online time, and the composition of the website accessed by the user, which constitutes a multi-dimensional behavior for a single user. The distribution of the online time is shown in the area chart. The types of website accessed by the user are shown by histogram and the pie chart simultaneously. (2) The monitor of single-user behavior displays the user's browsing log and posture classification by a scroll screen. Simultaneously, when a user accesses a website, the user identity score marked by user behavior authentication is displayed and updated in the line chart. (3) The monitor of multi-user displays the multi-user browsing log in a scrolling manner. Simultaneously, when multi-user access a website, the user identity scores marked by user behavior authentication are displayed and updated in the histogram.

The online monitoring subsystem of network transaction is demonstrated clearly in the above description, as shown in Fig. 5.7.

Fig. 5.7   Monitoring interface

5.5 Subsystem of Traffic Online Analysis and Service

This section introduces the design of traffic online analysis and service subsystem in mobile information service platform for networks. The traffic data has the characteristics of heterogeneity, dynamics, diversity, and distribution. The subsystem collects multi-source data, conducts comprehensive analysis and process, and provides information services for ordinary users and municipal administration [8, 9]. The information services can be accessed [10] through mobile terminal application or web page. This subsystem mainly provides services such as data collection and preprocessing, data transmission and storage, and traffic information service.

Specifically, the process of the business system is shown in Fig. 5.8. The data source of the system includes three types. The first type is the data directly collected by the sensing device, such as GPS, vehicle detector, car camera. The second type is city traffic data with privacy processing by municipal administration or enterprise. The third type is the traffic and related data obtained through the Internet, such as the location information published by Weibo. The basic process of the business system is as follows.

(1) The Web browser is a local thin client. There is no application installed locally except for the application plugin in the Web browser. The browser downloads the corresponding web page from the server to express various application functions. The Web sever receives the request from the Web browser. Then the request is forwarded to the service processing unit. Clients using specialized local client applications are fat clients, such as PDA, mobile phone, vehicle navigation terminal. The request from PDA, mobile phone or vehicle display terminal is also processed by the service processing unit [11].

(2) These requests are forwarded to the task manager, which is responsible for task scheduling. Available information can be obtained by inquiring the service registry, searching the location of the corresponding service (or the computing program) and other related information. Then the corresponding processing program is started for calculation.

(3) The resource manager provides available resource information for the scheduled tasks by querying the resource information table.

(4) The corresponding calculation program accesses the database or data file through the data access management unit.

(5) The task manager forwards the calculation result to the terminal through the service processing unit or the Web server. The corresponding service result will be displayed on the terminal.

(6) System management and maintenance module can acquire the information of software and hardware, including code, data, location, permissions, and other related information, and realize system management and maintenance, such as user management, code management, data management, resource management.

In addition, Figs. 5.9 and 5.10 show the services types provided by the online analysis and service subsystem to municipal administration and ordinary users.

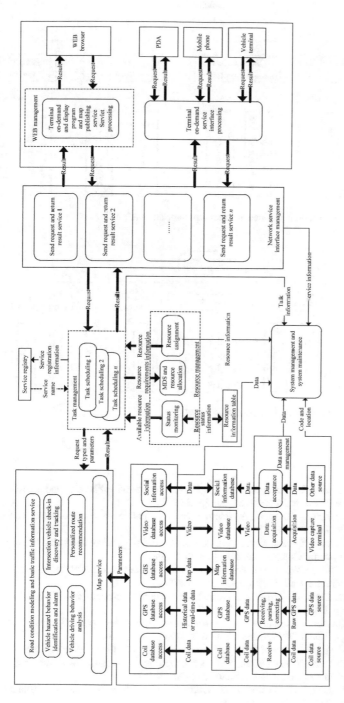

Fig. 5.8 The business process of the system

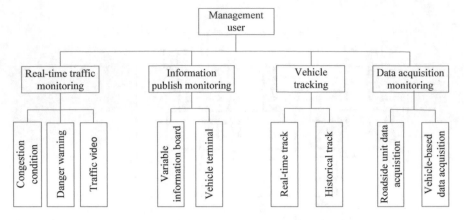

Fig. 5.9 Traffic information services for municipal administration

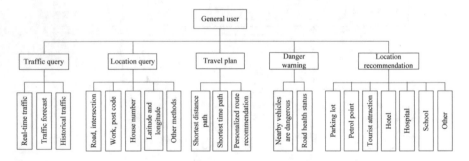

Fig. 5.10 Traffic information services for ordinary users

References

1. C. Jiang, H. Chen, C. Yan et al., Network Information Service Platform and Search Service Based on the Platform: 201210445457.4 2015-07-29
2. C. Jiang, H. Chen, C. Yan et al., An Internet-Based Resource Allocation System and Method: 201110270819.6, 2016-08-10
3. Y. Zhou, C. Jiang, Y. Fang, Research of scheduling of independent tasks onto heterogeneous computing systems. Comput. Sci. **35**(8), 90–92 (2008)
4. C. Jiang, Z. Ding, J. Wang et al., Big Data resource service platform for the Internet Financial Industry. Chin. Sci. Bull. **59**(36), 3547–3554 (2014)
5. C. Jiang, H. Chen, C. Yan et al., Trusted Authentication System and Method for Online Transactions: 201410499859.1, 2018-04-17
6. C. Jiang, H. Chen, C. Yan et al., Data Visualization System for User and Software Behavior Monitoring of Online Transactions: 201410513131.X, 2017-08-25
7. C. Jiang, W. Yu, *Risk Control Theory of Online Transactions* (Science Press, Beijing, 2018)
8. C. Jiang, Z. Ding, Y. Fang et al., Key technology and application of urban transportation intelligent road network. Autom. Panor. **5**, 76–78 (2015)
9. C. Jiang, Y. Zhang, H. Chen et al., A Traffic Guidance Method Based on Dynamic Road Network: 201310128165.2, 2015-06-03

10. C. Jiang, Z. Zhang, H. Chen et al., Method and System for Realizing Self-Displaying Road Condition Information for Users: 201310173301.X, 2015-07-22
11. C. Jiang, Z. Zhang, *Advanced Computing Technology for City Traffic* (Science Press, Beijing, 2014)

Chapter 6
Intelligent Transportation

Abstract In this chapter, utilizing tensor decomposition, similarity analysis, HMM, GMM and other data analysis tools, we analyze the feature of vehicle behaviors and traffic flows to select routes and identify dangerous behaviors of surrounding vehicles. We further expand the applications of intelligent transportation information services and improve peoples' travel experiences.

6.1 Related Applications and Technologies

As an important part of smart city, the intelligent transportation system [1] is based on road facilities. Advanced information technologies, electronic sensor technologies, and computer processing technologies are applied to solve the practical needs of transportations. Then, a comprehensive, real-time, accurate and efficient transportation system is established. In essence, the intelligent transportation system is formed by transforming and upgrading traditional transportation systems with high and new technologies. The intelligent transportation system is an important symbol of urban transportation entering the information age. In recent years, the development of Internet of Vehicles and autonomous driving has further promoted the expansion of intelligent transportation.

Intelligent transportation applications have always been the needs of government agencies, such as the traffic management bureau, the municipal administration, the public security system. Most functions of intelligent transportation applications are related to traffic light control, traffic accident treatment, traffic flow prediction, pedestrian warning, etc. In the early time, the famous intelligent transportation systems included Australia's SCATS, Japan's VICS, UK's SCOOT, US's TRAVTEK, ADVANCE, FASTTRAC, etc. In recent years, some international technology companies have gradually made their efforts on intelligent transportation. For example, in 2016, the transportation department of the US and Alphabet's subsidiary company Sidewalk Labs jointly announced a development program of traffic information platform named Flow.

The platform will collect traffic information through sensors deployed on the streets. Real-time monitoring of traffics in smart city is realized by using Wi-Fi-enabled phone booths and geographic information data of map service companies. Through the Watson IoT platform, IBM uses the Internet of Vehicles technology to automatically identify the area of high frequency of accidents. When the vehicle enters this area, it will receive speed limit prompt and warning. In this platform, data analysis and optimization technology is used to manage vehicle monitoring, alleviate congestion and improve traffic efficiency. Microsoft proposed the concept of urban computing, fully utilizing heterogeneous data in the city to solve the problems, such as environmental degradation, traffic congestion, increased energy consumption, and backward planning.

In China, Ali proposed the concept of "urban brain". The whole urban traffic data is accessible to "urban brain", so the "urban brain" can get the location of traffic jams and accidents. Besides, Tencent, Baidu, and other companies have also invested in related application of intelligent transportation such as smart bus, automatic driving.

In recent years, with the popularity of mobile devices, the demand for intelligent transportation information services is no longer limited to the government. The general public began to have an urgent need for traffic information services.

In response to such demands, the concept of Mobility as a Service (MaaS) came into being. Consulting the service model of cloud computing, MaaS was first proposed and defined in 2014 by the Chairman of the Finnish Intelligent Transportation Association, Mr. Sampo Hietanen. At the 2015 World Intelligent Transportation Conference, MaaS became a popular theme in the transportation field. Today, MaaS has become the main direction of the next generation transportation system. MaaS further emphasizes the integration of information, travel, payment and management, transforming transportation system from decentralized management to cooperative control. Maas not only uses mobile vehicles as part of the travel chain, but also converts road allocation into a service.

This kind of service is also provided by the client application, such as Didi, Uber. MaaS can realize passengers' destination prediction before issuing tickets, recommendation of pickup points, intelligent dispatch of tickets, path planning, safe driving and so on.

In addition to the APP for transportation, there are still some APPs for vehicle safety are closely related to traffic data, such as mobile phone application "OnStar", safe driving APP "Jimu QDrive", BlueDrive, Dash Car, CACAGOO, Automatic. These applications can realize the functions of collision warning, lane departure warning, and front vehicle startup warning on the mobile phone.

Our published book "Advanced Computing Technology for City Traffic" [2] focuses on the innovation of the multi-source traffic data integration and fusion, real-time analysis of road networks [3], the optimal travel plan [4, 5], rapid load balancing and so on. Our proposed methods have been successfully applied to "Shanghai Traffic Information Service Grid " to serve Shanghai Expo and Shenzhen Universiade.

Based on our previous work, we now have some new achievements of intelligent traffic information services. Through the analysis of vehicle trajectories in intelligent transportation [6–8], the problem of path estimation accuracy [9–18] and behavior prediction [19–25] of vehicles are solved. Getting rid of overdependence [26–33] on hardware devices (e.g. cameras, sensors, and radar), driver's driving status and habits can be extracted through historical data. At the same time, real-time warning is realized by utilizing neighbor discovery and wireless communication architecture.

This chapter mainly involves optimal path selection, driving records, and safe driving. Firstly, the prediction method of dynamic road condition and the shortest path approximation algorithm are given to provide travel planning services.

Then, this chapter analyzes the characteristics of nodes in high-speed mobile networks (e.g. Internet of Vehicles) and their demands for service applications. We also explore the vehicle behaviors in Internet of Vehicles, and present a text-searchable logbook system for urban drivers to recall and record the occasional events on the road. At last, combined with the application scenario of safe driving, a service application framework for real-time identification of dangerous driving behaviors is proposed.

6.2   Road Condition Prediction and Optimal Route Selection

Prediction of road condition plays an important role in making travel plans. Road condition prediction refers to the prediction of road congestion. There are many parameters that characterize the road condition, including traffic flow, traffic density, average speed, etc. Common prediction methods include method based on linear theory, methods based on non-linear theory, method based on hybrid theory, and traffic flow simulation. However, there are many factors that cause changes in road condition. Simply relying on a prediction model or historical road condition cannot accurately predict road condition, unless the road model is combined with the appropriate prediction method [34]. Therefore, this section introduces a road condition prediction method based on non-linear time sequences. Usually, travelers pay more attention to travel time in the prediction of road condition. Therefore, considering the traffic flow and congestion, this section introduces a approximation algorithm of the shortest path under dynamic networks.

6.2.1   Road Condition Prediction Based on Non-linear Time Series

(1)   Road Condition Prediction Based on Neighborhood Difference

The real-time traffic condition cannot be accurately reflected by the model merely using historical data. One of the methods for predicting traffic conditions is the neighborhood difference method. Firstly, we construct d time periods according to the GPS data collected in real-time and compare with that of the predicted model. Then we can adjust the model according to the difference and predict the road condition of the next time period.

Suppose that the current road condition can be reflected by vehicle speed, which is a $d-$ dimensional vector $X(t)$, $X(t) = (x(t), x(t - \tau), \cdots, x(t - (d - 1)\tau))$.

If the road condition model is $Y(t)$, $Y(t) = (y(t), y(t - \tau), \cdots y(t - (d - 1)\tau))$. $Y(t)$ is the historical vehicle speed. Then the prediction of road condition in the next period is $y'(t + \tau) = y(t + \tau) + \Delta(t)$. Note $\Delta(t)$ is the difference between $X(t)$ and $Y(t)$.

(2)   Model Construction of Current State

The basis of the neighborhood difference method is the reconstruction of time sequence. The key data has the following items: sampling interval $\Delta\tau$, delay time τ, embedding dimension d, etc. That is to say, the time span of the "current state" needs to be determined. Here, the sampling interval $\Delta\tau$ is the time interval for collecting GPS data. The description of how to construct the current state of vector d is given below.

Assume that a one-dimensional time sequence $\{x(i\,\Delta\tau)\} = \{x_i\}$, $1 \le i \le N$ has been observed. A d-dimensional vector cluster is generated by using the delay technique:

$$X_1 = \left(x_1, x_{1+p}, \cdots, x_{1+(d-1)p}\right)$$
$$X_2 = \left(x_{1+j}, x_{1+j+p}, \cdots, x_{1+j+(d-1)p}\right)$$
$$\cdots$$
$$X_k = \left(x_{1+(k-1)j}, x_{1+(k-1)j+p}, \cdots, x_{1+(k-1)j+(d-1)p}\right)$$

Suppose the delay time $\tau = p\Delta\tau$, the embed dimension d, and the data length $N = (k - 1)j + (d - 1)p$, usually $j = 1$. The key to the reconstruction of time delay method is to choose the appropriate delay time. The following three principles can be used to determine the delay time:

① The delay time can be determined by the first zero or minimum point of the autocorrelation function.

Estimating the first zero or minimum points of $R_x(\tau) = \frac{1}{N-p} \sum_{i=1}^{N-p} x_i x_{i+p}$, which minimizes the correlation between $x(t)$ and $x(t + \tau)$.

② The delay time can be determined by the first minimum points of mutual information.

If $a_0 \le x(t), x(t + \tau) \le a_n$, $[a_0, a_n]$ is divided into n sub-intervals, $[a_0, a_1], [a_1, a_2], \ldots, [a_{n-1}, a_n]$. Define the probability distribution of $\{x(t)\}$,

$$P_i(x(t)) = \frac{S(a_{i-1} < x(t) \le a_i)}{k}, \quad i = 1, 2, \ldots, n.$$

$S(\cdot)$ is the number of all sample points satisfying the inequality, and the conditional probability distribution is defined as follows:

$$P_j(x(t+\tau)|x(t)) = \frac{S(a_{j-1}\langle x(t+\tau) \le a_j | a_{i-1} < x(t) \le a_i)}{\sum_{i=1}^n S(a_{i-1} < x(t) \le a_i)}, \qquad j = 1, 2, \ldots, n.$$

Shannon entropy $H(x(t)) = -\sum_{i=1}^n P_i(x(t)) \ln P_i(x(t))$ describes the uncertainty of $x(t)$. Given $\{x(t)\}$, the uncertainty of $\{x(t+\tau)\}$ is as follows:

$$H(x(t+\tau)|x(t)) = -\sum_{j=1}^n P_j(x(t+\tau)|(x(t)) \ln P_j(x(t+\tau)|x(t)).$$

Then the mutual information is defined as:

$$\begin{aligned} I(x(t), x(t+\tau)) &= H(x(t+\tau)) - H(x(t+\tau)|x(t)) \\ &= H(x(t)) - H(x(t)|x(t+\tau)). \end{aligned}$$

The formula shows that the smaller I is, the correlation between $x(t)$ and $x(t+\tau)$ will be smaller. Therefore, the first minimum of points of I can be used to determine τ [35].

③ The delay time can be determined by the first maximum point of joint entropy.

Assuming the distribution of joint probability:

$$P_{ij}(x(t), x(t+\tau)) = \frac{R(a_{i-1} < x(t) \le a_i, a_{j-1} < x(t+\tau) \le a_j)}{k},$$

$$i, j = 1, 2, \ldots, n.$$

where $R(\cdot)$ is the number of data pairs satisfying the inequality. Then, in order to make the joint probability as uniform as possible, the joint probability of Shannon entropy

$$H(x(t), x(t+\tau)) = -\sum_{i=1}^n \sum_{j=1}^n P_{ij}(x(t), x(t+\tau)) \ln P_{ij}(x(t), x(t+\tau))$$

is in maximum value. That is, the overall uncertainty of $x(t)$ and $x(t+\tau)$ is the greatest.

For the determination of dimension, we can adapt the method of Ref. [36]. That is, given the lower dimension embedding space (e.g. $n = 2$), construct the n-dimension embedding vector $X_1 = (x_i, x_{i+p}, \cdots, x_{i+(d-1)p})$ by $\{x_i\}$ and calculate the correlation integral of the embedding vector $C(\varepsilon, n)$.

$$C(\varepsilon, n) = \frac{1}{N^2} \sum_{i,j} \theta(\varepsilon - \|X_i - X_j\|),$$

where $\theta(\cdot)$ is the Heaviside function $\theta(y) = \begin{cases} 0, \ y < 0 \\ 1, \ y \geq 0 \end{cases}$.

The correlation integral denotes the probability that two points are located in the ε-neighborhood.

Define the correlation dimension of the sequence as

$$D_c(n) = \lim_{\varepsilon \to 0} \lim_{N \to \infty} \frac{\lg C(\varepsilon, n)}{\lg \varepsilon}.$$

When ε is small, $\lg C(\varepsilon, n)$ and $\lg \varepsilon$ are approximately linear for a given n, and the slope is $D_c(n)$. When n increases, $D_c(n)$ increases with n, and the increasing rate decreases. When n increases to a certain value, $D_c(n)$ converges to the saturation value D, and the minimum n of D is the embedding dimension d.

(3) Road Condition Prediction Algorithm

Assuming that the road condition model is $Y(t)$, the prediction method is described as follows:

① According to the above method, the current state of the road can be constructed by a d-dimensional vector.

$$X(t) = (x(t), x(t - \tau), \cdots, x(t - (d - 1)\tau));$$

② According to the sampling period of current state and Y, we have

$$Y(t) = (y(t), y(t - \tau), \cdots, y(t - (d - 1)\tau));$$

③ Calculating $Z(t) = X(t) - Y(t) = (z(t), z(t - \tau), \cdots, z(t - (d - 1)\tau));$

④ Calculating $E(t) = \sum_{i=0}^{d-1} \frac{z(t - i\tau)}{d};$

⑤ Calculating the prediction value $y'(t + \tau) = y(t + \tau) + E(t)$.

6.2.2 Approximation Algorithm for Dynamic Shortest Path Problem

(1) Dynamic Single Source Shortest Path

The dynamic network generally means that the arc in the network is dynamically changing. There are four possible forms: the addition and deletion of arcs, and the increase and decrease of the weight of the arc. If these four changes are allowed, the network is a called full-dynamic network. If only the increase of weight and the deletion of arc (or the decrease of weight and the addition of arc) are allowed, the network is called a semi-dynamic network. In fact, the addition of arc is a special case of arc weight decrease (the arc weight is reduced from ∞ to a finite value). Similarly, the deletion of the arc is a special case of arc weight increase (the arc weight is increased to ∞). So we only need to study the change of arc weight. Therefore, it is necessary to study the case that the arc weight changes [37, 38].

Suppose the full-dynamic network of the non-linear arc weight function is based on the known states. In the case of dynamic networks, the weight function $c_{ij}(t)$ can be defined as the runtime from node i to j, where t is the moment of entering arc (i, j). The length of path (time) depends on the detailed process. If there is a path $P = \{(i_1, i_2), (i_2, i_3), \cdots, (i_k, i_{k+1})\}$, the starting time is t_1, then the length is

$$l(P) = c_{i_1 i_2}(t_1) + c_{i_2 i_3}(t_2) + \cdots + c_{i_k i_{k+1}}(t_k).$$

where

$$t_2 = t_1 + c_{i_1 i_2}(t_1),$$
$$t_3 = t_2 + c_{i_2 i_3}(t_2),$$
$$\cdots$$
$$t_k = t_{k-1} + c_{i_{k-1} i_k}(t_{k-1}).$$

The essence of the Dynamic Single Source Shortest Path (DSSSP) is to find an o-d path P and minimize this newly defined length $l(P)$.

This kind of dynamic problem can't utilize the existing dynamic programming SP algorithm. Let's first look at the example shown in Fig. 6.1, where the length of each arc is constant except $c_{34}(t)$, where

$$c_{34}(t) = \begin{cases} 1, & 0 \leq t < 1 \\ 4, & 1 \leq t < 2.5 \\ 2, & 2.5 \leq t < 5 \end{cases}.$$

The shortest path from node 1 to 4 is (1, 2, 3, 4) and the length is 5. The length of the other two roads (1, 3, 4) and (1, 4) both are 6. But in the shortest path (1, 2, 3, 4), the sub-path (1, 2, 3) is not the shortest. So the "Optimization Principle" doesn't fit in this example, that is, it cannot be solved by dynamic programming. Generally speaking, the composite structure of this kind of problem is too complex to give a solution.

Fig. 6.1 An example of a dynamic network

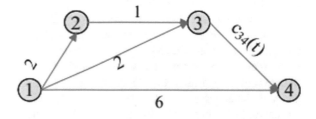

Because traditional static SP algorithms (e.g. Dijkstra) cannot be directly transplanted to dynamic networks, many researchers are devoted to finding effective approximation algorithms.

(2) Approximation Algorithm of DSSSP Based on Stable Domain

It has been proved that the decision form of DSSSP problem is NP-complete, then DSSSP problem is NP-hard, so finding a polynomial-time algorithm of DSSSP is nearly impossible. Therefore, a practical approximation algorithm or heuristic algorithm is needed.

A general non-linear function can be approximated by a linear function in a relatively short time interval. So let's start with a simple case that $c_{ij}(t)$ is a linear function. Suppose that the length of the arc $(i, j) \in R$ is linear,

$$c_{ij}(t) = c_{ij}^0 + a_{ij}t.$$

When $t = 0$, $c_{ij}(t) = c_{ij}^0$, which is the initial length of the arc. Then the shortest path tree T^0 is obtained by the Dijkstra algorithm. When t gradually increases, the optimal solution (the shortest path tree) also changes, but it is stable in the segment. So the variation range of t can be divided into several intervals, in which the shortest path tree is unchanged. When $t = 0$, the potential of the shortest path tree T^0 is $\{\pi_i^0\}$. Suppose the path from node o to node x in tree T^0 is P_x^0.

When the time is t, according to the recursive algorithm, the potential in T^0 is $\pi_x^0(t) = \pi_x^0 + \left(\sum_{(i,j) \in P_x^0} a_{ij}\right)t$, which is a linear function of t.

The sufficient condition that T^0 is the optimal solution is

$$\pi_j^0(t) - \pi_i^0(t) \le c_{ij}^0 + a_{ij}t, \quad \forall(i, j) \in R \tag{6.1}$$

The variable of this linear inequality is t. The solution is $0 \le t \le t_1$. Thus, when $t \in [0, t_1]$, T^0 is the optimal solution. So $[0, t_1]$ is the stable domain of T^0. At this point, if the potential of node i satisfies $\pi_i^0(t_1) < t_1$, T^0 is the optimal solution form node o to node i. Therefore, the shortest path from o to i in T^0 can be fixed, and the length of the arc will not change. The sub-tree formed by these nodes is called invariant sub-tree. Then, for the other parts of the tree T^0, we consider the change when t increases.

When $t > t_1$, there must be an inequality which is not satisfied the formula (6.1), such as $\pi_j^0(t) - \pi_i^0(t) \ge C_{ij}(t)$. Then the path P_j^0 from node o to j in T^0 is no longer the shortest, it can be replaced by $P_i^0 \cup \{(i, j)\}$. In this way, a new shortest path tree is obtained, which is recorded as T^1. Similarly, the potential function $\{\pi_i^1\}$ in T^1 can be obtained. Note that only the potential of node j and its successor changes. For the other nodes, $\pi_i^1 = \pi_i^0$. Therefore, it is not necessary to recalculate all of them. Furthermore, the stable domain $[t_1, t_2]$ of T^1 is obtained by using a linear inequality similar to (6.1). At the same time, nodes satisfying $\pi_i^1(t_2) \le t_2$ are added to the invariant sub-tree to fix the corresponding shortest path. By analogy, the corresponding optimal solution can be obtained until the endpoint potential (shortest path length) satisfies $\pi_u^m \leq t_{m+1}$, then the program ends. The path started from o to u can be found in all the invariant sub-tree.

When the arc length is a linear function, the above algorithm is equivalent to the linear programming method, and each of the shortest path trees $T^0, T^1, \cdots$ is equivalent to the basic feasible solution. The computational complexity analysis is as follows: Dijkstra algorithm needs to be called once when solving T^0, and the time complexity is $O(n^2)$. When calculating the stable interval in each iteration, there are at most m times divisions and m times comparisons to solve the linear inequality (6.1), where m is the number of arcs, so the time complexity is $O(m)$. The calculation of the algorithm depends on the step of t. The step of t can be adjusted so that at least one node in each iteration enters the invariant sub-tree. In this way, the number of iterations is n. So the time complexity of this algorithm is $O(mn)$.

For the case where the arc length is a non-linear function, it can be approximately replaced by a segmental linear function. The time is divided into several linear sub-domains $[t^0, t^1], [t^1, t^2], \cdots, [t^{k-1}, t^k]$, so the arc length is linear function in each linear sub-domain. Therefore, the above linear algorithm can be invoked for each linear sub-domain, and each linear sub-domain can be divided into stable domains. Then, the overall solution can be obtained by connecting each stable domain in turn. When switching between linear sub-domains, it is often necessary to recalculate the stable domain. The number of iterations for solving inequality (6.1) is $n + k$, and k is the number of linear sub-domain. Then the time complexity of the algorithm is $O(mK)$, where $K = max\{n, k\}$. The number of linear sub-domain depends on the specific form and precision of the non-linear weight function which can be selected subjectively. So the DSSS approximation algorithm based on stable domain is quasi-polynomial.

6.2.3   Experiments and Evaluation

The performance of the approximation algorithm is verified by experiments. Firstly, the relevant formulas and definitions used in the experiment are given.

To simplify the experiment, the cosine function is used to represent the non-linear variation of the arc weight in the network. Suppose the weight $c_{ij}(t)$ of the arc (i, j) is changed according to the following formula:

$$c_{ij}(t) = c_{ij}^0 + \frac{5}{c_{ij}^0} - \frac{5}{c_{ij}^0} cos\left(\frac{\pi t}{20}\right).$$

where c_{ij}^0 is the initial weight of the arc (i, j).

The approximation algorithm in this section performs linearized calculations according to the following formula:

$$c_{ij}(t) = \begin{cases} c_{ij}^0 + \frac{t-40m}{2c_{ij}^0}, & t \in [2m \cdot 20, (2m+1) \cdot 20] \\ c_{ij}^0 + \frac{20}{c_{ij}^0} + \frac{t-40m}{2c_{ij}^0}, & t \in [(2m+1) \cdot 20, (2m+2) \cdot 20] \end{cases}, m = 0, 1, 2, \dots.$$

The following formula is given to measure the performance of the approximation algorithm,

$$E_V = \sum_{j \in V} (L_{oj} - O_{oj}) / \sum_{j \in V} O_{oj}.$$

where L_{oj} is the length of the "shortest path" from the o to j, and O_{oj} is the length of the actual shortest path from o to j.

The enumerated method and the approximation algorithm are used to calculate the optimal path for the randomly generated one-way network. Then we calculate the cost of the approximation algorithm and the error ratio of the "shortest path". According to the maximum degree 3, 4, 5, and 6, the nodes are divided into 4 groups, each contains 12 networks, and the number of nodes is $11, 12, \dots, 22$. The experiment of 48 networks in four groups is called one round. The whole experiment lasted 30 rounds, so a total of 48×30 randomly generated one-way networks were involved in the experiment. The average calculation cost and the shortest path error ratio are shown in Figs. 6.2 and 6.3.

The experimental results show that:

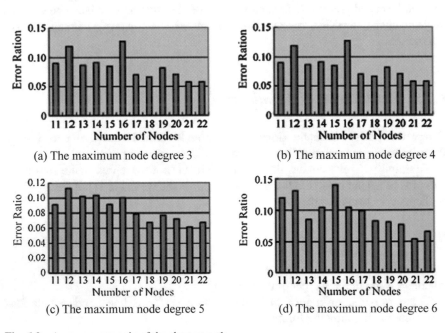

(a) The maximum node degree 3   (b) The maximum node degree 4

(c) The maximum node degree 5   (d) The maximum node degree 6

Fig. 6.2   Average error ratio of the shortest path

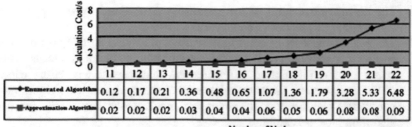

(a) Calculation cost of the shortest path with the maximum node degree3

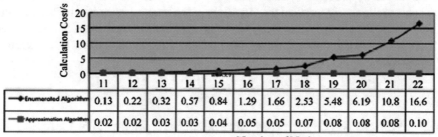

(b) Calculation cost of the shortest path with the maximum node degree 4

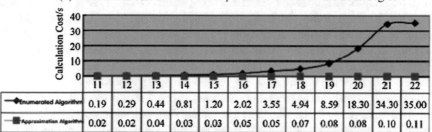

(c) Calculation cost of the shortest path with the maximum node degree 5

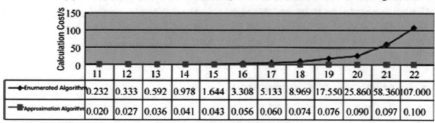

(d) Calculation cost of the shortest path with the maximum node degree 6

Fig. 6.3 Comparisons of shortest path calculation costs

① The average error ratio of the shortest path obtained by the approximation algorithm in this section is about 0.1
② The calculation cost of the approximation algorithm in this section is much smaller than the enumeration method. As the number of nodes increases, the calculation cost of the approximation algorithm increases slowly. With the increase of the node degree, the calculation cost of the approximation algorithm does not change significantly. By contrast, the calculation cost of the enumerated algorithm increases rapidly.
③ As the number of nodes increases, the average error ratio of the shortest path obtained by the approximation algorithm decreases. Of course, the simulation only preliminarily verified the efficiency of the method described in this section. Because the change of arc weight is quite complicated in practical problems, it is necessary to select a suitable segmented linear function according to the specific situation.

6.3 Vehicle Behavior Analysis Based on Sparse GPS Data

With the increasing number of vehicles and expansion of city, time spent on the road for urban drivers is prolonged. Long-time continuous driving easily distracts drivers, incurring fragment memories about occasional events on the road, especially for taxi drivers. In addition, practical GPS data is very sparse because existing vehicle equipment is not perfect enough. Hence, we purpose a text-searchable system named iLogBook to infer the trajectory of the vehicle through sparse GPS data and help the driver recall events on the road. For example, Fig. 6.4 shows the GPS log of a taxi from about 12 pm to 7 pm. The marks in red are GPS points, and the road segments in yellow are possible trajectories that the taxi traveled. It can be seen that the GPS points are sparse on some road segments, which makes it is hard to infer the trajectory. In addition, the driver passed through so many locations in the afternoon that it is difficult to remember all the details. Naturally, the driver may question about his own experience, such as "Which park did I see at about 1 pm yesterday?".

6.3.1 Overview of iLogBook

In this section, we take an overview of the iLogBook system. The main objective is to realize accurate inference of the vehicle's trajectory with sparse GPS data and help the driver recall the events on the road.

Two main modules comprise the system: data processing module and semantic analysis module, as shown in Fig. 6.5. In the data processing module, the system maps the discrete GPS points to the road segments at first. Then, two tensors are established to store information about traveling time and turning actions based on historical data.

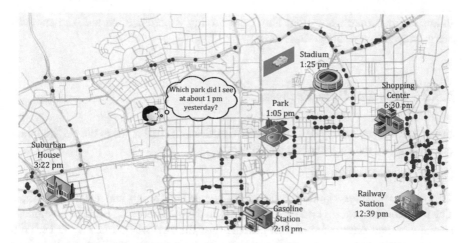

Fig. 6.4 A driver's query

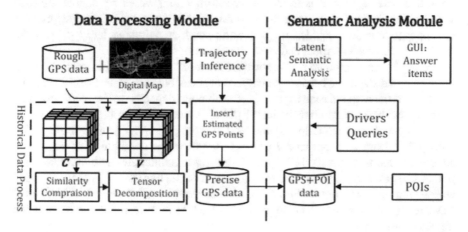

Fig. 6.5 The framework of iLogBook system

The non-zero ratio of each original tensor is less than 1%, since the mapped data is rough. Hence, a tensor recovery approach, including similarity comparison and tensor decomposition, is applied to the tensors to overcome the sparse problem. According to the results after tensor recovery, the system establishes an HMM in each sub-paths to infer the optimal trajectory for each driver. At last, additional estimated GPS points are inserted into the processed GPS data to enhance the precision in the optimal trajectory. From the data processing module, a corresponding intensive trajectory is obtained with the precise GPS points for each vehicle.

Next, the semantic analysis module will convert the GPS information to semantic information. In the module, the system establishes a relationship between trajectory GPS data and roadside POIs. The text searchable function is implemented by LSA to answer the driver's questions about the driving experience. At last, the answers are displayed in a webpage-based GUI.

6.3.2 Original Data Process

In this section, we mainly describe the difficulties and challenges in the original data processing and the corresponding solutions.

(1) Problem Description

The original trajectory data is composed of discrete GPS points and instant velocities. The fundamental process is to map the points on the road network. Each road segment is one-way and only contains two crosses. For the two-way situation, as Fig. 6.6 shows, we divide r_i into two road segments according to the traffic flow directions (it is easy to know a road segment is either in east-west direction or north-south one). If a road segment r is in the east-west direction, we let r^+ denote the road segment that the traffic flow runs toward east, while r^- denotes the road segment in the opposite direction. Besides, if r is in north-south direction, we let r^+ denotes the north-direction road segment and r^- is the opposite.

We apply the map-matching algorithm proposed in Ref. [39] to map the GPS points on road segments because it analyzes the possible situations. Specifically, the direction of the mapped road segment for each point depends on the recording time of the points before and after the target point. However, the problem still remains. Inaccuracy and scattered mapped data lead to wrong mapping results. In Fig. 6.7a, GPS points from 3:13 pm to 3:20 pm are far from the neighbor road segments. Moreover, among the mapped GPS points, the time intervals between two consecutive points are various from seconds to minutes, even hours, like the GPS points recorded at 3:10 pm and 3:11 pm in Fig. 6.7b. Due to the fast movement, a vehicle may travel a long distance during an interval. This leads to the uncertainty problem in the trajectory inference.

Fig. 6.6 An example of two-way road segments

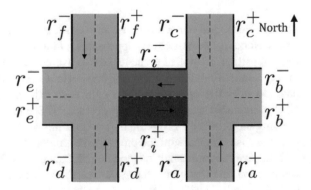

Fig. 6.7 Examples in a local area

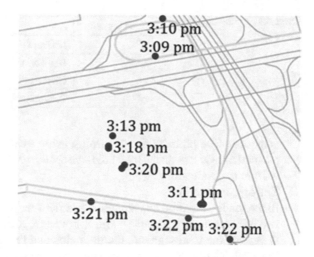

Therefore, we propose a hybrid estimation method, integrated similarity comparison, tensor decomposition and IIMM, to overcome inaccuracy and uncertainty problems in the data processing. After data processing, we obtain a series of GPS points for each driver, which can describe the trajectory precisely.

(2) **Historical Data Process**

One of the basic steps in the system is to extract driver's actions from map-matching data. Two tensors are established to store potential driver habits: time consumption and the veer probability, which is based on the historical data. Time consumption means the average duration that it takes a driver to travel through a road segment at a certain period of time. Veer probability represents the ratio of the turning actions (turn left, turn right, go straight and turn around) at the cross of a road segment.

① Time Consumption

We define a certain time period as a slot of one hour. Then, one day can be divided into 24 slots. For each driver, in a time slot, there are three situations for the mapped GPS points on a road segment: several points, one point, and none. On most road segments, there are several points mapped, like r_{bc} in Fig. 6.7b. We calculate the average velocity between each pair of two consecutive GPS points and get time consumption at the slot with these average velocities. Especially, if there is only one point or none mapped on the road segment, we set the value to be 0.

② Veer Probability

To estimate a driver's veer probability, we build an action-neighbor list for each road segment to bind the neighboring road segments with the vehicles' turning actions. Table 6.1 gives the action-neighbor list for r_i^+ according to the example in Fig. 6.6. From a driver's mapped data, we can extract the fuzzy trajectory, which is a sequence of the road segments. According to the fuzzy trajectory, we are able to glean the times that the driver travels from a road segment to its

Table 6.1 Action-neighbor list of r_i^+

Road segment	Action	Neighbors	Value
r_i^+	Left turn	r_c^+	$Pr(r_i^+ \rightarrow r_c^+)$
r_i^+	Right turn	r_a^-	$Pr(r_i^+ \rightarrow r_a^-)$
r_i^+	Go through	r_b^+	$Pr(r_i^+ \rightarrow r_b^+)$
r_i^+	Turn around	r_i^-	$Pr(r_i^+ \rightarrow r_i^-)$

neighbors. The probabilities of turning actions can be calculated. If no data or the total time is less than a threshold, we set the probability to be 0 (the threshold is 10 in the evaluation).

③ Tensor Construction

In the model, the time consumption and the veer probability are determined by two 3-dimensional coordinates: (d, r, t) and (d, r, a), where d, r, t and a denote the driver, the road segment, the time slot, and the turning action, respectively. We establish the relationship between the potential habit information (the time consumption and the veer probability) and the property elements (road, driver, time and action). Since tensor is defined in the vector space to build linear maps between geometric vectors and scalars, we introduce two 3-dimensional tensors to store the information. We let $\mathcal{C} \in \mathbb{R}^{M \times N \times 24}$ denote the time consumption tensor and $\mathcal{V} \in \mathbb{R}^{M \times N \times 4}$ denote the veer probability tensor, where M and N are determined by the size of the drivers and the road segments in the dataset, respectively.

④ Similarity Comparison

However, there still remains a problem that no data is matched at the road segment in the tensors due to the sparsity of historical data. In the experiment, there are more than 3000 road segments with no matched vehicle data. To overcome this problem, we exploit a cosine similarity metric to compare the similarity between a specific road segment and the others in the road network. Four features of a road segment are collected into a vector f_r: the direction, length, intersection type, and average traffic flow. Then, we fill the tensor ($\mathcal{C}$ or $\mathcal{V}$) by the following equation.

$$\mathcal{T}(:, i, :) = \frac{\sum_{j=1 \& j \neq i}^{N} s_{ij} \cdot \mathcal{T}(:, j, :)}{\sum_{j=1 \& j \neq i}^{N} s_{ij}},$$

where $s_{ij} = \frac{f_i \cdot f_j}{\|f_i\| \|f_j\|}$, and i, j label two different road segments, respectively.

⑤ Tensor Decomposition

Nevertheless, for each driver, the original data may exist large amount of zero value in each segment and time slot. The original non-zero ratio of tensor $\mathcal{C}$ is 0.307% and that of tensor $\mathcal{V}$ is 0.995% in the evaluation. After similarity comparison, the two ratios improve to 0.502% and 1.21%, respectively. To recover the empty values, we apply a tensor decomposition method based on Tucker

Decomposition. The basic idea is to replace the original tensor with the multiplication of a core tensor and several factor matrices [40]. The core tensor and the factor matrices are initialized with a smaller positive number at first. Next, the core tensor and matrices are calibrated until convergence through the comparison between the non-zero entries in the original tensor and core tensor and the corresponding multiplication (core tensor multiply the factor matrices). At last, the zero entries in the specific tensor can be filled by the multiplication after calibration. In the model, the physical meaning of the tensor decomposition is to fit a specified driver's behaviors by combining with other drivers' behaviors. Based on Tucker, we decompose the tensor C into four parts: core tensor $\mathcal{X}$, and factor matrices D_C, R_C and T. The process is shown in Fig. 6.8, where $\mathcal{L}_C$ denotes the objective function. By the function, the update tensor C' will compare each non-zero entry (d', r', t') with the original tensor C in an iteration until their difference is less than the threshold. By the same logic, the tensor V is decomposed into core tensor $\mathcal{Y}$, and factor matrices D_V, R_V and A. Thus, we get two full tensors C_{res} and V_{res} after decomposition.

⑥   Check Matrix

Though we fill the empty entries in two tensors, the errors still exist among these filled entries. Taking no account of the restrictions in the common environment leads to unreasonable entries. In tensor C_{res}, an unreasonable situation occurs when the traffic is heavy at a road segment, but the estimated traveling time is short.

Besides, the driver's familiarity with the local region affects both driving time and turning actions. To prevent the miscalculation, we introduce three check matrices in the decomposition. We divide the map into 8 regions to ensure that each entry in the matrices is non-zero. One is the traffic flow matrix F_T, which reflects the traffic flow at a region during a time slot. Another is the action frequency matrix F_A, which records the number of each action in a region. The last one is familiarity matrix F_D, which stores the frequency that a driver appeared in a region. These three matrices are built on real traffic data. In Fig. 6.8, F_D and F_T denote the familiarity matrix and the traffic flow matrix, respectively. Moreover, G_C and H_C are the auxiliary matrices. In each iteration, $\|F_D - D_V \times G_V\|^2$ and $\|F_A - A \times H_V\|^2$ will be added into the objective function, where $\|.\|^2$ denotes the L_2 norm.

Fig. 6.8 The principle of tensor decomposition

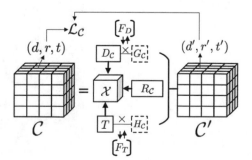

Similar to the decomposition of tensor $\mathcal{C}$, the action frequency matrix and the familiarity matrix are added to the decomposition of tensor $\mathcal{V}$. We decompose the tensor $\mathcal{V}$ into core tensor $\mathcal{Y}$, factor matrices $D_{\mathcal{V}}$, $R_{\mathcal{V}}$ and A, where A denotes the action factor. Besides, compared with the decomposition of tensor $\mathcal{C}$, the traffic flow matrix F_T is replaced by the action frequency matrix F_A. Note that both $\|F_D - D_{\mathcal{V}} \times G_{\mathcal{V}}\|^2$ and $\|F_A - A \times H_{\mathcal{V}}\|^2$ are considered in the objective function, where $G_{\mathcal{V}}$ and $H_{\mathcal{V}}$ are the auxiliary matrices.

(3) Trajectory Inference

With the historical data stored in $\mathcal{C}_{res}$ and $\mathcal{V}_{res}$, we build an HMM to infer the precise trajectory for each driver. In Ref. [41, 42], HMM exhibits great accuracy in map matching. These studies generate transition probability through the mapped candidates from sample GPS points. Here, we design the model from another perspective using two tensors. In the first step, we divide the trajectory data into segmentations with a fix time interval. Then, in each sub-trajectory, we build a set that contains all possible trajectories. Utilizing the tensor $\mathcal{C}_{res}$, we eliminate the unreasonable trajectories, and collect possible road segments in an area. Table 6.2 gives an example of a fragment in a driver's time consumption tensor. Associated with the time moment in Fig. 6.9, $\{r_1^-, r_2^-, \ldots, r_7^-\}$ are collected in the area.

Besides, tensor $\mathcal{V}_{res}$ is used to construct the transition matrix and the generation matrix. In the model, the relevant road segments are regarded as the hidden states, while the recorded GPS points are the observation states. The transition probability incorporates the veer probability and the action-neighbor list among neighboring road segments. For example, the transition probability from r_i^+ to r_c^+ in Fig. 6.6 is $Pr(r_i^+ \rightarrow r_c^+) = \mathcal{V}_{res}[:, r_i^+, 0]$, where 0 means left turn. Otherwise, the transition probability is 0. The generation probability depends on the mapped coordinate of the GPS point. If the coordinate is in the midpiece of the road segment, the probability is

Table 6.2 Time consumption tensor fragment

Road segment	r_1^-	r_2^-	r_3^-	r_4^-	r_5^-	r_6^-	r_7^-
Duration (s)	3.3	3.9	3.5	3.2	4.3	3.7	2.1

Fig. 6.9 An example of the fuzzy trajectory

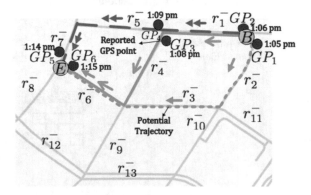

1 from this road segment or 0 from others. In contrast, if the coordinate is around the beginning point or endpoint of the road segment, the probability will be generated in four cases:

(a) for the mapped road segment, the probability is one minus distrust degree. The distrust degree is a training parameter that reflects the error ratio in map matching;
(b) for the neighboring road segments in the area, the probability is the product between distrust degree and the veer probability from the mapped road segment to its neighbors;
(c) for those adjacent but not neighboring road segments in the area (like r_3^- and r_4^- for the target road segment r_6^- in Fig. 6.9), they share equally the remaining probability;
(d) for others, the probability is 0. For instance, Table 6.3 gives a part of the tensor $\mathcal{V}_{res}$ about the road segments in Fig. 6.6. The generation probability of GP_3 is (0.09, 0, 0, 0.7, 0.21, 0, 0) in the order of the road segments, when the distrust degree is 0.3. For details, GP_3 is mapped to road segment r_4^-. The probability of r_1^- depends on the second case, and that of r_5^- is based on the third case.

The main advantage of our model is to solve the uncertainty problem in path inference due to the deviation of the GPS points at the junction points (crosses). As illustrated in Fig. 6.9, it is hard to distinguish which is the appropriate trajectory. But with the transition matrix and the generation matrix, the optimal trajectory can be inferred by applying the Viterbi algorithm [43].

(4) Estimated GPS Point Insertion

The last step is to insert additional GPS points into the mapped data to construct precise trajectory data. Two types of GPS points are inserted: cross points and midway points. Cross points are those ones at the cross that connect the adjacent road segments in the driver's optimal trajectory. Meanwhile, the midway points are those ones that refer to only one road segment. To confirm the location of the midway points, we uniformly divide a road segment into several sub-segments with a certain length. If there is no point mapped in the sub-segment, we insert midway points in geometric midpoint of the road segment. The inserting time is estimated through the distance of the tensor $\mathcal{C}_{res}$, the around GPS points and the length of inserted point. As Fig. 6.10 shows, those green points are the inserted and estimated GPS points.

Table 6.3 Veer probability tensor fragment

a	r						
	r_1^-	r_2^-	r_3^-	r_4^-	r_5^-	r_6^-	r_7^-
0	0.3	0.3	0.2	0.4	0.9	0.5	0
1	0	0.3	0.6	0.3	0	0.4	0.4
2	0.6	0.3	0.2	0.2	0	0	0.4
3	0.1	0.1	0	0.1	0.1	0.1	0.2

Fig. 6.10 Semantic analysis

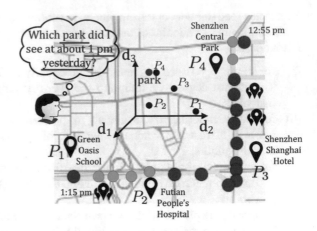

6.3.3 Semantic Analysis of GPS Data

On the basis of the data processing, we obtain the precise GPS trajectory data including the measured coordinates and the estimated coordinates for each driver in the dataset. Since the GPS log does not contain semantic information, a semantic analysis module is designed in the system to translate the trajectory data and provides a text-searchable function for drivers. We will describe the utilization of POI and the comprehension of the query in the following content.

(1) **POI Utilization**

The direct way to make a GPS point has the semantic meaning is to take advantage of the POIs (Points of Interest) information. A POI is marked with name, location and address of the roadside building, like Shenzhen Central Park, (22.5374, 114.0709), and No. 1 at Huaxi Road, Shenzhen, China in Fig. 6.10. To bind the precise GPS points with POI information, we draw a circle for each GPS point and gather the related POIs into a relevance vector. In the evaluation, the radius of the circle is the distance from the nearest GPS point. Then, a database is designed on the basis of MongoDB to store the precise GPS points and their corresponding relevance vectors.

(2) **Query Comprehension**

Though we have a precise trajectory data associated with POI information, it is still not enough to answer the drivers' fuzzy queries. To well comprehend the query is a key point. In the system, we apply the method based on LSA, since it is easy and works well compared with other complicated analysis approaches. When a driver types a query into the iLogBook, the system divides the query into words at first. Then, it screens those words that refer to the fuzzy location or time by a stop-word list and a semantic library. The library is constructed by the fuzzy time and location words, where the location words are those in the road names and the POI names. Especially, the location words are collected from the digital map and Baidu POI. If the query contains the time words or the location words, the system will select the items matching the time or the location condition in the database established in previous section. The database returns the relevant POIs in the driver's trajectory with the time or the location restriction. Otherwise, the system searches for the total relevant POIs in the driver's trajectory. We collect these POIs into an interest vector I.

Then, a semantic space is established to find the appropriate POIs with the help of the basic idea of LSA. We build a word list W, by dividing the name and the address of each POI in I into words. The POI named "Shenzhen Center Park" is divided into three words: Shenzhen, Center, and Park, which are collected into the word list. In addition, the word list is in English, due to the POIs utilized in the evaluation are translated into English. According to the interest vector I and the word list W, we construct a word-interest matrix, denoted as $\mathcal{Z}$. $\mathcal{Z}$ is a Boole matrix and $\mathcal{Z} \in \mathbb{R}^{|W| \times |I|}$, where $|W|$ is the size of the word list and $|I|$ is that of the interest vector. If the word appears in the name of the interest vector, the value is set to 1. Otherwise, the value is set to 0. The value combining the word "park" and the POI "Shenzhen Center Park" in $\mathcal{Z}$ is 1. Next, we decompose the matrix $\mathcal{Z}$ into the multiplication of three parts: a left orthogonal matrix $\in \mathbb{R}^{|W| \times l_W}$, a diagonal matrix $\Sigma \in \mathbb{R}^{l_W \times l_I}$ and a right orthogonal matrix $V \in \mathbb{R}^{|I| \times l_I}$, where l_I and l_W are low positive integers. We choose the first three values in each row of U as the semantic coordinate for each word. Similarly, we choose the first three values in each column of V^T as the semantic coordinate for each POI. Thus, the semantic space is constructed. In the example, (u_1, u_2, u_3) denotes the coordinate of the word "park", while (v_1, v_2, v_3) and (v'_1, v'_2, v'_3) denote that of the POI "Shenzhen Center Park" and the POI "Green Oasis School", respectively. In addition, the cost of building such a semantic space depends on the number of POIs selected in the database. Since the step is taken charge by the server-side, the time consumption could be controlled within 1 s.

We calculate the Euclidean distance between the word and the interest to obtain the correlation degree. In a word, the system searches for the words (not time and stop words) in the query and returns the closest POI for each in the semantic space. As shown in Fig. 6.10, the red and green points are GPS points, and the black are POIs. The system selects the GPS points combining with relevant POIs based on the time key words "1 pm, yesterday" in the query. Then, it finds the POI named "Shenzhen Central Park" in the semantic space, which is the nearest POI to the keyword "park". We compose the answers with the location words, the time words (if existed) and the selected POIs in sentences. Otherwise, the system will return "No item has been found!". Especially, if two POIs are very close, and have the same distance to a keyword, both of them will be picked up in the response.

6.3.4   Dataset

In this section, we give a brief introduction to the original data in the evaluation.

(1)   **Dataset**

The dataset contains 13,798 taxicabs' GPS points from April 18th to April 26th, 2011 in Shenzhen, China. The number of total GPS points is $171,332,738$. Due to the interference of the changeable environment, the sampling intervals of the GPS points for each taxicab are different. For each taxicab, the dataset stores the vehicle's license plate number, longitude location, latitude location, instantaneous velocity, direction and passenger status in an item.

(2)   **Digital Map**

Besides, the latitude range of the digital map utilized in the evaluation is from 22.4416615 to 22.6642819, and the longitude range is from 113.8327646 to 114.4025082. The background in Fig. 6.11 is the road network of the map. There are total 16,087 road segments, including 23,909 nodes.

(3)   **Point of Interest**

Furthermore, Baidu POI of Shenzhen are used in the evaluation, the total number of the POIs is $165,872$. Since the system is based on English, the information of POIs is translated into English.

(4)   **Ground Truth**

Ground Truth: To validate the performance of the data processing, we choose ten taxicabs with the densest GPS points, and mark their trajectories manually as the ground truth. Because their precise trajectories can be figured out with dense GPS points, but others cannot due to sparse GPS points recorded.

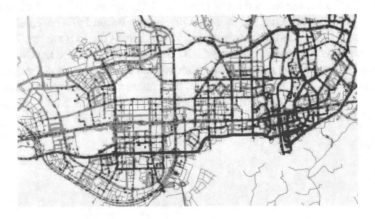

Fig. 6.11 GPS points mapping of three taxicabs

6.3.5 Experiments and Evaluation

We evaluate our system from two aspects. One is the source GPS data processing since it is the core step to support the system. The other one is semantic analysis. It translates GPS data into semantic information. First, we demonstrate the webpage based GUI of our system. Then, we give an introduction about the dataset and the ground truth in the evaluation. The detailed numerical results about data processing and semantic analysis are displayed in the next. Besides, a discussion about the scalability of our system will be given at last.

(1) **System Prototype**

We show the web page-based GUI in the system prototype, which is designed to improve the users' experience. Two GUI pages are included in the system: the query interface and the answer interface, as illustrated in Fig. 6.12a and b. The driver types query on the query page, and the system expresses the answer items on the answer page.

(2) **Data Processing**

According to Sect. 6.3.4, there are four steps in the source GPS data processing. Figure 6.11 gives a macro view of three taxicabs' GPS data on the road network. Among them, the most GPS sampling points are green, while the red and blue points reflect the average matching result of the dataset. The total number of the mapped GPS points is 77, 607, 953, and the mapping ratio is 45.3%. The average number of GPS points in a road segment is around 4,824. These express the sparsity of the data. With the help of the ground truth, we train the distrust degree parameter, which is determined by the accuracy of the map matching. Through experiments, e obtain the average accuracy ratio is 69.7% when we set the distrust degree to be 0.3 in the trajectory inference.

① GPS point mapping

According to Sect. 6.3.4, there are four steps in the source GPS data processing. Figure 6.11 gives a macro view of three taxicabs' GPS data on the road network.

(a)   (b)

Fig. 6.12 GUI prototype of iLogBook system

Among them, the most GPS sampling points are green, while the red and blue points reflect the average matching result of the dataset. The total number of the mapped GPS points is 77, 607, 953, and the mapping ratio is 45.3%. The average number of GPS points in a road segment is around 4,824. These express the sparsity of the data. With the help of the ground truth, we train the distrust degree parameter, which is determined by the accuracy of the map matching. We obtain the average accuracy ratio is 69.7% when we set the distrust degree to be 0.3 in the trajectory inference.

② Tensor Construction

Table 6.4 gives the statistic information about the tensors and the matrices constructed in Sect. 6.3.4. The size of the veer probability tensor is $13, 798 \times 16, 087 \times 4$, and that of the time consumption tensor is $13, 798 \times 16, 087 \times 24$. The ratio of the non-zero entries in the tensor C is 0.307%, and that in the tensor V is 0.995% before applying the similarity comparison method. Moreover, we detect that there are 3,025 road segments with no taxicab's data record in tensor C and V. As analyzed in the previous section, we fill the zero entries with the similarity function. Thus, the ratio of the non-zero entries increases to 0.944% in the tensor C and 1.42% in the tensor V, respectively.

③ Tensor Decomposition

After the decomposition, the zero entries can be recovered in each tensor. To validate the effect of the three check matrices, we use the values of a marked taxicab in tensor C and tensor V as the ground truth. Then, we set the values of this taxicab to be 0 before tensor decomposition. The performance is measured by calculating the mean absolute error (MAE) compared with the non-zero entries of this taxicab in both tensors. Besides, the sizes of the three check matrices are shown in Table 6.4. The size of the matrix F_D is $13, 798 \times 8$, that of the matrix F_T is 8×24 and that of the matrix F_A is 8×4.

The MAE between the original tensor decomposition (OTD) and the updated tensor decomposition (UTD) of tensor C is shown in Fig. 6.13a, and that of tensor V is shown in Fig. 6.13b. Specially, we choose the data from 6 am to 8 pm when we validate the performance of the time consumption. The "L", "R", "S" and "U" in Fig. 6.13b mean left turn, right turn, go straight and U-turn, respectively.

Table 6.4 Statistics of the tensor/matrix

Tensor or matrix	Size	Non-zero ratio (%)
V	$13, 798 \times 16, 087 \times 4$	0.995
C	$13, 798 \times 16, 087 \times 24$	0.307
F_D	$13, 798 \times 8$	100
F_T	8×24	100
F_A	8×4	100

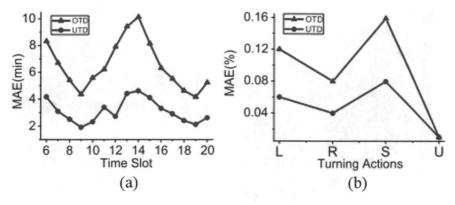

Fig. 6.13 MAE between OTD and UTD

④ Trajectory Inference

In the trajectories inference step, there are 13,798 fuzzy trajectories, the total length is about 5, 340, 457 km. The connection ratios of the trajectories for each taxi driver in the dataset are expressed in Fig. 6.14a, which reflects the fuzziness of the trajectories. In Fig. 6.14a, we find the values for all taxi drivers fall on the interval [0.1, 0.5]. This means that we need to infer the optimal sub-trajectories in almost 60% parts for each fuzzy trajectories.

As analyzed in Sect. 6.3.2, we divide each trajectory into several sub-trajectories with a fix time interval. Figure 6.14b gives the average number of the road segments in each sub-trajectory with three different time intervals: 30 min, 15 min, and 10 min. Considering the requirement of precision, we divide each driver's trajectory with 10 min interval. As shown in Fig. 6.14b, there are average 7.6 road segments and 21.4 GPS points in each sub-trajectory with 10 min interval. Then we collect the possible road segments into an area in each sub-trajectory. Figure 6.14c shows the average number of the road segments in each area, compared with the original ones in each sub-trajectory under 10 min time interval. We obtain the average road segments in each area is 13. Therefore, there are average 13 hidden states and 21 observation states in each HMM.

To evaluate the performance of the HMM method, we input parts of the GPS data into the model among marked taxicabs, comparing the estimated road with the real road. The accuracy of the trajectory inference among the marked taxicabs is shown in Fig. 6.14d, where the sample interval is twice as long as the original one. The result shows that the average accuracy is about 97%.

⑤ Estimated Points Insertion

At last, we show the percentage of estimated GPS point insertion in Fig. 6.15a, which means the ratio that the estimated GPS points occupied in the processed GPS points set. In the evaluation, we insert the estimated GPS points with three fixed lengths: 50 m, 100 m, and 200 m. Figure 6.15b shows the queries' accuracy of a marked vehicle under three lengths. From the figures, we find that more than 50% estimated

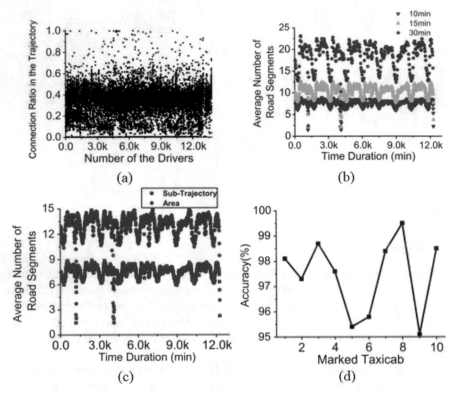

(a)

(b)

(c)

(d)

Fig. 6.14   Statistic results for trajectory inference

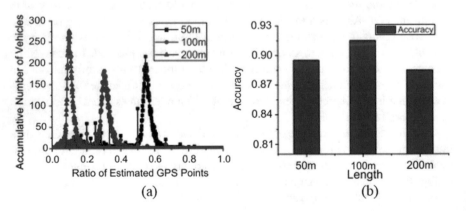

(a)

(b)

Fig. 6.15   Statistic result of the estimated GPS points

point insertion when the length is 50 m. Though the precise level is higher with a smaller length, more estimated points may bring wrong query answers. Hence, in the semantic analysis, we insert the points every 100 m.

(3)   **Semantic Analysis**

As we have analyzed in Sect. 6.3.3, the semantic modules to combine the roadside POIs in the trajectories with the drivers' queries. According to the map, there are an average 7.88 POIs contained in each road segment. Figure 6.16a gives a distribution of the POIs among the road segment. Except those that are too short or lack of POI information, most road segments involve $2 - 15$ POIs. On the other point of view, Fig. 6.16b displays the statistic result for the POI combining with the vehicles' trajectories in the dataset. Since a fraction of the trajectories is out of the selected map, the number of the POIs combined with those vehicles is limited. Generally, the range of the total POIs involved in the trajectory for a vehicle is from 2×10^4 to 5×10^4.

In Sect. 6.3.3, we design a semantic space on the basis of the relevant POI information due to individual driver's queries. The total number of words associated with the semantic analysis is 580, 552. We design a query list with 200 daily queries for mentioned 10 marked drivers, like "Which hotel did I see at 4 pm, April 19th?". Since their precise trajectories are marked, we have the standard answers about the POIs in their routes. The performance is shown in Fig. 6.17a. We find the average accuracy is over 90%. Besides, we display the average time consumption for answering the queries among marked drivers in Fig. 6.17b. This step is applied on a PC with 6 GB memory and Intel i5 1.70 GHz dual-core processor.

In addition, we randomly choose 20 queries from the list and apply them for the unmarked drivers. We calculate the ratio that the system could return the exact POIs. Figure 6.17c gives the results. We find our system iLogBook could response most parts of the queries for about 60% vehicles in the dataset, since some drivers' trajectories are beyond the map.

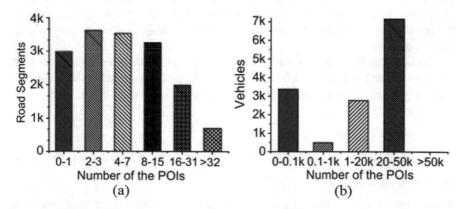

Fig. 6.16 Statistic result of the roadside POIs

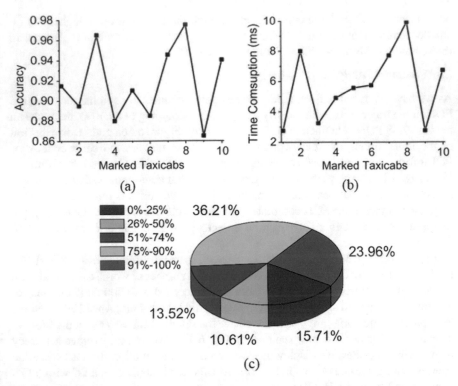

Fig. 6.17   Statistic result of the daily queries

(4)   **Scalability**

According to the description in previous section, our approach depends on two datasets: trajectory data and map data (e.g., roads and POIs). The trajectory data and the road network determine the constructions of two tensors (time consumption tensor and veer probability tensor), while the POI data works on the semantic space construction. Obviously, the rapid growth of the datasets affects the results of the modules in our approach directly. Hence, the scalability of our approach is an inevitable issue.

To overcome the issue, we would like to integrate an update mechanism into the system to take the data growth into account. In the mechanism, we divide time into several periods, and our system updates once in each period. In detail, three steps are contained:

① Map Data Update

At periodic intervals, our system updates its map dataset, including roads and POIs.

② Tensor Reconstruction

In each period, a new trajectory data stream comes. The map-matching and historical data process steps are applied to generate two tensors based on the new trajectory data and the updated road network at first. Then, we calibrate values in the tensors from two aspects: if a road segment belongs to the old road network, a weighted average method is utilized to update the values in the tensors; otherwise, the values stay the same. The update equation of the tensor is shown as follows:

$$\mathcal{T}_i(:, j, :) = \begin{cases} \gamma \mathcal{T}_{i-1}(:, j, :) + (1 - \gamma)\mathcal{T}_{t_i}(:, j, :) & j \in \mathcal{R} \\ \mathcal{T}_{t_i}(:, j, :) & j \notin \mathcal{R} \end{cases},$$

where $\mathcal{T}_i, \mathcal{T}_{t_i}$ denote the results after ith update and that during t_i period, respectively. j denotes a road segment and $\mathcal{R}$ is the road network. γ is a harmonic parameter.

③ GPS Point Reassociation

According to mentioned two steps, the results of path inference and GPS points filling would change as well. Hence, in the semantic analysis module, the updated precise GPS points and bound POIs' information will be reassociated.

6.4 Identification and Warning of Hazard Behaviors Based on Neighboring Vehicles

Driving safety is a persistent concern for urban dwellers who spend hours driving on road in ordinary daily life. According to the Global Road Safety Report 2015 published by WHO, more than 1.2 million people worldwide die from traffic accidents every year. Traditional driving hazard detection solutions heavily rely on onboard sensors (e.g., front and rear radars, cameras) to identify the behavior of surrounding vehicles through image processing. However, this method is limited by the camera's viewing angle and the quality of the shooting, as well as the bad weather. Through the research on neighbor discovery, internet of vehicle architecture, and GPS data in previous chapters, a system based on sparse GPS data and a centralized communication architecture will be introduced. This system can recognize dangerous behaviors by analyzing the vehicle's behaviors when driving and sent warning messages to cars nearby. In this section, based on the study of adjacent vehicle hazard behavior identification and early warning, a system called APP will be introduced to identify the vehicle's dangerous behaviors in real-time and alert the driver.

6.4.1 System Model and Design Goal

As shown in Fig. 6.18, the system is mainly divided into two modules: training and matching. The training module is used to refine sparse historical data and identify dangerous behaviors and normal behaviors. As shown in the sub-figure marked A of Fig. 6.21, reported behavioral data of two taxicabs are so coarse-grained to extract the behavior. In addition, tortuous road segments influence the accuracy of the driving direction estimation, as illustrated in the sub-figure marked B of Fig. 6.19. The

Fig. 6.18 System scenario

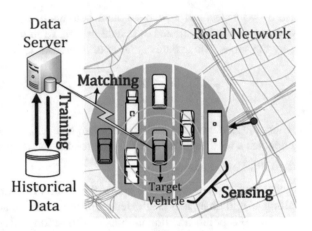

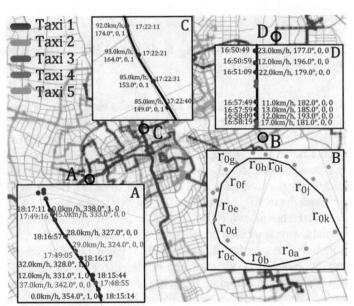

Fig. 6.19 Local examples of the sparse challenge

matching module utilizes a centralized network architecture to identify the behavior of vehicles around the target vehicle in real-time and return dangerous vehicles to the target vehicle for early warning. Further, the vehicle itself can sense the dynamics of surrounding vehicles to reduce the load of the centralized network and enhance real-time performance. In this section, we will briefly introduce the composition of the system model and the system design goals .

(1) **System Model**

There are two main entities and Wireless communication technology involved in the system as follows:

① The Server

In addition to processing historical data to identify dangerous behaviors, the server also collects various data and provides services via wireless communication. It is often the case that a driver constantly accesses to such a server with his/her smart device for certain services, e.g., online navigation.

② Vehicles

A vehicle is equipped with multiple sensors, e.g., a GPS receiver, motion sensors, etc., used to monitor its behavior on the road. The coarse-grained sensory data is packaged into the GPS trace and reported to the server via wireless communication.

③ Wireless communication

In APP, at current stage, data transmission between the server and vehicles is based on cellular networks such as 3G/4G/5G. Due to the communication cost, vehicles report their GPS trace data at a low frequency. In the future, new techniques such as V2X technology (vehicle-to-vehicle, vehicle-to-infrastructure, and vehicle-to-pedestrian) would also be considered.

In this section, the dangerous behaviors are not exactly equivalent to illegal driving behaviors. The dangerous behavior defined here is an act that poses a threat to vehicles nearby, such as frequent lane changes, traveling at a speed that does not match the surrounding vehicle (too fast or too slow). For example, as shown in the sub-graph labeled C of Fig. 6.21, the speed limit of the elevated road is 80 km/h. Obviously, this car is over-speed. In sub-graph D, the direction of the sample vehicle changes quickly. Because the angle of the road segment is $179°$, it can be inferred that the car is constantly changing lanes. Although this is not illegal, it poses a threat to other vehicles.

(2) Design Goals

This auxiliary system is named APP (Augmented Proactive Perception) ,Its purpose is mainly divided into three parts:

① Proactively alert urban drivers of potential dangerous neighbor vehicles via historical and real-time GPS data on the road.

② Recognize the dangerous behaviors accurately and in time due to fast mobility and ephemeral neighboring relationship among the vehicles on the road.

③ Service can be ensured in low communication cost.

6.4.2   Overview of APP System

In this section, we take an overview of the system framework. As shown in Fig. 6.20, the system consists of two modules: training module, and matching module. The training module is to fill the driving behaviors at each road segment via the rough historical GPS trace data, which is taken charge of by the data sever. In the model, a four-dimension coordinate (acceleration, brake, direction, and velocity) is constructed from the mapped data to describe the driving behaviors on each road segment.

① Acceleration describes the acceleration of the vehicle on the road segment.
② The number of brakes indicates the frequency that the vehicle is at the braking status on the road segment.
③ The directional indicates the variance of the differences between the direction of the recorded point and the angle of the segment.
④ Velocity indicates the average velocity on a road segment.

It can be seen that each behavior vector is composed of three fixed attributes: driver, road segment and time point. So use four 3D tensors to store 4 features in the behavior vector. However, the initial tensor is very sparse, the proportion of non-zero values is less than 12%, and the values are not accurate enough. In order to solve the problem of sparse data and inaccuracy, the same tensor decomposition method as in Sect. 6.3 will be used to fill and correct the tensor. Different from the Sect. 6.3, in addition to the tensor decomposition and check matrix, it is necessary to accurately process the road segments to solve the problem of many road segments rather than

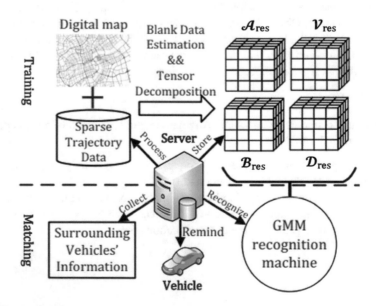

Fig. 6.20   System framework

one. After the data is filled, driver's behavior vector can be obtained on each road segment, which is convenient for identifying dangerous behaviors.

On the other hand, the matching module is mainly divided into two steps. The first step is to identify the behavior vectors on each segment to distinguish dangerous behaviors from normal behaviors. The second step is to match the behavior uploaded by the vehicle and alert the target vehicle with dangerous behaviors around it. A GMM based approach is utilized to cluster the recovered data on each road segment and time slot into two categories: dangerous and normal. Historical data is used to train parameters of GMM. The cooperation of these two modules and the internal relationship architecture is shown in Fig. 6.20.

6.4.3 Data Training

In this section, we first give the problem description in the training of the source GPS trace data. Then, we show the solutions step by step.

(1) Problem Description

An item in the source historical GPS trace data mainly contains six elements: GPS point, time, instant velocity, direction, brake, and highway. Especially, highway and brake are Boolean values to reflect whether a vehicle is on highway and braking state, respectively. For example, the sub-graph of Fig. 6.19 labels several items. The basic step is to match the raw GPS data onto each road segment in a digital map. In this Chapter, the road network is a set of road segments, and each one is one-way and contains only two intersections. As Fig. 6.21a shown, the roads are divided into segments by hollow points.

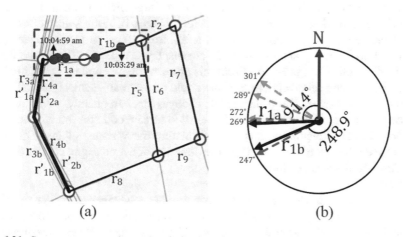

(a)   (b)

Fig. 6.21 Segment segmentation and optimization of angle data optimization

The biggest challenge is data coverage. The historical GPS trace data is far away to provide enough driving information at a certain time period on each road segment. So it is more difficult to recognize the dangerous behaviors since the abnormal behaviors are in the minority. For instance, Fig. 6.19 shows five cab's trajectories during a day, where different colors denote different cabs. The data was recorded almost every 10 s. Obviously, the trajectory is clear (could tell the driving route), but it is not real to make the cab's data cover all the time and map. What is worse, there are several road segments with no data mapped. Besides, the changing direction of a road segment affects the vehicles' direction data which makes it hard to excavate precise behaviors, e.g., r_0 in the lower right of Fig. 6.19 and r_1 in the upper left of Fig. 6.21a. Hence, we propose a hybrid solution, including direction data refinement, blank data estimation, and tensor decomposition to enhance the dataset with precise items. Among them, the direction of the road segment in the road network is provided by the public electronic map dataset.

(2) **Behavior Definition**

Here, we introduce four attributes to describe the driving behavior based on map-matching data: velocity, acceleration, direction, and brake.

① Velocity

The instant velocity data is attached to each item. For a vehicle, velocity is directly related to safety. Both driving too fast and too slow will create a threat to normal behaviors. In this chapter, we define the velocity attribute as the average speed on a road segment.

② Acceleration

Acceleration: Besides the speed, big acceleration also brings dangers. We define the acceleration attribute as the average acceleration on a road segment.

③ Direction

The direction is defined as the clockwise rotation angle between the road (or vehicle) direction and the North of map. In Fig. 6.21a, the solid points in the rectangle are map-matching points of a taxi from 10 am to 11 am on April 1st, while their corresponding directions are displayed in Fig. 6.21b. In the figure, the direction of r_{1a} is $268.6°$. From this observation, we find that the directions $269°$, $247°$ are relatively close to the angle of the road segment, which meets the common sense. But if the vehicle changes lanes frequently, deviations will become large. Meanwhile, the behavior will threaten others' safety. Hence, we describe the direction attribute by calculating the variance of the differences between the record directions and the direction of a road segment. The detail is shown in the next section.

④ Brake

There is a brake tag in a data item, which reflects whether the target vehicle is under braking condition or not. On a road segment, we define the brake attribute as the frequency of the braking conditions. The frequency of the brakes on a given section of a car is calculated through dividing the number of recorded points in the brake state by the total number.

(3) **Direction Data Refinement**

As mentioned in previous section, the value of direction attribute is affected by the changes of the road direction. In this chapter, we give a refinement method to obtain a more accurate value. Three steps are contained:

① split a road segment into several straight sub-segments;
② calibrate the direction value on each sub-segment;
③ combine the results together.

In a digital map, a road consists of several GPS points. We filter two types of points: cross and inflection. The cross point, denoted as intersection in physically, is utilized to divide a road into road segments, while an inflection point separates a road segment into two sub-segments with different directions. The cross points are easy to obtain. Besides, we find the inflection points of a road segment using the following equation.

$$|\Theta(p_i, p_b) - \Theta(p_i, p_e)| > \varepsilon, \tag{6.2}$$

where $\Theta(p_i, p_j)$ denotes the oblique angle of the line segment with ending points p_i and p_j, and ε denotes the bias threshold.

For example, as illustrated in Fig. 6.21a, the hollow points are cross points. Hence, the roads in the area are divided into 9 road segments and 16 sub-segments. r_i denotes the i-th urban road segment, while r_i' denotes the i-th highway road segment.

Then, on each sub-segment, the mapped points calculate the differences between their directions and the sub-segment's direction. Figure 6.21b shows the example data. On sub-segment r_{1a}, there three mapped points, and their directions are 272°, 289°, and 301°, respectively. The absolute differences are 3.4, 20.4 and 32.4. By the same logic, that of the points on r_{1b} is 20.1 and 1.9. At last, we calculate the mean square deviation of the differences to obtain the value of direction attribute. In the example, it is about 377. In addition, as displayed in the bottom right of Fig. 6.19, definition in Eq. (6.2) also could handle the special case that the road segment is an arc (appears in highway).

(4) **Data Filling**

After raw data preprocessing, including map-matching and direction data refinement, we obtain the driving behavior data from four dimensions on each road segment at a certain time slot. However, on most road segments, the scale of the behavior data is not enough to distinguish dangerous behaviors from normal ones. To solve this problem, we apply a tensor decomposition based method to enhance behavior data on each road segment

① Tensor Construction

Each action in the behavior data is determined by a 3D coordinate (u, r, t), where u, r and t denote the driver, the road segment, and the time slot, respectively. Since a tensor describes linear relations between scalars and geometric vectors, we can link the driving behaviors (scalars) with the inherent property elements (vector) by tensors. Hence, four 3D tensors $(\mathcal{A}, \mathcal{B}, \mathcal{D}, \mathcal{V})$ are constructed to store the behavior data of different attributes. The size of each tensor is $M \times N \times L$, where M, N, and L denote the number of drivers, the road segments and the time slots, respectively. In the evaluation, we set the time slot to be one hour.

② Blank Data Estimation

After construction, we find that there are several road segments with no data mapped due to the sparsity of the data. In the evaluation, the count is 185 in total 478 road segments. To solve the problem, we fill the blank data by comparing the Euclidean distances between the target road segment and the others with a similar shape. A feature vector f is included to collect the intrinsic properties for each road segment. The vector consists of three elements: average direction, length, and intersection type. Then, we update each tensor by the following equation:

$$T(:, i, :) = \frac{\sum_{j=1 \& j \neq i}^{N} \theta_{ij} \cdot T(:, j, :)}{\sum_{j=1 \& j \neq i}^{N} \theta_{ij}}, \tag{6.3}$$

where labels i and j denote two different segments, and θ_{ij} denotes the Euclidean distance between f_i and f_j, $\theta_{ij} = \frac{f_i \cdot f_j}{\|f_i\| \|f_j\|}$.

③ Tensor Decomposition

To provide enough behavior data on a road segment, we decompose the tensors by Tucker Decomposition to fill the empty entries [44]. A target behavior tensor T is decomposed into four parts: core tensor $\mathcal{C}$, and three factor matrices U, R and T, as the following equation shows:

$$\mathcal{T}_{rev} = \mathcal{C} \times U_1 \times R_2 \times T_3,$$

where 1, 2 and 3 denote the multiply order, and $Trev$ denotes the recovery tensor.

④ Initial State

The value of each part is random. Then, during every iteration, a recovery tensor T_{rev} is constructed by the multiplication of these four parts. Through the comparison of the non-zero entries between the source tensor and the recovery one by an objective function, the values in each part will be converged. When the iteration converges, the filled tensor T_{rev} is obtained. Figure 6.22 gives the main process of the decomposition, where $\mathcal{L}$ denotes the objective function. Each non-zero entry (u, r, t) in source tensor T is compared with corresponding entry (u', r', t') until convergence (the difference is below a threshold). Thus, we get four filled tensors $\mathcal{A}_{rev}$, $\mathcal{B}_{rev}$, $\mathcal{D}_{rev}$, and $\mathcal{V}_{rev}$.

⑤ Check Matrix

Nevertheless, there are irrational values among the filled entries in the tensors, due to the neglect of additional limitations, e.g., environment and familiarity. To guarantee

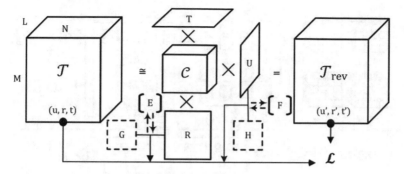

Fig. 6.22 Description of tensor decomposition

the accuracy of the recover entries, two check metrics are involved in the tensor decomposition: traffic environment matrix E and driver familiarity matrix FF, as shown in Fig. 6.22. In the system, the digital map is divided into 4 zones to fill the check matrices with non-zero entries. E collects the traffic flow at each zone during a time slot, which size is $L \times 4$. Meanwhile, F counts the drivers' appearance at each zone, which size is $M \times 4$. The objective function of each tensor is updated with two additional items: $\|F - U \times G\|^2$ and $\|E - T \times H\|^2$, where $\|.\|^2$ denotes the L_2 norm, and G, H are auxiliary matrices.

6.4.4 Behavior Matching

According to the previous definition of dangerous behaviors and the processing of behavioral data, behavior data of each vehicle on a road segment at a certain time slot can be obtained. Next, we need to distinguish between dangerous behaviors and normal behaviors, and then identify unknown behaviors.

(1) Danger Extraction

In the first step, we cluster the behavior data on each road segment into two categories: dangerous and normal. Since it is hard to demarcate the border of the dangerous behaviors, Gaussian Mixture Model (GMM) is applied to distinguish whether the driver's behavior is dangerous in the system due. In addition, the distribution of the natural world usually can be described by Gaussian model, including the vehicular networks. And GMM has a good ability to demarcate the border

The basic idea of the GMM clustering method is to regard the distribution of the data as the mixture of several Gaussian distributions, and separate each out by the parameters trained through Expectation-Maximization (EM) algorithm [45]. Figure 6.23 displays the process. From the recovered behavior data, each tensor extracts a vector with M elements, which means a behavior on a road segment during a certain time slot. Then, we construct a behavior matrix S, which size is $4 \times M$.

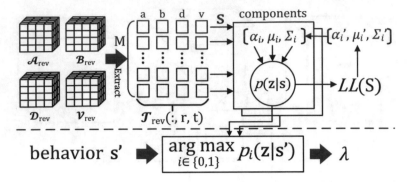

Fig. 6.23 Description of GMM

Each row vector in S respects a driver's driving behaviors, named behavior vector. Since two categories (dangerous and normal) are enough in the system, we mix 2 Gaussian distributions, called components, to fit the distribution of the behavior vectors. A component consists of three parameters α, μ, Σ and a probability $p(z|s)$, where α, μ, Σ denote the mixture coefficient, center vector, and covariance matrix, respectively. Specially, $\sum_{i=0}^{1} \alpha = 1$ and covariance matrix is a 4×4 matrix. z is a random variable to denote the tag of the component of a vector s, where $z \in \{0, 1\}$. The calculation of $p(z|s)$ is based on Bayesian theorem, combining with mentioned three parameters. In the first iteration, $\alpha_0 = \alpha_1 = 0.5$, and two center vectors are randomly selected from the behavior matrix. Besides, as Fig. 6.23 shown, a likelihood function $LL(S)$, integrated with $p(z|s)$, is utilized to train the parameters in each component. The training process is handled by EM algorithm, which object is to maximize the likelihood function during every iteration. After convergence, we obtain the probability distributions for the dangerous and normal behaviors at each road segment during a certain time slot, which separates these two behaviors out.

(2) **Danger Recognition**

With the parameters obtained in the distinguish step, the system could recognize an unknown behavior vector through trained models, shown in the lower part of Fig. 6.23. When a new behavior vector s' comes, the system use λ to label the behavior according to the result of $arg\,min_{i \in 0,1} p_i(z|s')$. The physical meaning is to put the behavior into the corresponding categories with the maximum probability.

6.4.5   Experiments and Evaluation

We first describe the evaluation methodology, including dataset description, metrics definition, and experimental settings. Then, we show the choices of the parameters in the system. At last, we validate the efficiency of our system from two impacts: data sparseness, and road types

(1) Dataset Description

We give a brief introduction of the datasets, digital map, and ground truth:

① Dataset

The dataset records 13,676 taxicabs' running items from April 1st to Apr. 30th in 2015 in Shanghai, which size is about 300G. Each item stores the information of highway, GPS point, record time, direction, instant velocity, brake state and so on. Besides, the average record time interval is about 10 s.

② Validation Dataset

The validation dataset is used to test the effectiveness of the GMM model described in previous section. The dataset is a demo set collected by an insurance company from Jul. 4th to Dec. 31st in 2016 in Shanghai, including 100 vehicles' traveling data, and its size is about 4 MB. In the dataset, each item not only includes the elements similar to the dataset, but also contains an additional element named insurance compensation ratio. The compensation ratio of insurance could reflect whether the vehicle has suffered accidents or not.

③ Digital Map

The map we utilized in the experiment is generated by OpenStreetMap [8], which is the area with the red dotted borders in Fig. 6.24a. Besides, 478 road segments are contained in the map.

④ Ground Truth

In the experiment, we manually mark 10 taxicabs' behaviors in the dataset as the ground truth. 3 of them are selected from a blacklist with 27 taxicabs, which is published by the Traffic Management Bureau. The other 7 taxicabs are those with the maximum mapped items in the selected map. To mark the behavior, we first give a threshold parameter ω. A behavior will be regarded as dangerous, if any one value in the behavior vector does not satisfy the following equation

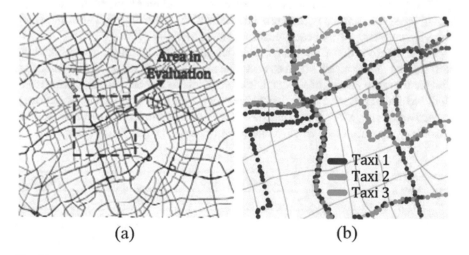

(a)   (b)

Fig. 6.24 Examples of map-matching

where $\omega \in (0, 1)$ and χ denotes the element (a, b, d, v) in the behavior vector (shown in Fig. 6.23). From the observations of the behavior vectors on each road segment, we find when $\omega = 0.1$, dangerous behaviors can be marked efficiently. Besides, in the validation dataset, we regard those with non-zero compensation ratio as the dangerous vehicles

⑤ Metrics Definition

We evaluate the performance of dangerous behaviors recognition from two metrics: precision and recall. The calculation of precision is defined as $\frac{tp}{tp+fp}$, and that of recall is $\frac{tp}{tp+fn}$, where tp, fp, and fn denote the true positives, the false positives, and the false negatives, respectively. Specifically, the true positives are the count that right recognizing dangerous behaviors.

(2) **Data Processing Results and Parameter Choice**

We first show the results in data processing, then we give the choice of the parameters in our system.

① Map-Matching

The fundamental step is map-matching. Figure 6.24b shows the map-matching of the three taxis. It can be seen that the recorded points are dense, which is also helpful for analyzing the behavior of the vehicle. The total count of the mapped items is 120, 172, 806.

② Data Filling

Where T denotes the tensor $(A, B, D, or\ V)$, while E and F denote the check matrices.

Table 6.5 displays the statistical information of the behavior attribute tensors and check matrices. Since the size of four tensors is the same $(13, 676 \times 478 \times 24)$, we let T denote the target attribute tensor. The ratio of the non-zero entries in tensor T is 11.57%. Moreover, we find that there are 185 road segments with no data recorded. We fill these zero entries with blank data estimation, which is defined in Eq. (6.3). Thus, the non-zero ratio of each tensor increases to 18.88%.

The non-zero ratio of the tensor after decomposition is 100%. We validate the performance of two check matrices using the mean absolute error (MAE) compared with the non-zero entries of a marked taxicab, which is selected as the ground truth. First, we decompose the four attribute tensors with and without check matrices, respectively. Then, MAE is calculated between the real nonzero values in the original tensors and the estimated values in the recovery ones. The size of the matrix E is 13,

Table 6.5 Statistics of the Tensor/Matrix	Tensor/matrix	Size	Non-zero ratio (%)
	T	$13, 676 \times 478 \times 24$	11.57
	E	$13, 676 \times 4$	100
	F	4×24	100

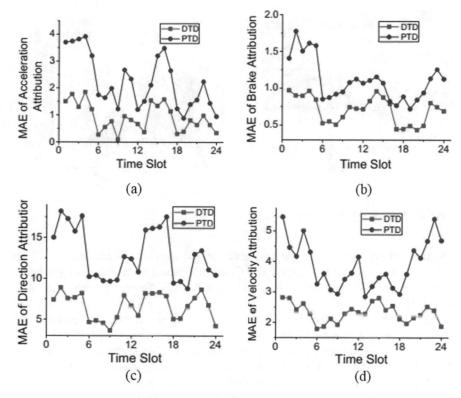

Fig. 6.25 MAE between PTD and DTD

676×4, while that of the matrix F is 4×24. We name the decomposition method integrated with check matrices derivative method (DTD), while the primary method (PTD) is without check matrices. The MAEs between the PTD and the DTD of four attribute tensors are shown in Fig. 6.25. Clearly, the check matrices give a great favor in the tensor decomposition.

③ Parameter Settings

The threshold ε in Eq. (6.2) is set to be $1°$. Hence, the 478 road segments in the selected map can be divided into 1,870 sub-segments. We evaluate the performance of direction data refinement using the average value of the taxicabs' directions mapped on a road segment as the reference. Figure 6.26a illustrates the directions of a road segment with 21 sub-segments and that of the taxicabs mapped on it. Note that labels "RD", "AD", "SD" and "SAD" denote road segment direction, average direction, segmental direction, and segmental average direction, respectively. Note that "RD" and "SD" (calculate the direction only between beginning node and end node) come from the digital map, while "AD" and "SAD" are calculated (obtain the average value from the direction data) by the taxicabs' data. Obviously, only using the directions of the road segments may cause errors in the direction attribute calculation.

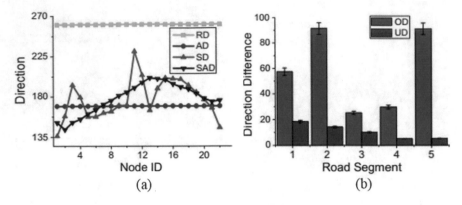

Fig. 6.26 Dangerous behavior recognition results

Figure 6.26b compares the original difference (OD) and updated difference (UD) by 5 road segments in the map. Original difference means the absolute average difference between "RD" and "AD", while updated difference denotes that between "SD" and "SAD".

As described in previous section, we set $\alpha_0 = \alpha_1 = 0.5$ when we initialize the parameters in GMM. Meanwhile, two center vectors are randomly selected among 13,676 behaviors on each road segment at a certain time slot. The covariance matrices Σ_0 and Σ_1 are initialized as the identity matrices, which have the same size 2×2. Figure 6.27a shows the average percentages of the dangerous taxicabs at each time slot after the clustering of GMM based method. We find that less dangerous behaviors occurred during rush hour than others. Moreover, to validate the credibility of the GMM-based approach in the system, we first do not input the behavior data of the 10 marked taxicabs into the GMM in the danger extraction step. After a trained GMM obtained, we analyze its performance among the total behaviors of the

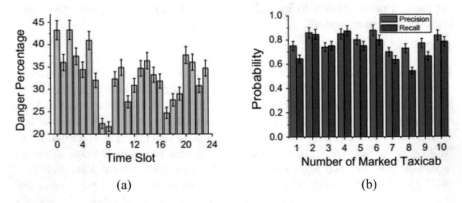

Fig. 6.27 Results of direction refinement

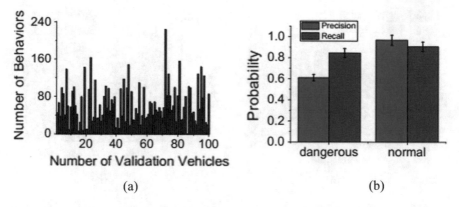

Fig. 6.28 Dangerous behavior recognition

marked taxicabs, which is shown in Fig. 6.27b. The average precision that a taxicab's dangerous behaviors can be right recognized is about 81%.

④   Dangerous Vehicle Recognition

In this section, we give the results about the dangerous vehicle recognition by the GMM based method described in previous section. A validation dataset is included in the evaluation. The dataset contains 6,370 behaviors of 100 vehicles. Figure 6.28a shows the count distribution of the vehicles' behaviors. The minimum count is 1, while the maximum is 223.

During the recognition, we utilize the GMM based method to distinguish each behavior. Then, for each vehicle, their behaviors are classified into two categories: dangerous and normal. Thus, if the count of the dangerous one is bigger than the normal one, the vehicle will be marked "dangerous". Otherwise, we mark it "normal".

As the ground truth mentioned in previous section, 13 vehicles' compensation ratio is not equal to zero, which are regarded as dangerous vehicles. Figure 6.28b gives the recognition results of the dangerous vehicles in the validation dataset. We find that most (over 80%) dangerous vehicles could be recognized. Meanwhile, the precision of the normal vehicles recognition is high (about 97%), which means our system gives a strict bound for those vehicles with safety behaviors.

(3)   **Case Study**

In this section, we design two different experiments to study the impacts of the data sparseness and the road type on the system, respectively

①   Impact of Data Sparseness

In our system, the data sparseness is described as the non-zero ratio in the source historical dataset. We adjust the ratio by random removing the non-zero entries in the original behavior tensors. 5 levels are divided in the experiment: 20%, 40%, 60%, 80% and 100%. Each level reflects the ratio of the remaining non-zero entries in original ones. For example, when the level is 20%, the non-zero entries

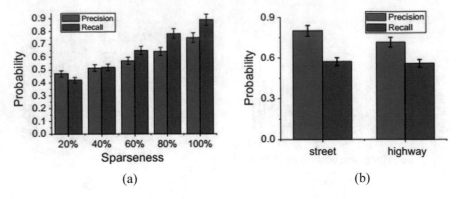

Fig. 6.29 Results of case study

ratio is $11.57\% \times 20\% = 2.314\%$ in the original tensors. Then, we calculate the recall and precision of a marked taxicab's total behaviors. The result is shown in Fig. 6.29a. It is easy to observe that behavior recognition tends to random distribution when the data is too sparse.

② Impact of Road Types

Next, we keep the original training tensor and compare the performances under urban street and highway two different road types. In the experiment, we select two road segments with different types (street or highway) and regard a marked taxicab's behaviors on both ones as the ground truth. The result is displayed in Fig. 6.29b. The performance in highway shows more recall but less precision due to the high mobility.

References

1. J.W. Yin Zhu, Y. Zhou, *Intelligent Transportation System* (Chinese People's Public Security University Press, Beijing, 2010)
2. Z.Z. Changjun Jiang, *Advanced Urban Communications Technology* (Science Press, Beijing, 2014)
3. Z. Zhang, Y. Shi, C. Jiang, *Parallel Implementing of Road Situation Modeling with Floating GPS Data*. Lecture Notes in Computer Science, vol. 3842 (2006), pp. 620–624
4. C. Y. Changjun Jiang, Y. Chen, A path planning method and system based on distributed dynamic road network: 201610387934.4, 2019-01-25
5. Y. Z. Changjun Jiang, Y. Chen, A trajectory reduction algorithm based on road attributes and real-time road conditions: 201310156627.1, 2015-04-15
6. S. Yang, C. Wang, L. Yang, et al., iLogBook: enabling text-searchable event query using sparse vehicle-mounted GPS data. IEEE Trans. Intell. Transp. Syst. 1–11 (2018)
7. Z. Xiao, C. Wang, W. Han et al., Unique on the road: re-identification of vehicular location-based metadata, in *Proceedings of SecureComm*, Guangzhou, China (2016), pp. 496–513
8. S. Yang, C. Wang, H. Zhu, et al., APP: augmented proactive perception for driving hazards with sparse GPS trace, in *Proceedings of ACM Mobihoc*, Catania, Italy (2019), pp. 21–30

9. P. Banerjee, S. Ranu, S. Raghavan, Inferring uncertain trajectories from partial observations, in *Proceedings of International Conference on Data Mining*, Shenzhen, China (2014), pp. 30–39
10. T. Hunter, P. Abbeel, A. Bayen, The path inference filter: model-based low-latency map matching of probe vehicle data. IEEE Trans. Intell. Transp. Syst. **15**(2), 507–529 (2014)
11. G. R. Jagadeesh, T. Srikanthan, Robust real-time route inference from sparse vehicle position data, in *Proceedings of IEEE ITSC*, Qingdao, China (2014), pp. 296–301
12. J.D. Lafferty, A. Mccallum, F. Pereira, Conditional random fields: probabilistic models for segmenting and labeling sequence data, in Proceedings of ICML, Williamstown, MA, USA (2001), pp. 282–289
13. P.E. Newson, J. Krumm, Hidden Markov map matching through noise and sparseness, in *Proceedings of ACM SIGSPATIAL, Seattle*, WA, USA (2009), pp. 336–343
14. M. Rahmani, H.N. Koutsopoulos, Path inference from sparse floating car data for urban networks. Transp. Res. Part C-emerging Technol. **30**, 41–54 (2013)
15. Y. Wang, Y. Zheng, Y. Xue, Travel time estimation of a path using sparse trajectories, in *Proceedings of ACM SIGKDD*, New York, NY, USA (2014), pp. 25–34
16. H. Wei, Y. Wang, G. Forman et al., Fast Viterbi map matching with tunable weight functions, in *Proceedings ACM SIGSPATIAL*, Redondo Beach, California (2012), pp. 613–616
17. H. Wu, J. Mao, W. Sun et al., Probabilistic robust route recovery with Spatio-Temporal dynamics, in *Proceedings of ACM SIGKDD*, San Francisco, California, USA (2016), pp. 1915–1924
18. K. Zheng, Y. Zheng, X. Xie et al., Reducing uncertainty of low-sampling-rate trajectories, in *Proceedings of IEEE ICDE*, Washington, DC, USA (2012), pp. 1144–1155
19. D. Feldman, A. Sugaya, C. Sung et al., iDiary: from GPS signals to a text-searchable diary, in *Proceedings of ACM SenSys*, Rome, Italy (2013), p. 60
20. J. Krumm, D. Rouhana, Placer: semantic place labels from diary data, in *Proceedings of ACM UbiComp*, Zurich, Switzerland (2013), pp. 163–172
21. C. Parent, S. Spaccapietra, C. Renso et al., Semantic trajectories modeling and analysis. ACM Comput. Surv. **45**(4), 42 (2013)
22. A. Vu, J.A. Farrell, M.J. Barth, Centimeter-accuracy smoothed vehicle trajectory estimation. IEEE Intell. Transp. Syst. Mag. **5**(4), 121–135 (2013)
23. Z. Yan, D. Chakraborty, C. Parent et al., SeMiTri: a framework for semantic annotation of heterogeneous trajectories, in *Proceedings of EDBT/ICDT*, Uppsala, Sweden (2011), pp. 259–270
24. M. Ye, D. Shou, W. Lee, et al.On the semantic annotation of places in location-based social networks, in *Proceedings of ACM SIGKDD*, Uppsala, Sweden (2011), pp. :520–528
25. K.S. Yen, S.M. Donecker, K. Yan et al., Development of vehicular and personal universal longitudinal travel diary systems using GPS and new technology. Report, California Department of Transportation, Division of Research and Innovation (2006)
26. G.S. Aoude, V.R. Desaraju, L.H. Stephens et al., Behavior classification algorithms at intersections and validation using naturalistic data, in *Proceedings of .IEEE IVS*, Baden-Baden, Germany, (2011), pp. 601–606
27. V. Coroama, The smart tachograph – individual accounting of traffic costs and its implications, in *Proceedings of IEEE PerCom*, Pisa, Italy (2006), pp. 135–152
28. H. Eren, S. Makinist, E. Akin et al., Estimating driving behavior by a smartphone, in *Proceedings of IEEE IVS*, Alcala de Henares, Spain (2012), pp. 234–239
29. H. Liu, T. Taniguchi, Y. Tanaka et al., Visualization of driving behavior based on hhidden feature extraction by using deep learning. IEEE Trans. Intell. Transp. Syst. **18**(9), 2477–2489 (2017)
30. J.G. Smith, S.K. Ponnuru, M. Patil, Detection of aggressive driving behavior and fault behavior using pattern matching, in *Proceedings of IEEE ICACCI*, Jaipur, India (2016), pp. 207–211
31. T. Umedu, K. Isu, T. Higashino et al., An intervehicular-communication protocol for distributed detection of dangerous vehicles. IEEE Trans. Veh. Technol. **59**(2), 627–637 (2010)
32. C. You, N.D. Lane, F. Chen et al., CarSafe app: alerting drowsy and distracted drivers using dual cameras on smartphones, in *Proceedings of ACM Mobisys*, Taipei, Taiwan (2013), pp. 461–462

33. J. Yu, H. Zhu, H. Han et al., SenSpeed: sensing driving conditions to estimate vehicle speed in urban environments. IEEE Trans. Mob. Comput. **15**(1), 202–216 (2016)
34. C.J. Jiang, Z.H. Zhang, G.S. Zeng et al., Urban traffic information service application grid. J. Comput. Sci. Technol. **20**(1), 134–140 (2005)
35. Z.H. Zhang, C. Jiang, F. Yu, Road situation modeling and parallel algorithm implementation with FCD based on principle curves, in *Proceedings of Eighth International Conference on High-performance Computing in Asia-pacific Region*, Beijing, China, 2005:181–186
36. P. Grassberger, I. Procaccia, Measuring the strangeness of strange attractors. Physica D **9**(1–2), 189–208 (1983)
37. Z. Zhang, Fast algorithm of dynamic shortest paths based on discrete varying-weight networks. Comput. Sci. **37**(4), 238–240 (2010)
38. L. Lin, C.G. Yan, C.J. Jiang, X.D. Zhou, Complexity and approximate algorithm of shortest paths in dynamic networks. Chin. J. Comput. **30**(4), 608–614 (2007)
39. M.A. Quddus, W.Y. Ochieng, R.B. Noland, Current map-matching algorithms for transport applications: state-of-the art and future research directions. Transp. Res. Part C-emerging Technol. **15**(5), 312–328 (2007)
40. H. Tan, G. Feng, J. Feng et al., A tensor based method for missing traffic data completion. Transp. Res. Part C-emerging Technol. **28**, 15–27 (2013)
41. Y. Lou, C. Zhang, Y. Zheng, et al.Map-matching for low-sampling-rate GPS trajectories, in *Proceedings of ACM SIGSPATIAL*, Seattle, WA, USA (2009), pp. 352–361
42. C.Y. Goh, J. Dauwels, N. Mitrovic et al., Online map-matching based on Hidden Markov model for real-time traffic sensing applications, in *Proceedings of ITSC*, Anchorage, AK, USA (2012), 776–781
43. G.D. Forney, The viterbi algorithm. Proc. IEEE **61**(3), 268–278 (1973)
44. A. Cichocki, Era of big data processing: a new approach via tensor networks and tensor decompositions, in *Proceedings of SISA*, Nagoya, Japan (2013), pp. 1–30
45. A.P. Dempster, N.M. Laird, D.B. Rubin, Maximum likelihood from incomplete data via the EM algorithm. J. R. Stat. Soc. Ser. B-Methodol. **39**(1), 1–22 (1977)

Chapter 7
Smart Tourism

Abstract In this chapter, we first analyze and summarize the current hotspot platforms and Apps of smart tourism at home and abroad. On this basis, we focus on the key application layer technology, the POI recommendation technology, in smart tourism. In view of the problems of sparse check-in data and long tensor factorization time, the recommendation method that can accurately recommend the POIs to the users and reduce the calculation time is given according to the similar characteristics of users, time slots and POIs. In addition, besides the recommendation of the single POI, a personalized POI sequence recommendation method is given, which further improves users' experience of smart tourism POI services.

7.1 Related Applications and Technologies

As an important branch of smart city, smart tourism uses new technologies such as cloud computing and Internet of Things to actively perceive and timely release information on tourism resources, tourism activities and tourists' needs. The purpose is to enable people to obtain the information in real time, arrange and adjust work and travel plans, so as to achieve the intelligent perception and the convenient utilization of various types of tourism information. The applications of smart tourism in the tourism industry chain include: tourism information platforms, smart scenic spots, online travel enterprises, smart travel agencies, smart hotels, and smart travel traffic [1].

With the rise of the concept of smart city, smart tourism has developed rapidly abroad. As early as 2005, the Steamboat Ski Resort in Colorado, USA, first introduced a feedback system equipped with RFID locating devices specially designed for tourists, called Mountain Watch, which is the origin of smart tourism. The feedback system can not only monitor the location of tourists in real time, recommend ski routes for tourists, and feedback consumption situation, but also provide users with safe and convenient technology services. In 2009, with the support of the EU, the two companies in the UK and Germany collaborated to develop an intelligent guide software called iTacitus. Based on the AR technology, visitors can experience history "in person" through sounds, lights and videos. When a tourist is in a certain place,

© Springer Nature Singapore Pte Ltd. & Science Press 2020
C. Jiang and Z. Li, *Mobile Information Service for Networks*,
https://doi.org/10.1007/978-981-15-4569-6_7

if the mobile phone camera is aimed at the historical remains in front of the eyes, the image recognition software of the mobile phone and the GPS can immediately determine the precise location of the tourist. Then, the scene of the historic site will be displayed by iTactius from the perspective of the visitor, and the defective part of the site can also be displayed by the virtual reconstruction technology. Moreover, the software also has the function of route planning with custom-made exclusive travel plans for tourists. In the same year, South Korea launched the "I Tour Seoul" smart travel service system. It can provide a handheld mobile travel information service platform for tourists, which offers relevant attractions, restaurants and tourist routes according to users' current locations. In 2012, the Belgian capital Brussels launched the "Tag City" project based on smartphones. This project uses the close-range and high-frequency wireless communication chips to make barcoded stickers and pastes them in museums, places of interest, shops and restaurants throughout the streets of Brussels. Visitors only need to download the barcode scanners on the i-nigma website with their smartphones, and they can scan the "Tag City" stickers anytime and anywhere in Brussels, to easily access relevant historical and cultural introductions, shopping discounts and route navigation. In addition, the well-known online travel platforms of the United States, Priceline, Expedia, and Sabre, can provide smart travel services such as travel ticketing, route planning, and hotel reservations. They are comprehensive travel platforms.

In China, Zhenjiang City of Jiangsu Province first proposed the concept of "Smart Tourism" and launched the "Smart Tourism" project in 2010. In 2011, Nanjing launched the "Smart Tourism" construction, and the "Nanjing Tourist Assistant" and other clients were successfully developed and put into use. In the same year, Shanghai launched the mobile phone guide iTravels, which can display information about tourist attractions in a multimedia way, as well as comprehensive service information based on geographic location services. The "Strait Intelligent Tourism" project initiated by Fujian Province has the functions of online electronic trading, offline payment verification terminal system and interconnected distribution system. In 2015, China issued the "Guiding Opinions on Promoting the Development of Smart Tourism" and "Several Opinions on Further Promoting Tourism Investment and Consumption", indicating the importance attached to the construction of smart tourism. Since the beginning of smart tourism in China, all provinces and cities around the country have continuously built smart tourism products with their own distinctive brands. Besides the government-led tourism information publishing platforms or Apps, there are various online travel companies in China, such as Ctrip, Qunar, Feizhu, Tuniu, Yimu, Yilong, Maotuying, and Tongcheng Travel Network. They provide technology infrastructures to travel service providers through mobile clients and online platforms, and provide the deep searching and smart recommendation for travel routes of domestic and international airfare, hotels, vacations, travel group purchases and travel information for travelers anytime, anywhere through the full platform coverage of websites and mobile clients. They can help travelers find cost-effective products and provide better travel information and convenient booking services. The Qyer and the Mafengwo provide users with comprehensive travel services such as travel guides, travel specials and reservations.

Among the above travel platform systems and App products, one of the most important technologies for smart tourism is the location recommendation. The location recommendation is the basis for a series of application-level issues such as the travel route selection, the travel product recommendation, and the crowd forecast. This chapter will focus on location-based and personalized location recommendations, as well as location sequence recommendations [2–8] in travel services.

In location-based recommendations, an important concept is Point of Interests (POI), which is a meaningful place in the physical world, such as a park or mall. It is usually represented as a location with a coordinate and a category marker, so there are a lot of POIs in the physical world. In this chapter, a "location" defaults to one POI. When a user visits a location, he/she can make a tag to generate a record and publish it in the virtual space, which we call Check-in. The popularity of location-aware devices such as mobile phones and GPS navigation systems has facilitated the rapid development of location-based services such as Weibo, Foursquare, and Gowalla. Such huge geo-tagged data from mobile devices creates opportunities for us to provide better services to users by understanding and analyzing their interests and behaviors.

In academia, researchers have provided a variety of location recommendation methods. For example, in literature [9], two typical types of travel recommendation methods were proposed: the public recommendation and the personalized recommendation. Among them, the public recommends the most interesting location in a geographic space to users, ignoring the user's personalized preferences. The personalized recommendation is to use a tree-shaped hierarchical diagram to model the user's access sequence, and apply the Hyperlink-Induced Topic Search (HITS), so as to infer the user's preference degree for specific locations in a certain area. In addition, many personalized location recommendation methods have been proposed one after another. For example, in literature [10], an enhanced collaborative filtering method was used to implement restaurant recommendations. In literature [11], a location-based and preference-related recommendation system was proposed to recommend a range of attractions within a certain region. In the literature [12, 13], user preferences, social influences, and geographic influences were all applied to location recommendations. However, although a user has visited many POIs in the physical world, his/her check-in records left in cyberspace are minimal. Based on these sparse check-in data, how to provide accurate service recommendations to users is a problem worth studying.

In addition, besides a single location recommendation, we sometimes want to be recommended as a sequence of locations. In order to recommend a sequence of locations to users, the researchers conducted researches based on two types of data: the GPS trajectory data and the social media data with geotags. Since the former researches mainly use historical GPS trajectories to infer popular paths [14–18], they are not able to flexibly provide personalized paths. With the popularity of mobile devices and location-based social networks, the path planning using geo-labeled social media data has received close attention from industry and academia. Many researchers have used mobile social application data to conduct researches on path planning [19–25], such as the recommendation methods of personalized location sequence named BFA and TripMine⁺ [26, 27]. In addition, some literatures proposed a variety of different path planning models and algorithms. In the literature [28], both geo-labeled social media data and GPS trajectories data were used. In literature [29], the users' call record data was used and the dynamic Bayesian network method was adopted to fuse the similar users' mobile modes to predict the users' next POIs. But this method could only predict the location that has occurred in history, but failed to predict new locations. Literature [30] designed a POI prediction method based on deep learning. However, none of the above methods can quickly implement the planning of constrained POI sequences. In the personalized POI sequence recommendation, the total money and total time spent on accessing the location are treated as a cost, and they are placed in the constraint. And the quality characterized by the POI sequence score and diversity is considered as a benefit. Therefore, in this sense, the personalized POI sequence recommendation problem can be attributed to the orienteering game problem [31]. However, the personalized location sequence recommendation problem has unique features simultaneously:

(1)   If a location is accessed in different time periods, its benefits are different;
(2)   In the planning process, the POIs sequence diversity is considered, which needs to be obtained by calculating the similarity between the POI that has not been visited and each POI that has been selected.

For the above features, it is not possible to directly solve the personalized POI sequence recommendation problem by using the existing operational research methods. Therefore, it is necessary to design a new planning algorithm for solving the problem.

In this chapter, based on the above-mentioned accurate location recommendation problem based on sparse check-in data and personalized location sequence recommendation problem, a personalized location recommendation method based on the collaborative tensor factorization and the partition based collaborative tensor factorization are given respectively in Sects. 7.2 and 7.3 to solve the problem of time-consuming for the precise recommendations and the tensor factorization based on sparse data. A method for recommending the POI sequences based on maximum edge correlation is given in Sect. 7.4. In the recommendation process, both the correlation of POI sequences, and their diversity are considered, and the planning process of the POI sequences can be quickly completed.

7.2   Location Recommendation Based on Collaborative Tensor Factorization

Personalized location recommendation methods aim to provide users an ordered location list according to some explicit or implicit interests of users [32]. In reality, although a user has visited many points of interest in the physical world, his/her check-in record left in cyberspace is minimal. Thus, making an accurate recommendation based on these sparse check-in data is a big challenge, which is a problem worth studying.

There have been many researches trying to solve this problem. For example, many methods based on Collaborative Filtering (CF) and Matrix Factorization (MF) have attracted the attention of many researchers [33–37]. These methods usually can obtain high prediction accuracy and scalability. However, they usually do not consider other context factors like time factor which is necessary to improve the accuracy of personalized location recommendation.

In this section, a general framework of the collaborative tensor factorization is presented, which can be used for the multivariate relationship prediction and context-based recommendation. Based on the framework, a n-order tensor and a plurality of context characteristic matrices are simultaneously decomposed with the proviso that the tensor must share at least one factor with each of the characteristic matrices [38]. In this section, the personalized location recommendation is modeled as the prediction problem of missing values in tensors. In addition, we consider not only the association among users, locations and time slots, but also the relationship between category distribution, time distribution, and the correlations between two POIs. On this basis, the predicted value is used as a score of a user to a certain location within a certain time period, and the location is accurately recommended to the user according to the score.

Specifically, the user's check-in behavior is first modeled as a third-order tensor of user-POI-time, which describes the relationship between different users, time periods and locations. At the same time, from three different angles of the time distribution, the category distribution and the position correlation feature, the features are extracted and the corresponding feature matrices are constructed. Then, the collaborative tensor factorization method is used to reconstruct the user's location preference. Finally, the user check-in data set of the Weibo position website is used to conduct experiments and evaluate the proposed method. The experiments show that, compared with the "user-POI" matrix factorization method, the collaborative factorization method of the "user-POI-time" tensors and the three contextual feature matrices can give more accurate score prediction results, thereby obtaining more accurate location recommendation results.

7.2.1 Collaborative Tensor Factorization Method

Tensor factorization method has been widely used in urban computing [39]. For example, in order to realize different kinds of recommendations, a context-aware tensor factorization method is used by leveraging additional information, such as the activity-activity correlation and geographical features of a location [40–42]. Urban refueling behavior is inferred together with POI data, traffic features, and gas stations' contextual features [43, 44]. Travel time of a road segment without being traversed by trajectories in current time slot is also estimated through a context-aware tensor factorization approach. Based on the tensor factorization method, the fine-grained noise situation of different times of day for each region of NYC is inferred by using the 311 compliant data together with social media, road network data, and POIs [45]. To the best of our knowledge, the personalized location recommendation method of collaborative tensor factorization has not been presented yet.

In order to improve the effectiveness of personalized location recommendation, many contexts are considered in the model and many context-ware recommendation models are proposed. Zheng et al. [46] use GPS data and comments at various locations to discover interesting locations and possible activities that can be performed for recommendation. Cheng et al. [47] fuse matrix factorization with geographical and social influence for POI recommendation. However, a general framework is needed to model different contexts.

First, here give the definition of commonly used symbols: R is the set of real numbers, R^+ is the set of positive real numbers, $N = \{0, 1, 2, \ldots\}$ is the natural number set, and, $N^+ = N \backslash \{0\}$, $N_k = \{0, 1, 2, \ldots, k\}$, $N_{k^+} = \{1, 2, \ldots, k\}$, $k \in N^+$.

Below we first give the definitions of location, check-in and the problem description of the location recommendation, then give a model of the location recommendation problem.

Definition 7.1 Point of Interests (POI)

$P = [P_{id}, L_1, L_2, C_1, C_2, \cdots, C_k]$ is a point of interest (POI),where

(1) P_{id} is a unique identifier for the POI;
(2) L_1 and L_2 respectively denote the latitude and longitude of the POI;
(3) C_1-C_k denote k categories which the POI belongs to.

A POI is a significant venue/location in physical world, like a shopping mall or a theatre. Usually, a POI belongs to one or more categories such as Entertainment, Vehicles, Education, Food and Dining, Government, Shopping, Sports, and Travel etc.

Definition 7.2 Check-In

$c_i = [UC_{id}, U_{id}, P_{id}, T]$ is a check-in, where

(1) UC_{id}, U_{id} and P_{id} are the unique identifiers of a check-in, a user, and a POI, respectively;
(2) T is a time stamp.

In location location-based social networks (LBSNs) such as Foursquare and Weibo, a user can mark a POI while arriving there, and thus a check-in is made.

Definition 7.3 POI Recommendation

Given a set of check-ins denoted by CI $= \{ci_1, ci_2, \ldots, ci_n\}$, an ordered list of top-k POIs LP $= (P_1', P_2', \ldots, P_k')$ is provided to a user.

The goal of POI recommendation is to provide a POI recommendation list to a user according to user preferences about different POIs in different time slots. In order to obtain a user's preferences about different POIs in different time slots, we formulate this problem to predict missing ratings. It is assumed that the check-in frequency characterizes a user's visiting preference. The higher the check-in frequency, the

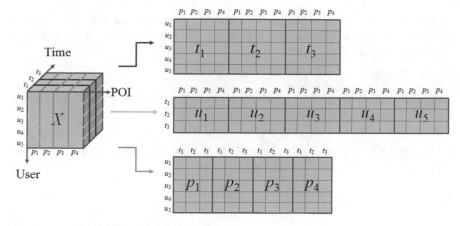

Fig. 7.1 An example of "User-POI-Time" tensor

more the POI is preferred by a user [48]. Based on this assumption, the check-in frequency of a POI can be used to estimate a user's visiting preference for this POI.

In the location recommendation, the most important issue is the prediction of the user's score on one POI. In this section, the location prediction problem is characterized by the recover problem of missing values in the tensor and is implemented by a method based on the tensor factorization.

An example of a tensor model is given below. Figure 7.1 shows an example of three-mode tensor $X \in R^{5 \times 4 \times 3}$. Its three modes represent users, POIs and time slots, respectively. The "user-POI-time" tensor can be flattened in three ways to obtain matrices comprising its modes, as shown in the right side of the Fig. 7.1. Each entry's value $X(i, j, k)$ of X denotes the check-in frequency of user u_i in POI p_j in time slot t_k. Given X, the distribution of check-ins over different POIs of a user u_i during a time slot t_k can be obtained by retrieving the vector $X(i, j, k)$, $\left(j \in N_4^+\right)$. Users can also be ranked at t_k according to p_j based on $X(i, j, k)$, $\left(j \in N_5^+\right)$. POIs can be ranked according to overall check-in $\sum_{i=1}^{5} \sum_{k=1}^{3} X_{ijk}$.

The following describes the method of collaborative tensor factorization.

(1) n-Mode Tensor Factorization

In order to fill the missing entries in the original tensor, the n-mode tensor factorization is a commonly used method. Given an n-mode tensor $X \in \mathbb{R}^{D_1 \times D_2 \cdots \times D_n}$, a common approach of filling the missing entries of tensor X is to factorize X into the multiplication of a core tensor $G \in \mathbb{R}^{k_1 \times k_2 \cdots \times k_n}$ and a set of (low-rank) matrices $M_1 \in \mathbb{R}^{D_1 \times k_1}, M_2 \in \mathbb{R}^{D_2 \times k_2}, \cdots, M_n \in \mathbb{R}^{D_n \times k_n}$ based on X's non-zero entries. It is used to recover the original tensor, and each of these elements can be calculated by the following formula:

$$\hat{x}_{d_1, d_2, \dots, d_n} = G \times_1 (M_1)_{d_{1*}} \times_2 (M_2)_{d_{2*}} \times_3 \cdots \times_n (M_n)_{d_{n*}} \quad (7.1)$$

Next, the loss function, the regular term and the optimized objective function of the n-mode tensor factorization are analyzed in turn, and then its factorization algorithm is given.

① Lost Function

First, analogous to the matrix factorization [49, 50], the loss function of the n-mode tensor factorization is defined as

$$\Phi(\hat{x}, x) = \frac{1}{\|D\|_1} \sum_{d_1, d_2, \dots, d_n} D_{d_1, d_2, \dots, d_n} l(\hat{x}_{d_1, d_2, \dots, d_n}, x_{d_1, d_2, \dots, d_n}) \tag{7.2}$$

where,

$$D_{d_1, d_2, L, d_n} = \begin{cases} 1 & if \ x_{d_1, d_2, L, d_n} \ is \ observable \ in \ X \\ 0 & else \end{cases} \tag{7.3}$$

In Eq. (7.2), $l : \mathbb{R} \times x \to \mathbb{R}$ represents the loss term for a single element, calculated with the distance between the observed and predicted values of the element. $\hat{x}_{d_1, d_2, \dots, d_n}$ can be obtained by formula (7.1). The overall loss Φ is only defined on the observable values in the tensor X. The loss function l can have the following options,

(1) Quadratic Error

$$l(\hat{x}, x) = \frac{1}{2}(\hat{x} - x)^2, \quad and \quad \partial_{\hat{x}} l(\hat{x}, x) = \hat{x} - x$$

(2) Absolute Error

$$l(\hat{x}, x) = |\hat{x} - x|, \quad and \quad \partial_{\hat{x}} l(\hat{x}, x) = sgn[\hat{x} - x]$$

(3) ε-Sensitive Loss

$$l(\hat{x}, x) = \max(0, |\hat{x} - x| - \varepsilon), \ and \ \partial_{\hat{x}} l(\hat{x}, x)$$
$$= \begin{cases} sgn[\hat{x} - x] \ if \ |\hat{x} - x| > \varepsilon \\ 0 \qquad\qquad else \end{cases}.$$

Not all loss function options are listed here. For example, possible loss functions include Huber loss and Hinge loss functions [51], which are useful in exploring implicit information [52].

② Regularization

Simply minimizing a loss function often leads to overfitting problems. Therefore, in order to avoid it, the L_2 norm of the factor is usually added as a regular term. For matrices, the norm is also generally considered to be the Frobenius norm, which is denoted by the symbol $\|\cdot\|_F$. For the sake of simplicity, the text is replaced by $\|\cdot\|$.

$$\Omega[M_1, M_2, \ldots, M_n] := \frac{1}{2}\left[\lambda_1\|M_1\|^2 + \lambda_2\|M_2\|^2 + \cdots + \lambda_n\|M_n\|^2\right] \qquad (7.4)$$

In a similar way, for the core tensor G, we can also use the L_2 norm as a regular term.

$$\Omega[G] := \frac{1}{2}\left[\lambda_0\|G\|^2\right] \qquad (7.5)$$

Here, we can also use the L_1 norm as a regular term to find a sparse solution [53, 54].

$$\Omega[M_1, M_2, \cdots, M_n] := \sum_{d_1, k_1}\left|(M_1)_{d_1, k_1}\right| + \sum_{d_2, k_2}\left|(M_2)_{d_2, k_2}\right| + \cdots + \sum_{d_n, k_n}\left|(M_n)_{d_n, k_n}\right|$$

$$(7.6)$$

When L_1 norm is used as a regular term, and a sparse model can be obtained with it. However, the optimization is not trivial for a lot of hidden parameters needed in the process of optimization. Therefore, the L_2 norm is often used as a regular term.

③ Optimization

Combining the loss function and the regular term, the objective function of the optimization problem is

$$L(G, M_1, M_2, \cdots, M_n)$$
$$= \Phi\left(\hat{X}, X\right) + \Omega[G] + \Omega[G, M_1, M_2, \cdots, M_n]$$
$$= \frac{1}{\|D\|_1}\sum_{d_1, d_2, \cdots, d_n} D_{d_1, d_2, \cdots, d_n}\, l\left(\hat{x}_{d_1, d_2, \cdots, d_n}, x_{d_1, d_2, \cdots, d_n}\right)$$
$$+ \frac{1}{2}\left[\lambda_0\|G\|^2\right] + \frac{1}{2}\left[\lambda_1\|M_1\|^2 + \lambda_2\|M_2\|^2 + \cdots \lambda_n\|M_n\|^2\right] \qquad (7.7)$$

Currently, there are many ways to minimize the value of the objective function in Eq. (7.7). In the matrix factorization, the subspace descent method is a very popular method, which can also be used for the tensor factorization. In the subspace descent method, when optimizing one of the components, keep the remaining components fixed, and then iteratively optimize each part of the model like this in turn. For example, while maintaining the matrix and tensor of other than M_1, the optimization of matrix M_1 operation is performed. Then, when the matrix and tensor of other than M_2 are kept unchanged, the matrix M_2 is optimized, and so forth. This method can converge quickly, but the optimization process needs to be set to batch form.

When the size of the data set grows, it is less feasible to solve the factorization problem by using the batch optimization. Instead, a simple online algorithm is used. Given a $x_{d_1, d_2, \cdots, d_n}$, the algorithm performs Stochastic Gradient Descent (SGD) in the factors $(M_1)_{d_1*}, (M_2)_{d_2*}, \ldots, (M_n)_{d_n*}$. In order to calculate the update process in the

SGD, it is necessary to calculate the gradient of the objective function with respect to each component. First, give the gradient of the loss function for each component, as follows,

$$
\begin{aligned}
&\partial_{(M_1)_{d_1*}} l\left(\hat{x}_{d_1,d_2,\cdots,d_n}, x_{d_1,d_2,\cdots,d_n}\right) \\
&= \partial_{\hat{x}_{d_1,d_2,\cdots,d_n}} l\left(\hat{x}_{d_1,d_2,\cdots,d_n}, x_{d_1,d_2,\cdots,d_n}\right) \times \partial_{(M_1)_{d_1*}} \hat{x}_{d_1,d_2,\cdots,d_n} \\
&= \left(\hat{x}_{d_1,d_2,\cdots,d_n} - x_{d_1,d_2,\cdots,d_n}\right) \times \partial_{(M_1)_{d_1*}} \left[G \times_1 (M_1)_{d_1*} \times_2 (M_2)_{d_2*} \times_3 \cdots \times_n (M_n)_{d_n*}\right] \\
&= \left(\hat{x}_{d_1,d_2,\cdots,d_n} - x_{d_1,d_2,\cdots,d_n}\right) \times \left[G \times_2 (M_2)_{d_2*} \times_3 \cdots \times_n (M_n)_{d_n*}\right]
\end{aligned} \tag{7.8}
$$

Similarly, calculate as follows,

$$
\begin{aligned}
&\partial_{(M_1)_{d_1*}} l\left(\hat{x}_{d_1,d_2,\cdots,d_n}, x_{d_1,d_2,\cdots,d_n}\right) \\
&= \left(\hat{x}_{d_1,d_2,\cdots,d_n} - x_{d_1,d_2,\cdots,d_n}\right) \times \left[G \times_2 (M_2)_{d_2*} \times_3 \cdots \times_n (M_n)_{d_n*}\right] \\
&\partial_{(M_2)_{d_2*}} l\left(\hat{x}_{d_1,d_2,\cdots,d_n}, x_{d_1,d_2,\cdots,d_n}\right) \\
&= \left(\hat{x}_{d_1,d_2,\cdots,d_n} - x_{d_1,d_2,\cdots,d_n}\right) \times \left[G \times_1 (M_1)_{d_1*} \times_3 \cdots \times_n (M_n)_{d_n*}\right] \\
&\qquad\qquad\cdots\cdots \\
&\partial_{(M_n)_{d_n*}} l\left(\hat{x}_{d_1,d_2,\cdots,d_n}, x_{d_1,d_2,\cdots,d_n}\right) \\
&= \left(\hat{x}_{d_1,d_2,\cdots,d_n} - x_{d_1,d_2,\cdots,d_n}\right) \times \left[G \times_1 (M_1)_{d_1*} \times_2 \cdots \times_{n-1} (M_{n-1})_{d_{n-1}*}\right] \\
&\partial_G l\left(\hat{x}_{d_1,d_2,\cdots,d_n}, x_{d_1,d_2,\cdots,d_n}\right) \\
&= \left(\hat{x}_{d_1,d_2,\cdots,d_n} - x_{d_1,d_2,\cdots,d_n}\right) \times \left[(M_1)_{d_1*} \otimes (M_2)_{d_2*} \otimes \cdots \otimes (M_n)_{d_n*}\right]
\end{aligned}
$$

In the above formulas, $\otimes$ denotes the Kronecker product of the matrix, also called the direct product or tensor product. The Kronecker product of the two matrices is still a matrix.

Therefore, the gradient of the entire objective function with respect to each factor can be calculated. Here give the following examples.

Owing to $\partial_{(M_1)_{d_1*}} \Omega[G] = 0$, and

$$
\begin{aligned}
\partial_{(M_1)_{d_1*}} [M_1, M_2, \cdots, M_n] &= \partial_{(M_1)_{d_1*}} \left\{\frac{1}{2}\left[\lambda_1\|M_1\|^2 + \lambda_2\|M_2\|^2 + \cdots + \lambda_n\|M_n\|^2\right]\right\} \\
&= \lambda_1 (M_1)_{d_1*}
\end{aligned}
$$

Thus,

$$
\begin{aligned}
\partial_{(M_1)_{d_1*}} L(G, M_1, M_2, \ldots, M_n) &= \partial_{(M_1)_{d_1*}} \left\{\phi\left(\hat{X}, X\right) + [G] + [G, M_1, M_2, \ldots, M_n]\right\} \\
&= \partial_{(M_1)_{d_1*}} \phi\left(\hat{X}, X\right) + \lambda_1 (M_1)_{d_1*}
\end{aligned}
$$

In addition, owing to $\partial_G \Omega[G] = \lambda_0 G$, and $\partial_G \Omega[M_1, M_2, \cdots, M_n] = 0$.

Then, $\partial_G L(G, M_1, M_2, \cdots, M_n) = \partial_G \Phi\left(\hat{X}, X\right) + \lambda_0 G$.

Therefore, based on the above calculations and inferences, an optimization process for the tensor factorization can be given, as shown in Algorithm 7.1. The algorithm only accesses one of the rows of the matrix $M_i \left(i \in N^+ \right)$ at a time, so the algorithm is easy to implement. In addition, given a subset of tensor elements that do not overlap, the algorithm is easily parallelized by performing independently updates. The scale of the algorithm is linear with the elements amount K and the dimension of the factor M_i in the tensor. Therefore, the complexity of the algorithm is $O(K D_1 D_1 \cdots D_n)$.

Algorithm 7.1   Factorization Algorithm of n-Mode Tensor

Input: tensor X , dimension $D_1, D_2, \cdots, D_n$, threshold ε

Output: core tensor G , matrix $M_i \left(i \in N^+ \right)$

1.   Initialize $X \in \mathbb{R}^{D_1 \times D_2 \times \cdots \times D_n}$, $G \in \mathbb{R}^{K_1 \times K_2 \times \cdots \times K_n}$, $M_i \in \mathbb{R}^{D_i \times K_i}$ $\left(i \in N^+ \right)$

2.   Set step size to η, $t = t_0$

3.   while $Loss_t - Loss_{t+1} > \varepsilon$

4.   For the observed values $x_{d_1, d_2, \cdots, d_n}$ in the tensor X, perform the following

   steps

5. $\eta \leftarrow \frac{1}{\sqrt{t}}$, $t \leftarrow t + 1$

6. $\hat{x}_{d_1, d_2, \cdots, d_n} = G \times_1 (M_1)_{d_1 *} \times_2 (M_2)_{d_2 *} \times_3 \cdots \times_n (M_n)_{d_n *}$

7. $(M_1)_{d_1 *} \leftarrow (M_1)_{d_1 *} - \eta \lambda_1 (M_1)_{d_1 *} - \eta \partial_{(M_1)_{d_1 *}} l(\hat{x}_{d_1, d_2, \cdots, d_n}, x_{d_1, d_2, \cdots, d_n})$

8. $(M_2)_{d_2 *} \leftarrow (M_2)_{d_2 *} - \eta \lambda_2 (M_2)_{d_2 *} - \eta \partial_{(M_2)_{d_2 *}} l(\hat{x}_{d_1, d_2, \cdots, d_n}, x_{d_1, d_2, \cdots, d_n})$

9.   ... ...

10. $(M_n)_{d_n *} \leftarrow (M_n)_{d_n *} - \eta \lambda_n (M_n)_{d_n *} - \eta \partial_{(M_n)_{d_n *}} l(\hat{x}_{d_1, d_2, \cdots, d_n}, x_{d_1, d_2, \cdots, d_n})$

11. $G \leftarrow G - \eta \lambda_0 G - \eta \partial_G l(\hat{x}_{d_1, d_2, \cdots, d_n}, x_{d_1, d_2, \cdots, d_n})$

12. Otherwise ,output G , matrix $M_i (i \in N^+)$

The general n-mode tensor factorization process is given above. For the sake of simplicity, the objective function of the decomposition error is often directly defined as,

$$L(G, M_1, M_2, \ldots M_n) = \frac{1}{2} \| X - G \times_1 M_1 \times_2 M_2 \times_3 \ldots \times_n M_n \|^2 + \frac{\lambda}{2} \left(\| G \|^2 + \sum_{i=1}^{n} \| M_i \|^2 \right)$$

$$(7.9)$$

where $\|\cdot\|$ denotes the l_2 norm; $\times$ denotes the matrix multiplication; $\times_i$ stands for the tensor-matrix multiplication and the subscript i represents the i-th mode of a tensor; $G \in \mathbb{R}^{K_1 \times K_2 \times \dots \times K_n}$ is a tensor, $M_i \in \mathbb{R}^{D_i \times K_i}$ is a matrix, and their multiplication is $(G \times_i M_i) \in \mathbb{R}^{K_1 \times \dots \times K_{i-1} \times D_i \times K_{i+1} \times \dots \times K_n}$. Where the elements in the multiplication of the matrix and the tensor satisfy

$$(G \times_i M_i)_{k_1 \dots k_{i-1} d_i k_{i+1} \dots k_n} = \sum_{k_i=1}^{K_i} x_{k_1 \dots k_{i-1} d_i k_{i+1} \dots k_n} m_{d_i k_i}.$$

The first part of Eq. (7.9) is to control the factorization error and the second one is a regularization penalty to avoid over-fitting. λ is a parameter denoting the weight of the regularization penalty. Note that $K_1 - K_n$ are usually very small. Using Algorithm 7.1, we can get a set of optimized matrices $M_1 - M_n$ by minimizing the objective function. Afterwards, we can recover the missing entries of X by the following formula (7.10).

$$X_{rec} = G \times_1 M_1 \times_2 M_2 \times_3 \dots \times_n M_n \qquad (7.10)$$

The above is the specific process of the n-mode tensor factorization. Below we will study how to achieve the collaborative factorization of tensors and multiple matrices.

(2) Collaborative Tensor Factorization (CTF)

Since the original tensor is very sparse, it is not accurate enough to fill the missing entries only by utilizing those non-zero entries. In the literature [55], a model of collective matrix factorization is proposed to improve the predictive accuracy by exploiting information from one relation while predicting another. Several matrices are simultaneously factorized, sharing parameters among factors when an entity participates in multiple relations. Based on this idea, we can factor a tensor by factorizing several feature matrices collaboratively and thus achieve a higher accuracy of filling in the missing entries of a tensor.

Given an n-mode tensor $X \in \mathbb{R}^{D_1 \times D_2 \times \dots \times D_n}$ and several feature matrices $F_1 - F_m$, we factorize X with feature matrices $F_1 - F_m$ collaboratively. It is worth noting that at least one mode of each feature matrix F_i should occur in X.

① If F_i shares one mode with X, $F_i \in \mathbb{R}^{D_i \times F_i}$ can be factorized into the multiplication of two matrices, i.e., $F_i = F_{i1} \times F_{i2}$, where $F_{i1} \in \mathbb{R}^{D_i \times K_i}$ and $F_{i2} \in \mathbb{R}^{K_i \times F_i}$ are low rank latent factors for F_i. Tensor X and matrix F_i share matrix F_{i1} or F_{i2};

② If the two modes of F_i both belong to X, $F_i \in \mathbb{R}^{D_i \times D_j}$ can be factorized into the multiplication of two matrices, i.e., $F_i = F_{i1} \times F_{i2}$, where $F_{i1} \in \mathbb{R}^{D_i \times K_i}$ and $F_{i2} \in \mathbb{R}^{K_i \times D_i}$ are low rank latent factors for F_i. Tensor X and matrix F_i share matrix F_{i1} or F_{i2}.

For the collaborative tensor factorization, the objective function can be defined as follows:

$$
L(G, M_1, \ldots, M_n, F_{11}, \ldots, F_{m1}, F_{12}, \ldots, F_{m2}) = \frac{1}{2} \| X - G \times_1 M_1 \times_2 \ldots \times_n M_n \|^2
$$

$$
+ \sum_{i=1}^{m} \frac{\lambda_i}{2} \| F_i - F_{i1} \times F_{i2} \|^2
$$

$$
+ \frac{\lambda_0}{2} \left(\| G \|^2 + \sum_{i=1}^{n} \| M_i \|^2 + \sum_{i=1}^{m} \left(\| F_{i1} \|^2 + \| F_{i2} \|^2 \right) \right)
$$

$$(7.11)$$

where $\| X - G \times_1 M_1 \times_2 \ldots \times_n M_n \|^2$ and $\| F_i - F_{i1} \times F_{i2} \|^2$ are respectively used to control the errors of factorizing X and F_i; $\| G \|^2 + \sum_{i=1}^{n} \| M_i \|^2 + \sum_{i=1}^{m} (\| F_{i1} \|^2 + F_{i2} \|^2)$ is a regularization penalty to avoid over-fitting; and λ_i $(i \in \mathbb{N}_m)$, are parameters denoting the weights of each part during the collaborative factorization. If $\lambda_i = 0$, the model in this section degenerates to the original tucker decomposition method [56–58]. Since at least one mode of feature matrix F_i is shared with X, for some $F_{ij} (i \in \mathbb{N}_m^+, j \in \mathbb{N}_2^+)$, it is identical with some $M_k (k \in \mathbb{N}_n^+)$.

In order to solve the optimization problem, we use gradient descent algorithm to find a local optimization. Specifically, we use an element-wise optimization algorithm [59], which updates each entry in the tensor independently. After the factorization, we can recover X by Eq. (7.10).

The implementation process of the collaborative tensor factorization algorithm is similar to that of the n-mode collaborative tensor factorization algorithm. However, the objective functions of the two are different, so that the calculation results of the derivation of each factor are slightly different. The more related content will not be described in this book. The specific steps can be referred to the Algorithm 7.1.

7.2.2 POI Recommendation Method Based on Collaborative Tensor Factorization

A POI recommendation method based on collaborative tensor factorization is proposed in this section. In this section, we first give the basic framework of the method, and then elaborates the construction method of the original tensor, the extraction process of the feature matrix, and the method of the collaborative tensor factorization algorithm, respectively.

(1) **Framework**

Figure 7.2 presents the framework of our POI recommendation method, which consists of three layers: (1) data collection and preprocessing; (2) tensor construction and factorization; and (3) personalized POI recommendation.

Firstly, we crawl users' check-in data and POI information from Weibo and Dianping websites, and then extract data through processing and filtering.

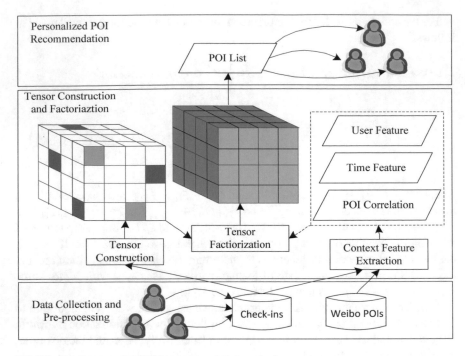

Fig. 7.2 The framework of POI recommendation method

Secondly, we construct a tensor and three feature matrices using the obtained data, and then recover the tensor by collaborative tensor factorization.

Finally, we can recommend an ordered POI list to a user according to his/her preference ratings to different POIs in different time slots which are queried from the recovered tensor.

Since the second layer is the key part of our method, we especially introduce it in details in the following sections.

(2) **Tensor Construction**

We model the preference of a user to a location in a time slot by a three-mode tensor $X \in \mathbb{R}^{N \times M \times T}$, where N, M and T denote the counts of users, POIs and time slots, respectively, as shown Fig. 7.1.

Mode-1 (Users): $U = [u_1, u_2, \ldots, u_i, \ldots, u_N]$ denotes N different users;

Mode-2 (POIs): $P = [p_1, p_2, \ldots p_i, \ldots, p_M]$ denotes M different POIs visited by users;

Mode-3 (Time slots): $T = [t_1, t_2, \ldots, t_i, \ldots, t_T]$ denotes T different time spans.

We divide a day into the same time slots, and thus the number of slots in the time dimension is fixed. A day is divided into 24 time slots, e.g., "8 am–9 am" is one slot. After projecting the check-ins over a long period into one day, we can calculate the check-in frequency for every time slot of a day over a long period. Thus, an entry

$X(i, j, k)$ stores the check-in frequency (i.e., preference rating) of user u_i in p_j in t_k over a long period of time. The value of each entry in tensor X is normalized to $[0, 1]$ for the convenience of factorization.

(3) Feature Extraction

Since the constructed "user-POI-time" tensor X is over sparse, factorizing X solely based on its own non-zero entries cannot produce the accurate results. To deal with this problem, we extract and utilize three feature matrices that can be used as contexts in the factorization process. They reflect features of user, time, and POI correlation. The three matrices are denoted by F_1, F_2 and F_3. F_1 describe the preference correlation between different users. F_2 describes the temporal correlation between different time slots. F_3 describes the co-occurrence correlation between different POIs.

① User feature $F_1 \in \mathbb{R}^{N \times L}$ is the "user-POI category" matrix where $F_1(i, j)$ denotes the number of check-ins of user u_i in POI category c_j. Matrix F_1 gives the distribution of users over different categories, such as Entertainment, Shop, and Hotel. It incorporates the similarity between two users in terms of their category preferences. Intuitively, users with similar category preference features could have a similar POI check-in situation.

② Time feature $F_2 \in \mathbb{R}^{T \times N}$ is the "time-user" matrix where $F_2(i, j)$ denotes the number of check-ins created in time slot t_i by user u_j. Matrix F_2 reveals the correlation between different time slots in terms of the distribution of check-ins of different users. Two time slots sharing a similar user distribution could have a similar check-in situation.

③ POI correlation feature $F_3 \in \mathbb{R}^{M \times M}$ is the "POI-POI" matrix where $F_3(i, j)$ describes the co-occurrence correlation between POIs p_i and p_j. It is calculated by $F_3(i, j) = |U^i \cap U^j|$. Notice that $U^i(U^j)$ denotes the set of users who have checked in $p_i(p_j)$ and $|U|$ is the number of elements in the set U. Then the value of each entry in matrix F_3 is normalized to $[0, 1]$. Once the correlation is determined, we can infer the visit probability of other POIs for a user through the user's check-in history.

(4) Collaborative Tensor Factorization

Based on the tensor construction and feature extraction methods introduced above, we can obtain a tensor ("user-POI-time" tensor $X \in \mathbb{R}^{N \times M \times T}$) and three feature matrices: "user-POI category" matrix $F_1 \in \mathbb{R}^{N \times L}$, "time-user" matrix $F_2 \in \mathbb{R}^{T \times N}$, and "POI-POI" matrix $F_3 \in \mathbb{R}^{M \times M}$.

The tensor X and three feature matrices $F_1 - F_3$ are simultaneously factorized. The three feature matrices have correlations with different modes of the tensor, respectively. F_1 shares factor M_1 with X, F_2 shares factor M_2 with X, and F_3 shares factors M_2 and M_3 with X. Using the collaborative tensor factorization method described in Sect. 7.2.1, the objective function of our model can be defined as follows:

$$L(G, M_1, M_2, M_3, F_{11}, F_{12}, F_{21}, F_{22}, F_{31}, F_{32}) = \frac{1}{2}\|X - G \times_1 M_1 \times_2 M_2 \times_3 M_3\|^2$$

$$+ \sum_{i=1}^{3} \frac{\lambda_i}{2} \|F_i - F_{i1} \times F_{i2}\|^2$$

$$+ \frac{\lambda_0}{2}\left(G^2 + \sum_{i=1}^{3}\|M_i\|^2 + \sum_{i=1}^{3}(\|F_{i1}\|^2 + F_{i2}\|^2)\right)$$

$$(7.12)$$

Since F_1-F_3 share factors with X in the factorization, we have that $F_{11} = M_1, F_{12} \in \mathbb{R}^{K_1 \times C}$, $F_{21} = M_2$, $F_{22} = M_2^T$, $F_{31} = M_3$, $F_{32} = M_1^T$. Thus the objective function is:

$$L(G, M_1, M_2, M_3, F_{12}) = \frac{1}{2} X - G \times_1 M_1 \times_2 M_2 \times_3 M_3\|^2 + \frac{\lambda_1}{2} F_1 - M_1 \times F_{12}\|^2$$

$$+ \frac{\lambda_2}{2} F_2 - M_2 \times M_2^T \|^2 + \frac{\lambda_3}{2} F_3 - M_3 \times M_1^T \|^2$$

$$+ \frac{\lambda_0}{2}(\|G\|^2 + \sum_{i=1}^{3}\|M_i\|^2 + F_{12}\|^2)$$

$$(7.13)$$

Then we use an element-wise gradient descent optimization algorithm to solve the optimization problem.

Finally, we can recover X by $X_{rec} = G \times_1 M_1 \times_2 M_2 \times_3 M_3$. Every user's preferences about different POIs in different time slots (i.e. the recovered values) can be obtained, and thus an ordered POI list can be recommended to a user according to his/her preferences.

7.2.3 Performance Evaluation

(1) Experiment Design

① Experiment Environment
   The data processing process uses Java programming language and Matlab tools, MySQL database, machine configuration for Windows 7 64-bit operating system, Intel i7-2600 processor, 8 GB RAM. The tensor factorization is based on Matlab tensor toolkit TensorToolbox.
② Data Collection and Analysis
   This section introduces our datasets that are from two publicly accessed websites: Weibo and DianPing. And Weibo is a social network platform that is very popular among users. On this platform, users can easily obtain, spread and share information instantly, and can also build personal communities and establish friend relationships. Weibo website was formerly known as "Sina Weibo" and it had been internally tested since the beginning of August 2009. In 2012, it

officially launched Sina Weibo's "Location Service Interface" to provide third-party with multi-dimensional location services based on "location service" and "interest map". It also provide API interfaces for third-party developers to call and complete the location application development. Founded in 2003, DianPing is a consumer review website that is independent of third-party and can provide various information services including merchant information, consumer reviews and offers. In addition, it can also provide O2O trading services, such as group purchases, restaurant reservations.

The Weibo location service platform opens up APIs for developers to develop more applications for accessing Weibo services, which can be used to obtain data about Weibo locations. The Weibo location APIs refer to Twitter and provide sufficient data access interfaces for obtaining Weibo content, comments, user information, check-in and forwarding, social relationships, etc. In order to obtain experimental data, we designs a Weibo check-in data collection system, using the APIs to obtain data about the Weibo locations. The functional modules of the system mainly include: the user ID crawling module, the check-in data crawling module, the location information crawling module. The specific system architecture is shown in Fig. 7.3.

The Weibo location APIs used in the system mainly include related nearby read interfaces, user read interfaces and location read interfaces. See it in Table 7.1.

In total, we crawl 694 million check-ins created by 390,000 users in 90,000 POIs of Shanghai city from December 1st, 2012 to September 25th, 2014. For each POI, we crawl its description including identifier, geographic coordinates and categories. For the POIs without category labels, we supply the category information according to that from DianPing website. For each check-in, its description includes not only identifiers of check-in, user, and POI, but also a timestamp.

Since the check-in behaviors of every user usually happen in randomness and uncertainty, and the check-in data is too large and sparse, we extract a small dataset from the raw data in order to accurately evaluate our method. The specific data filtering steps are as follows:

First, we select all such users whose total check-in number is more than 500.

Secondly, from the selected data, we delete the check-ins which are created in the POIs that are in total visited less than 50 times.

After the preprocessing and filtering procedures, we eventually obtain a collection of 17,469 check-ins created by 131 unique users in 106 different POIs. After data statistics, the data of Weibo location is very sparse. More than 95% of users have less than 20 times of check-in, and more than 93% of the locations are checked in less than 10 times.

In this section, we set one hour as a time slot, and the size of the constructed "user-POI-time" is $131 \times 106 \times 24$. Even though the tensor is constructed based on this preprocessed dataset, it is still very sparse because only 0.98% entries of X have nonzero values.

③ Experiment Method

In order to evaluate our proposed POI recommendation model, we conduct experiments by using the extracted dataset. We compare our proposed method Collaborative

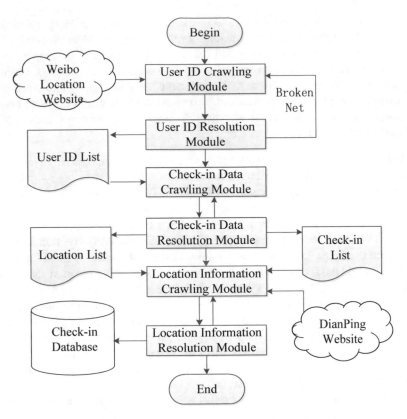

Fig. 7.3 The architecture diagram of Weibo location check-in data collection system

Table 7.1 The main APIs used by the data collection system

	Function	Interface
Nearby read interface	Obtain nearby location	place/nearby/poi
	Know people near the location of Weibo	place/nearby/user
User read interface	Obtain user information in the LBS location service	place/users/show
	Obtain POIs that users have checked in	place/users/checkins
	Obtain POI about someone who checked in at a place	place/pois/user
Location read interface	Obtain location details	place/pois/show
	Obtain location classification	place/pois/category

Tensor Factorization (CTF) with the Matrix Factorization approach with Time Slicing (TMF) [60]. Both methods all aim to obtain every user's ratings to every POIs in different time slots.

TMF method is completed as follows: (1) projecting all the check-ins into one day, (2) dividing all the check-ins into 24 subsets according to their timestamp, e.g., if the timestamp of a check-in is 8:08, then it belongs to the subset in time slot "8:00–9:00", (3) constructing 24 "user-POI" matrices of the check-ins in each time slots, and (4) filling the missing entries by matrix factorization for each "user-POI" matrix.

CTF method simultaneously factorizes the "user-POI-time" tensor with other three feature matrices by using the method presented in Sect. 7.2.1.

We employ two metrics for the performance evaluation. They are Root Mean Square Error (RMSE) and Mean Absolute Error (MAE), where y_{rec} is a recovered value, y is the ground truth, and n is the number of entries. RMSE and MAE can be calculated by the following equations:

$$RMSE = \sqrt{\frac{\sum_{i=1}^{n}(y_i - (y_{\text{rec}})_i)^2}{n}} \tag{7.14}$$

$$MAE = \frac{\sum_{i=1}^{n}|y_i - (y_{\text{rec}})_i|}{n} \tag{7.15}$$

In our experiments, we realize TMF with SVD (k = 10) and solve the CTF optimization problem using element-wise gradient descent optimization algorithm proposed in. In the experiments, we set $\varepsilon = 0.02$. In total, we conduct ten groups of experiments and each group contains ten sub-experiments. During each sub-experiment, we randomly select 70% of entries as training data, and the remaining 30% are used as validation data. After completing all the sub-experiments, we record the result of each group by computing the average RMSE and MAE of its ten sub-experiments.

(2) **Experimental Results and Analysis**

Using the data set extracted in the above experiments, the next experiments were carried out on the CTF approach and the TMF approach according to the experimental design. Table 7.2 presents the performance evaluation results of the two approaches.

The smaller the value of the evaluation indexes RMSE and MAE, the better the prediction result is. Therefore, we can see that CTF outperforms TMF from the Table 7.2. The reason is that the TMF method only uses the factorization of "user-POI" matrix which neglects the correlations among different time slots. In addition, CTF not only considers the time correlations in tensor but also leverages additional features of users, POIs and time slots.

Table 7.2 Performance comparison between TMF and CTF methods

	RMSE		MAE	
	TMF	CTF	TMF	CTF
1	0.55772	0.06847	0.47885	0.02297
2	0.55945	0.06966	0.48139	0.0227
3	0.55319	0.07097	0.47471	0.02318
4	0.54972	0.07168	0.47186	0.02346
5	0.55971	0.06396	0.4818	0.02154
6	0.55579	0.07152	0.47936	0.0234
7	0.55491	0.07023	0.47613	0.02306
8	0.55342	0.07068	0.47483	0.02321
9	0.55972	0.06961	0.48159	0.02266
10	0.5559	0.06566	0.47815	0.0216

7.3   Partition-Based Collaborative Tensor Factorization for POI Recommendation

The collaborative tensor factorization method given in Sect. 7.2 can provide more accurate recommendations. But from the statistics and the analysis on the collected Weibo location check-ins data, it can be concluded that the user check-in data is very few and very sparse. From December 1st, 2012 to September 25th, 2014, more than 95% of users have less than 20 times of check-in, and more than 93% of the locations are checked in less than 10 times. The original tensor constructed based on the user's check-in data is large in scale and sparse in data, so that it takes a long time to directly perform collaborative tensor factorization on the entire tensor. Moreover, since many users, timeslots, or POIs have similar characteristics, it is not necessary to directly process the entire tensor. Therefore, the information of similar objects can be used for recommendations, which is also the main idea of collaborative filtering.

In order to further improve the recommendation's accuracy and efficiency, PCTF (Partition based CTF) which takes into account the association degree between users (or timeslots, POIs) is proposed in this section. Firstly, we cluster the entities on each mode of the tensor, and divide the original tensor and the corresponding feature matrix based on the clustering result. Secondly, we recover the missing value of tensor by using the CTF over sub-tensors and corresponding feature matrices. Finally, POIs is recommended to users according to predicted results.

7.3.1   Problem Description

Before introducing the PCTF-based location recommendation algorithm, we first introduce the block-based tensor factorization and clustering algorithm which are closely related to the recommendation algorithm. Similar to Sect. 7.2, the relevant problem description is given here.

(1) **Block-based Tensor Factorization**

In practice, there are two toolboxes on MATLAB for tensor manipulation: one is the Tensor Toolbox for sparse tensors and another is an N-way Toolbox for dense tensors [61]. Besides, researchers propose various block-based algorithms and systems due to the significant cost of tensor factorization and apply parallelization strategies, such as Map-Reduce-based implementation [62], and sampling-based method [63] to perform tensor factorization [64]. In literature [65], a personalized tensor decomposition mechanism for considering the user's focus is proposed to improve the accuracy and reduce the overall decomposition time. Based on these works, we partition the tensor by clustering its every mode, factorize each sub-tensor with corresponding submatrices by using collaborative tensor factorization method, and then recover each sub-tensor. Finally, the original tensor is recovered by sub-tensor merging.

(2) **Clustering Algorithm**

Clustering algorithms are generally used in the unsupervised fashion. By clustering, a set of data instances can be grouped according to some notion of similarity. Such an algorithm needs only the set of object features as its input, but not all label information.

K-means clustering algorithm [66, 67] is a simple and popular method used to automatically partition a set of instances into k clusters. It proceeds by selecting k initial cluster centers and then iteratively refines them as follows:

① Each instance I_i is assigned to its closest cluster center.
② Each cluster center CC_i is updated to be the mean of its constituent instances.
③ The algorithm converges when there is no further change in assignment of instances to clusters.

(3) **Problem Description**

The problem solved in this section is still the prediction problem focused on the missing scores of the original tensor constructed by user's check-ins data. The goal is to further improve the accuracy of the prediction results and reduce the time required for the solution. Therefore, we partition the original tensor according to the idea of divide and rule. An example of tensor partition is given below.

If a tensor is very huge and sparse, the correlation degree between entries is usually different. For example, in the "user-POI-time" tensor in Fig. 7.1, similarities between users (or timeslots or POIs) are different. According to the idea of collaborative filtering, users (or time-slots or POIs) with similar features should bring stronger influences to each other. Thus, in order to recover more accurate entries, a tensor can be partitioned into several small sub-tensors according to its modes before collaboratively factorizing these tensors. For example, clustering the entities at each mode of the tensor shown in Fig. 7.1, users are partitioned into two sets $(\{u_1, u_2\}, \{u_3, u_4, u_5\})$, timeslots into two sets $(\{t_1\}, \{t_2, t_3\})$, and POIs into two sets

Fig. 7.4 An example of the tensor partition

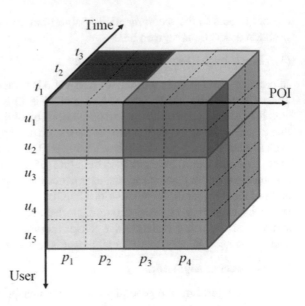

({p_1, p_2},{p_3, p_4}). Then the "user-POI-time" tensor can be partitioned into $2 \times 2 \times 2 = 8$ sub-tensors, as shown in Fig. 7.4.

7.3.2   POI Recommendation Method Based on PCTF

(1) Framework

In this section, we present a partition-based collaborative tensor factorization method to achieve the personalized POI recommendation. Figure 7.5 shows the framework of PCTF-based POI recommendation. In the picture, X_i, UF_i, PF_i and TF_i denote the i-th sub-tensor, the i-th sub-matrices of user feature matrix, POI correlation matrix and time feature, respectively. The framework consists of four layers: (1) data collection and pre-processing; (2) tensor construction and feature extraction; (3) tensor partition and factorization; and (4) personalized POI recommendation. The main functions of the four layers are described in turn below.

① Data Collection and Pre-Processing: we collect users' check-in data and POI information from Weibo and Dianping websites, and then extract data through processing and filtering.

② Tensor Construction and Feature Extraction: we construct a tensor and three feature matrices by using the obtained data.

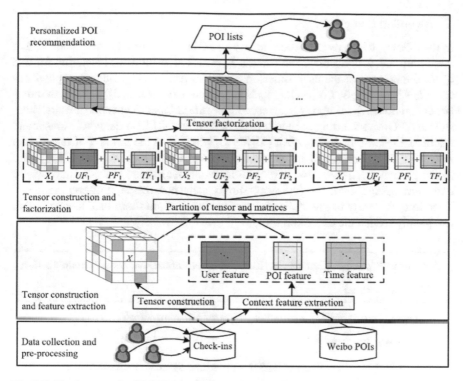

Fig. 7.5 The framework of PCTF-Based POI recommendation

③ Tensor Partition and Factorization: we partition the tensor and matrices through clustering every mode and then recover the tensor by using CTF over sub-tensors and sub-matrices.

④ Personalized POI Recommendation: we can recommend an ordered POI list to a user according to his/her preference ratings to different POIs in different time-slots which are queried from the recovered tensor.

(2) **PCTF Algorithm**

① PCTF algorithm

The result of performing CTF on one big tensor is not accurate due to the fact that correlation degrees between users (or time-slots or POIs) are not considered in CTF. Therefore, we partition the tensor into sub-tensors according to the related similarities and perform CTF on the corresponding sub-tensors and sub-matrices to predict the missing value of the entire tensor. This section describes the PCTF algorithm (Algorithm 7.2) where X is the "user-POI-time" tensor and F_1, F_2, and F_3 are user feature matrix, time feature matrix, and POI correlation feature matrix, respectively. Here, one object is denoted by a feature vector, and we use cosine distance to compute their similarities.

② Algorithm Complexity

In the follows, we analyze the complexity of PCTF algorithm. In the second line of Algorithm 7.2, it is necessary to use the K-means algorithm for clustering for one of the dimensions of the user, timeslots and POI. And the algorithm complexity is $O(I_1 N_u N N) + O(I_2 N_t T N) + O(I_3 N_p M M)$, where $I_i (i \in \{1, 2, 3\})$ denotes the number of iterations, N_u, N_t and N_p are respectively the number of clusters of users, time-slots and POIs. According to literature [33], if we use CTF on the whole tensor and matrices, the complexity is $O(\mathbb{K} K_1 K_2 K_3 r_u)$, where $\mathbb{K}$ is the number of ratings and $K_i (i \in \{1, 2, 3\})$ and r_u are the dimensionalities of the factors $M_i (i \in \{1, 2, 3\})$ and F_1, respectively. However, we have partitioned the tensor and matrices into several non-overlapping sub-tensors (correspondingly, some non-overlapping sub-matrices). Therefore, it is easy to parallelize by performing CTF on them independently that can greatly reduce the execution time.

Algorithm 7.2 Algorithm of partition-based collaborative tensor factorization (PCTF Algorithm)

Input: $X \in \mathbb{R}^{N \times M \times T}$, $F_1 \in \mathbb{R}^{N \times L}$, $F_2 \in \mathbb{R}^{T \times N}$, $F_3 \in \mathbb{R}^{M \times M}$

Output: $X_{\text{rec}} \in \mathbb{R}^{N \times M \times T}$

1. Compute user, time, and POI similarities by cosine distance over F_1, F_2 and F_3, respectively;

2. Cluster users into N_u clusters, time-slots into N_t clusters, and POI into N_p clusters by using K-means algorithm, the user, time-slot and POI similarities are used as the inputs of K-means, respectively;

3. Partition X into $N_u \times N_t \times N_p$ sub-tensors, denoted by $S_i (i \in [1, N_u \times N_t \times N_p])$;

4. Partition F_1, F_2 and F_3 into N_u, N_t and N_p sub-matrices, respectively;

5. **for** each sub-tensor S_i with the corresponding sub-matrices,

6.   factorize it using the CTF method;

7.   Recover each sub-tensor S_i to obtain a new tensor $S_{i_{rec}}$;

8. **end for**

9. Merge $S_{i_{rec}} (i \in [1, N_u \times N_t \times N_p])$ and obtain the whole tensor X_{rec};

10. **return** X_{rec}.

7.4   Maximal-Marginal-Relevance-Based POIs List Recommendation

In general, traditional trip recommendation systems provide the same venues or trips to different users by considering experts' suggestions or experienced users' opinions, but neglecting users' personalized preferences. Indeed, users themselves can plan a trip by obtaining detailed information from the Internet, such as the geographic features, attractive attributes, and the other travelers' comments about venues, but that will cost a great deal of time. Fortunately, the location-based services have been widely used, especially, the location-based social networks have become popular. It has accumulated a large number of user data with geospatial location tags such as check-ins, which provides new ideas for solving this problem. Meanwhile, there are some issues to recommend a personalized trip by using these check-in data:

(1) Diversity is an important factor that should be considered in trip planning. According to literature [68], people would also enjoy exploring previously unvisited places due to their novelty-seeking tendency, which is biologically embedded into human brains according to the uncovered genetic roots and relations to a dopamine system. Specifically, as reported in literature [69], more than 35% of location visits are generated in new places each day even after half a year. This novelty-seeking characteristic is adopted in a dining recommender system [70]. Intuitively, this neophilia characteristic is especially outstanding in trip recommendation, which is reflected as trip diversity. Trip score and diversity are both considered in a personalized trip recommendation (PTR) framework. However, under PTR, trip diversity is not fused into a trip planning procedure, and this can lead to unfairness and inflexibility.

Since trip diversity is an important factor in trip recommendation, how to accurately calculate it remains an open question. In practice, the POI categories have different granularities, which are usually represented by a category hierarchy. In Foursquare, a two-level category hierarchy structure is proposed, which contains eight categories and some subcategories for each category. For example, there are 45 subcategories in the category "Shop".

POI category also contains different levels. Hence, we consider two levels as shown in Fig. 7.6, called the 1st and 2nd-level ones to facilitate the discussion. Thus, any trip diversity calculation strategy considering no hierarchy of POI categories cannot lead to precise diversity evaluation results.

(2) How to efficiently provide a personalized trip according to user preferences is a big challenge in trip recommendation. In fact, we can classify a trip according to the time it takes and the number of locations it contains. Based on the former, there are two trip modes: short and long trips. A short trip is to plan a trip that will take several hours to travel, which is often preferred by office workers within the daytime of a weekend. On the contrary, a long one takes several days such as a honeymoon trip, holiday tour and global traveling. On the other hand, by considering the location count, trips can be divided into few and many-location trips. Usually, a prosperous city contains thousands of POIs. For example, on

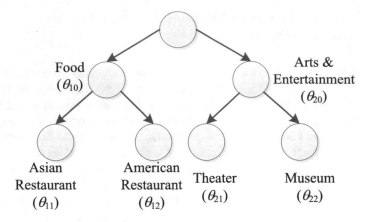

Fig. 7.6 An example of category hierarchy

the Dianping website which is a leading platform in China for providing local information, trading and consumer reviews, we have 412342 and 392499 POIs in Beijing and Shanghai, respectively. The complexity of Trip-Mine + is exponential with the problem size. By using this method, a short trip with less than ten locations can be designed in an acceptable time. But to plan a longer trip containing more than 15 locations, its computing time is beyond the tolerance of users. This issue motivates us to seek computationally tractable methods in intelligent optimization. An ant colony optimization (ACO) method [71–74] proposed by Dorigo et al. can fast solve hard combinatorial optimization problems and achieves good results. This work intends to improve it to an effective plan and recommends many-location trips.

Above all, this section focuses on personalized POIs list recommendation methods. We propose a Maximal-marginal-relevance-based Personalized Trip Recommendation (MPTR) model with the consideration of both trip relevance and trip diversity in its trip planning. Specially, a novel calculation method of POI similarity is presented based on a predefined category hierarchy, and then a new evaluation strategy is proposed to compute trip diversity. The results match well with actual situations. We propose an Ant-colony-optimization-based Trip Planning (ATP) algorithm to conduct trip planning.

7.4.1   Problem Description

First, the relevant problem description is given here. Table 7.3 below introduced the notations used in this section and the corresponding description definition.

The relevant definitions are given here. $G = (P, E)$ denotes a graph constructed for a travel region, where $P = \{p_0, p_1, , p_n\}$ is a POI set and $E = \{(p_i, p_j)|p_i, p_j \in P\}$ is a set of edges where $e_{ij} = (p_i, p_j), (i \neq j)$ represents the link between POIs

Table 7.3 Notions

Notions	Description
α	Weight of pheromone in computing the transition probability of an edge
β	Weight of a heuristic factor in computing the transition probability of an edge
$\Gamma = < p_1, p_2, \cdots, p_m >$	A trip that is a sequence of POIs
Γ_θ	The set of all POIs in trip Γ which belong to category θ
$\Gamma_k(t)$	The sequence of POIs that have been visited by ant k by time t
$\delta_{ij}(t)$	Pheromone-count on e_{ij} at time t
$\Delta_{ij}^k(r)$	Increment of pheromone on e_{ij} given by ant k during iteration r
$\Delta_{ij}(r)$	Increment of pheromone on e_{ij} during iteration r
$\eta_{ij}^k(t)$	A heuristic factor for the k-th ant to select e_{ij} at time t
θ_{xy}	The y-th subcategory of the x-th category
Θ	The set of all categories
Θ_Γ	The set of categories to which the POIs in trip Γ belong
λ	Weight of trip-relevance value in computing the trip-quality
ξ_Γ	Entropy of trip Γ
ρ	Evaporation rate of pheromone
τ_i	The stay time at p_i
τ_{ij}	The travel time from p_i to p_j
τ^r	The time spent at iteration r
ϕ_{ij}	Similarity between POIs p_i and p_j
Φ	A set of trips
ω	A positive constant denoting the initial pheromone-count on each edge
Ω	A positive constant denoting the released pheromone of each ant
B_{max}	The maximal budget given by a user
c_i	The money spent on POI p_i
C_Γ	The money spent on trip Γ
$\mathbb{C}(u, \theta)$	All check-ins of user u generated in the POIs of category θ
$\mathbb{C}(u, p_i, t)$	All check-ins of user u generated in POI p_i in time-slot t
d_{ij}	The distance between the categories of p_i and p_j
d_{max}	The maximal distance between categories
d_{min}	The minimal distance between categories
D_Γ	Diversity value of trip Γ
D_Γ^i	Diversity value of trip Γ based on the entropy of POI's i-level category
e_{ij}	The edge linking POIs p_i and p_j
$G = (P, E)$	An undirected graph with P as a set of nodes (POIs) and E as a set of edges
k	The k-th ant

(continued)

Table 7.3 (continued)

Notions	Description
K	The number of POIs in the trip that contains the most POIs among those satisfying the time and budget constraints
l_i	The level of the category of p_i
l_{max}	The maximal value of category level
$m = \lvert\Gamma\rvert$	The number of POIs in trip Γ
$n = \lvert P\rvert$	the number of elements in set P
N	The number of all ants
$N_i(t)$	The number of ants located in p_i at time t
$\mathbb{N}^+$	The positive integer set
$\bullet p_i$	The set of POIs that have been visited before p_i
$\mathbb{P}_{ij}^k(r)$	Transition probability from p_i to p_j for the k-th ant at time t
$Q_\Gamma^u(t)$	Quality value of trip Γ as given by user u where Γ starts at time t
r	The r-th iteration
R	The number of iterations
s_{i1}^u	The user-based POI score of p_i as given by user u
$s_{i2}^u(t)$	The time-based POI score of p_i as given by user u at time t
$s_i^u(t)$	The score of p_i as given by user u at time t
$S_\Gamma^u(t)$	The score of trip Γ as given by user u where Γ starts at time t
t_i	The arrival time at POI p_i
T_Γ	The time needed to travel trip Γ
T_{max}	The maximal time given by a user
u	A user
$U_k(t)$	The set of POIs in $\Gamma_k(t)$
$V_k(t)$	The set of POIs that have not been visited by ant k by time t

p_i and p_j. Travel Time denoted as $_{ij}$ is the time needed to travel from one POI p_i to another one p_j. All the edges are undirected with $\tau_{ij} = \tau_{ji}$. Stay Time denoted as τ_i indicates the time spent at p_i. A trip $\Gamma = p_0, p_1, , p_m$ is an ordered sequence of m POIs. In trip Γ, the start location denoted by p_0 is omitted for brevity. t_i denotes Arrival Time of p_i. It can be calculated as follows:

$$t_i = t_{i-1} + \tau_{i-1} + \tau_{i-1,i} \qquad (7.16)$$

where $i > 0$, and $p_i \in P$.

Fig. 7.7 An example of a
graph

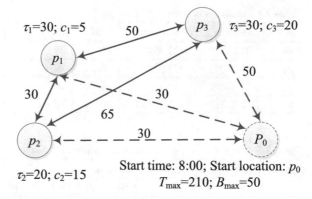

$\tau_1=30; c_1=5$ 50 p_3 $\tau_3=30; c_3=20$

p_1

50

30   30

65

30

p_2 - - - - - $\underline{30}$ - - - - -> P_0

$\tau_2=20; c_2=15$ Start time: 8:00; Start location: p_0
                           $T_{\max}=210; B_{\max}=50$

Given a user u, start time t and a trip Γ, Trip Score, denoted by $S_\Gamma^u(t)$, is calculated as follows:

$$S_\Gamma^u(t) = \sum_{i=0}^{m} s_i^u(t_i) \tag{7.17}$$

It represents the interest degree of trip Γ as given by user u where Γ starts at time t. Here $s_i^u(t_i)$ denotes the POI score of p_i as given by user u at time t. Trip Time, denoted as T_Γ, can be obtained as follows:

$$T_\Gamma = \sum_{i=1}^{m} \tau_i + \sum_{j=0}^{m} \tau_{j,j+1} \tag{7.18}$$

It represents the total time needed to travel trip Γ from start location p_0 and finally return to p_0. For brevity, we assume $p_{m+1} = p_0$ and $\tau_{m,m+1} = \tau_{m0}$.

Trip Cost, denoted by C_Γ, can be calculated as follows:

$$C_\Gamma = \sum_{i=1}^{m} c_i \tag{7.19}$$

It represents the total money spent on trip Γ, where c_i denotes the total money needed to visit POI p_i.

In the following, an example is given to show the above concepts. As shown in Fig. 7.7, there are 6 edges and 4 POIs, where p_0 is the start POI of user u. Attributes of $p_1 - p_3$ are shown in Table 7.4. θ_{xy} denotes the y-th subcategory of the x-th category, where $x, y(x, y \in \mathbb{N}^+)$ are labels for 1st-level category and 2nd-level one, respectively. For brevity, we assume that θ_{x0} denotes the x-th category at the 1st level. The departure time at p_0 is 8:00. The maximal values of time and budget are $T_{max} = 240\,min$ and $B_{max} = 50$, respectively. In the following discussion, their units are omitted for conciseness. The stay time at POI p_1 is $\tau_1 = 30$. The travel

Table 7.4 Attributes of three POIs $p_0 - p_3$

POI	Latitude	Longitude	Cost	Stay time	Category 1	Category 2
p_0	31.19722	121.4093	10	20	θ_{10}	θ_{11}
p_1	31.23237	121.4714	5	30	θ_{10}	θ_{11}
p_2	31.23668	121.49905	15	20	θ_{10}	θ_{12}
p_3	31.23312	121.47188	20	30	θ_{20}	θ_{22}

Table 7.5 The scores of $p_0 - p_3$ is made by users u_1 and u_2

POI	POI score in 24 different time-slots									
	$\cdots$	8:00–9:00		9:00–10:00		10:00–11:00		11:00–12:00		$\cdots$
		u_1	u_2	u_1	u_2	u_1	u_2	u_1	u_2	$\cdots$
p_0	$\cdots$	0.1	0.3	0.05	0.4	0.4	0.1	0.05	0.1	$\cdots$
p_1	$\cdots$	0.4	0.1	0.3	0.1	0.02	0.3	0.3	0.3	$\cdots$
p_2	$\cdots$	0.2	0.5	0.3	0.1	0.2	0.1	0.05	0.1	$\cdots$
p_3	$\cdots$	0.05	0.5	0.05	0.2	0.3	0.05	0.1	0.05	$\cdots$

time from p_1 to p_2 is $\tau_{12} = 30$. Thus we have $t_1 = 8 : 30$ and $t_2 = 9 : 30$. Assume that $s_1^u(8 : 30) = 0.4$ and $s_2^u(9 : 30) = 0.3$. Then for $\Gamma_1 = p_1, p_2$, its trip score is $S_{\Gamma_1} = 0.4 + 0.3 = 0.7$, trip time is $T_{\Gamma_1} = \tau_{01} + \tau_1 + \tau_{12} + \tau_2 + \tau_{20} = 140$, and the trip cost is $C_{\Gamma_1} = c_1 + c_2 = 20$.

Since each user's check-ins record is different, even for the same time period, they give different scores for the same POI. Table 7.5 illustrates the scoring of four different locations p_0-p_3 for different time periods about two different users u_1 and u_2.

In order to provide users with a sequence of POIs which meet their preferences and diversity, Trip Quality denoted as $Q_\Gamma^u(t)$ is defined as follows:

$$Q_\Gamma^u(t) = \lambda \times S_\Gamma^u(t) + (1 - \lambda) \times D_\Gamma \tag{7.20}$$

where $\lambda \in [0, 1]$ and $1 - \lambda$ respectively denote the weights of trip-relevance and trip-diversity values when computing the quality value of trip Γ as given by user u. λ can be adjusted flexibly by users according to their preferences.

The new trip recommendation model MPTR can be formulated accordingly. Given a user u, start time t, the maximal travel time T_{max} and the maximal budget B_{max}, and trip-relevance weight λ, a trip with the highest trip-quality can be provided. The model is formalized as follows:

$$\text{The recommended trip} = argmax_\Gamma \, Q_\Gamma^u(t)$$

$$\begin{cases} T_\Gamma \leq T_{max} \\ C_\Gamma \leq B_{max} \end{cases} \tag{7.21}$$

where $argmax_\Gamma Q_\Gamma^u(t)$ denotes the trip for which $Q_\Gamma^u(t)$ has the maximal value.

The above is the relevant problem description of the personalized POI recommendation. For this problem, the corresponding solution method is given below.

7.4.2 Personalized Trip Recommendation

(1) Trip-Mine + Algorithm

In Trip-Mine + , we call $\Gamma = p_1, p_2, \cdots, p_m$ a Valid Trip if $T_\Gamma \le T_{max}$ and $C_\Gamma \le B_{max}$, where T_{max} and B_{max} denote the maximal time that user u can spend and maximal budget that u can afford for trip Γ, respectively. A valid trip is called an Optimal Trip if there is no any other trip' such that $S_\Gamma^u(t) > S^u(t)$.

Trip Diversity ξ_Γ is evaluated by the entropy of trip Γ,that is called Trip Diversity based on Entropy (TDE) and computed by the following formula:

$$\xi_\Gamma = - \sum_{\theta \in |\Theta_\Gamma|} \left(\frac{|\Gamma_\theta|}{|\Gamma|} \times \log_{|\Theta|} \frac{|\Gamma_\theta|}{|\Gamma|} \right) \tag{7.22}$$

where $|\Theta|$ denotes the number of all POI-categories, $|\Theta_\Gamma|$ indicates the number of categories to which the POIs in Γ belong and $|\Gamma_\theta|$ denotes the number of all POIs in Γ which belong to category θ.

In the example shown in Fig. 7.7, Γ_1 is a valid trip because that $T_{\Gamma_1} = 140 \le T_{max}$ and $C_{\Gamma_1} = 20 \le B_{max}$. However, $\Gamma_2 = p_1, p_2, p_3$ is not valid since $T_{\Gamma_2} = 255 > T_{max}$.There are several valid trips in the map such as p_1, p_2 and p_2, p_3. The optimal trip is Γ_1 since its trip score is greater than any other valid ones. By Trip-Mine + , a trip with the highest score can be provided to users, but it has an exponential-time complexity.

As shown in Fig. 7.6, there are two categories at the 1st level and four ones at the 2nd level. θ_{11} and θ_{12} are subcategories of θ_{10},and θ_{21} and θ_{22} are subcategories of θ_{20}. $\Gamma_1 = p_1, p_2, \Gamma_3 = p_2, p_3$, and $\Gamma_4 = p_0, p_1$ are three trips. Diversity based on the entropy of level-1 category (D^1) is

$$D_{\Gamma_1}^1 = D_{\Gamma_4}^1 = -(2/2 \times log_2 2/2) = 0.0;$$
$$D_{\Gamma_3}^1 = -(1/2 \times log_2 1/2 + 1/2 \times log_2 1/2) = 1.0.$$

Diversity based on the entropy of level-2 category (D^2) is

$$D_{\Gamma_1}^2 = D_{\Gamma_3}^2 = -(1/2 \times log_4 1/2 + 1/2 \times log_4 1/2) = 0.5;$$
$$D_{\Gamma_4}^2 = -(2/2 \times log_4 2/2) = 0.0.$$

However, the diversity of Γ_1 should be higher than that of Γ_4 because p_0 and p_1 in Γ_4 both belong to the 2nd-level category θ_{11}. The diversity of Γ_3 should be higher than that of Γ_1 because p_1 and p_2 in Γ_1 both belong to the 1st-level category θ_{10}, which cannot be correctly reflected only by D_Γ^1 or D_Γ^2 at the same time. Therefore, a new diversity computation method considering category similarity is clearly required to distinguish them.

(2) **Method and Framework**

The maximal-marginal relevance (MMR) method [75] has been employed in retrieval to reorder documents and in summarization to generate summaries based on document diversity. PTR considers time and budget constraints in trip planning. Though top-k trips with the higher trip scores are re-ranked by trip diversity after route planning, such selection poses an unfairness issue since some trips with higher diversity but smaller trip scores are excluded in the first step. Focusing on this issue, this section fuses POI sequence correlation and diversity into POI trip planning based on the maximum edge correlation method, and we present a new method called MPTR. Below, we introduce the framework of MPTR. Our proposed framework has two modules: POI scoring (offline phase) and trip planning (online phase).

During the offline phase, POI similarity is calculated according to POI categories by using our proposed method to be described. In addition, POI scores of users at different time slots can be obtained by using some existing methods, such as ranking-by-preference (RBP) and normalized-by-time (NBT) methods.

RBP can provide a user-based POI score, which is to count the number of user's check-in POIs that belong to a given POI's category θ and normalize it to fall into $[0, 1]$. It can be calculated as follows:

$$s_{i1}^u = \frac{|\mathbb{C}(u, \theta)|}{\arg_{\theta' \in \Theta} \max(|\mathbb{C}(u, \theta')|)} \tag{7.23}$$

where θ denotes the category that POI p_i belongs to, and $|\mathbb{C}(u, \theta)|$ denotes the total number of check-ins generated by u in the POIs of category θ.

NBT can provide a time-based POI score, which is to sum up the numbers of check-ins for all time periods and then normalize it. It can be calculated as follows:

$$s_{i2}^u(t) = \frac{|\mathbb{C}(u, p_i, t)|}{arg_{t' \in \mathbb{T}} \max(|\mathbb{C}(u, p_i, t')|)} \tag{7.24}$$

where $\mathbb{C}(u, p_i, t)$ denotes the number of check-ins generated in POI p_i by user u in time-slot t that t lies in. $\mathbb{T}$ denotes the set of all time-slots. Here divide one day into 24 time-slots, i.e., one hour is one time-slot.

Thus, the POI score of p_i contributed by user u at time t can be obtained by the following equation.

$$s_i^u(t) = \gamma_1 s_{i1}^u + \gamma_2 s_{i2}^u(t) \tag{7.25}$$

where γ_1 and γ_2 are the weights of user-based and time-based POI scores, respectively. In this section, we set $\gamma_1 = \gamma_2 = 0.5$.

During the online phase, when users propose requests, constraints-satisfied trips with higher qualities should be provided. Different from PTR [21], the diversity and relevance of a trip are fused into trip quality according to users' preferences, and then trip quality is used as the objective function during the planning procedure. In order to improve the planning efficiency, ATP is proposed to provide users with feasible trips in a computationally efficient way.

In our study, trip relevance reflects the degree of users' interest in a trip, which can be calculated by a trip score. Trip diversity reflects differences among POIs in a trip, which can be provided by calculating POI similarity.

(3) Diversity Evaluation Strategy

In MPTR, trip relevance is denoted by a trip score obtained from formula (7.16). To compute trip diversity, we propose a new trip diversity evaluation strategy named TDS (Trip Diversity based on POI Similarity). First, we define POI similarity.

Definition 7.4 POI Similarity: Given two PIs p_1 and p_2, the similarity between them is defined as follows:

$$\phi_{ij} = \frac{l_i + l_j}{2 \times l_{max}} \times \frac{d_{max} - d_{ij}}{d_{max} - d_{min}} \tag{7.26}$$

where l_i and l_j respectively indicate the levels of the categories of p_i and p_j in the category hierarchy, l_{max} is the maximal value of category level, d_{ij} denotes the distance between the categories of p_i and p_j in the category hierarchy (i.e., the edge-count of the shortest path between these two categories), and d_{max} and d_{min} are the maximal and minimal values of distances between any two categories.

Assume that $\phi_{xy}^{x'y'}$ denotes the similarity between categories θ_{xy} and $\theta_{x'y'}$, then we can compute it by (7.26) in the same way. For example, in the two-level category hierarchy in (7.14), we have $d_{max} = 4$ and $d_{min} = 0$. Therefore, we have:

$$\phi_{11}^{10} = \frac{(1+2)}{(2 \times 2)} \times \frac{(4-1)}{(4-0)} = \frac{9}{16} = 0.5625,$$

$$\phi_{11}^{12} = \frac{(2+2)}{4} \times \frac{(4-2)}{4} = \frac{2}{4} = 0.5,$$

$$\phi_{11}^{20} = \frac{(1+2)}{4} \times \frac{(4-3)}{4} = \frac{3}{16} = 0.1825,$$

$$\phi_{11}^{22} = \frac{(2+2)}{4} \times \frac{(4-4)}{4} = 0.0,$$

$$\phi_{10}^{20} = \frac{(1+1)}{4} \times \frac{(4-2)}{4} = 0.25.$$

Based on POI similarity, Trip Diversity for trip Γ is as follows:

$$D_\Gamma = \begin{cases} \dfrac{\sum_{i=2}^{m}\left(1-\max_{p_j \in \bullet p_i} \phi_{ij}\right)}{|\Gamma|-1}, & \text{if} |\Gamma| > 1 \\ 0 & \text{, else} \end{cases} \qquad (7.27)$$

where $|\Gamma|$ denotes the POI-count in trip Γ and $\bullet p_i$ the set of POIs that have been visited before POI p_i in Γ.

For the example in Fig. 7.7, we have $D_{\Gamma_1} = 0.5$, $D_{\Gamma_3} = 1.0$ and $D_{\Gamma_4} = 0.0$ according to (7.27). Thus, the diversity value computed by the method makes more sense than that of the state-of-the-art methods since it can clearly distinguish the three trips.

(4) **MPTR Analysis**

In the MPTR method, when selecting the next POI in the POI sequence, we must consider not only the position scores but also the similarity between the POI to be selected and each POI included in the current POI sequence. Finally, the user is provided with the highest "Trip Quality" POI sequence.

MPTR is more flexible since both trip-relevance and trip-diversity are considered in trip planning, and their importance in deciding a trip can be adjusted flexibly via a weight λ by users to improve their experience. The trip-quality value of a trip provided by MPTR is greater than or equal to that of PTR [21], which is theoretically ensured by Theorem 7.1. However, MPTR also needs exponential time to obtain the best trip.

Theorem 7.1 If Γ_1 and Γ_2 are respectively the trips found via MPTR and PTR for user u, then $Q_{\Gamma_1}^u(t) \geq Q_{\Gamma_2}^u(t)$.

Proof: Suppose that $\Phi\ominus$ is a set of valid trips that satisfy a user's constraints. $Q_\Gamma^u(t) = \lambda \times S_\Gamma^u(t) + (1-\lambda) \times D_\Gamma$, where $S_\Gamma^u(t)$ is trip-relevance value and D_Γ trip-diversity one, and the objective of both PTR and MPTR is to find the trip with highest trip-quality value $Q_\Gamma^u(t)$.

With PTR, trip planning and re-ranking are included. First, top-k trips ordered by $S_\Gamma^u(t)$ are selected into a trip subset Φ' and $\Phi' \subseteq \Phi$. Then, reorder the k POIs sequences according to the combined values of $S_\Gamma^u(t)$ and D_Γ. However, with MPTR, $Q_\Gamma^u(t)$ is the objective function during trip planning.

Since Γ_1 and Γ_2 are respectively the trips found via MPTR and PTR, $\forall \Gamma' \in \Phi$, $Q_{\Gamma_1}^u(t) \geq Q_{\Gamma'}^u(t)$ and $\forall \Gamma'' \in ', Q_{\Gamma_2}^u(t) \geq Q_{\Gamma''}^u(t)$.

If $\Gamma_1 \in '$, then $\forall \Gamma'' \in ', Q_{\Gamma_1}^u(t) \geq Q_{\Gamma''}^u(t)$. We have $Q_{\Gamma_1}^u(t) = Q_{\Gamma_2}^u(t)$.

If $\Gamma_1 \in \Phi-'$, since $\Gamma_2 \in ', ' \subseteq \Phi$, then $\Gamma_2 \in \Phi$. We have $Q_{\Gamma_1}^u(t) \geq Q_{\Gamma_2}^u(t)$.

Therefore, the conclusion holds.

The below explain MPTR through an example given by Fig. 7.7. The procedure of using Trip-mine + is shown in Fig. 7.8. [5, 90, 8 : 30, 0.4(0.1), 1.0, 0.7(0.55)] on p_1 denotes the attributes about the trip p_1, where the money and time spent on it are 5 and 90, respectively, the arrival time at p_1 is 8:30, the trip score of p_1 as given by u_1 (u_2) is 0.4 (0.1), the diversity value of p_1 is 1.0, and the trip quality value of p_1 as given by $u_1(u_2)$ is 0.7 (0.55) when the weights of trip score and diversity are equal.

In this example, there are two users u_1 and u_2. Different POI scores on the same POIs at the same time are obtained through their different check-in records, as shown in Table 7.5. From p_0, one-POI trips can be obtained, i.e., p_1, p_2 and p_3. For each trip, we first judge whether it is a valid trip by calculating the money and time spent on it. If so, we calculate its score, diversity value and quality; otherwise we delete it. Then based on the valid one-node trips, we extend them to two-node trips, i.e., p_1, p_2, p_1, p_3, p_2, p_1, p_2, p_3,p_3, p_1 and p_3, p_2. Similarly, we judge whether a trip is a valid one or not and calculate the corresponding attributes for all valid trips. After that, three-node trips are obtained based on the valid two-node trips. The above procedure continues until there are no more POIs to be visited or $B_{max}(T_{max})$ is exceeded. The whole procedure is shown in Fig. 7.8, and 11 valid trips are finally obtained. According to the trip quality values of all the valid trips, p_2, $p_1 p_3$ $\left(Q^{u_1}_{p_2, p_1, p_3}(8:00) = 0.815\right)$ is recommended to u_1 as the exact solution, and p_3, p_1 $\left(Q^{u_2}_{p_3, p_1}(8:00) = 0.9\right)$ is recommended to u_2.

(5) Trip Planning Algorithm

Trip recommendation discussed above is an optimization problem. Its global optimal solution offers the highest trip quality. However, it is NP-hard. Though enumeration with a pruning method can plan a short trip with fewer locations in acceptable time [21], to plan a long trip containing over 15 locations costs than 5 days in our experiments. Thus it is unendurable for users. In order to improve its efficiency, this work adopts ACO to obtain an approximately-optimal solution efficiently. An ant-colony-optimization-based trip planning (ATP) algorithm is presented next.

① ATP

The symbols used in ATP are described as follows. t denotes time-counter, r denotes iteration-counter, τ^r denotes the time spent on the r-th iteration, R is the total number of iterations, $N_i(t)(i \in \mathbb{N}^+)$ denotes the number of ants located in POI p_i at time t, $N = \sum_{i=1}^{n} N_i(t)$ indicates the total number of ants, $\delta_{ij}(t)$ is the pheromone-count on e_{ij} at time t, k denotes the k-th ant, and $U_k(t)$ is the set of POIs that have been

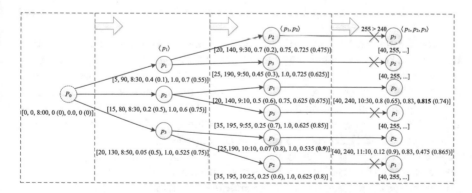

Fig. 7.8 Example of using MPTR

visited by ant k by time t. The ant will put POI p_i into $U_k(t)$ when it passes p_i by time t, and it will not choose p_i next time.

When an ant makes a choice for its next POI, pheromone on the edges and heuristic information should be computed at time t, the transition probability from p_i to p_j for ant k is denoted by $P_{ij}^k(t)$ and computed as follows:

$$P_{ij}^k(t) = \begin{cases} \frac{[\delta_{ij}(t)]^\alpha \times [\eta_{ij}(t)]^\beta}{\sum_{ps \in V_k(t)} [\delta_{is}(t)]^\alpha \times [\eta_{is}(t)]^\beta} & , \text{if} p_j \in V_k(t) \\ 0 & , \quad \text{else} \end{cases} \tag{7.28}$$

where $V_k(t) = P - U_k(t)$ denotes the POIs that are allowed to be visited for ant k after time t. $\delta_{ij}(t)$ denotes the pheromone on edge e_{ij} at time t. $\eta_{ij}^k(t)$ is a heuristic factor for ant k to select e_{ij} at time t. α and β denote the weights of pheromone and heuristic factor, respectively.

Assume that ant k starts a trip from POI p_0 at time t_0. At time t, it is located at POI p_i and has traversed a POI sequence $\Gamma_k = p_1, p_2, \cdots, p_i$. Then we have $U_k(t) = \{p_1, p_2, \cdots, p_i\}$. Thus the heuristic factor $_{ij}^k(t)$ can be computed as follows:

$$\eta_{ij}^k(t) = Q_{\langle \Gamma_k, p_j \rangle}^k(t_0) \tag{7.29}$$

where Γ_k, p_j indicates POI sequence $p_1, p_2, \ldots, p_i, p_j$, and its trip quality is used as the heuristic factor.

When all the ants have completed their travels, i.e., the r-th iteration is completed, the pheromone on each edge should be updated as follows:

$$\Delta_{ij}^k(r) = \begin{cases} \Omega \times Q_{\Gamma_k}^k(t_0) & k \, pass \, through \, e_{ij} \, in \, r \, iteration \\ 0 & else \end{cases} \tag{7.30}$$

$$\Delta_{ij}(r) = \sum_{k=1}^{N} \Delta_{ij}^k(r) \tag{7.31}$$

$$\delta_{ij}(t + \tau^r) = (1 - \rho) \times \delta_{ij}(t) + \Delta_{ij}(r) \tag{7.32}$$

First, for the trip that has been traversed by ant k during this iteration, its trip-quality value can be computed by (7.20). Second, the pheromone that is left by ant k during iteration r is obtained by (7.30), where Ω is a positive constant denoting the released pheromone of each ant. Third, the increment of pheromone on e_{ij} during iteration r can be calculated by (7.31), where N is the number of all ants. Finally, the pheromone on e_{ij} after iteration r can be computed by (7.32), where $\rho(0 < \rho < 1)$ denotes the pheromone evaporation coefficient, and naturally $(1 - \rho)$ indicates the persistence coefficient of pheromone. Equations (7.30)-(7.32) are derived from the classical ant colony optimization algorithm, and show an update process of the pheromone on each edge after the r-th iteration. After the pheromone updating is completed, the $r + 1$-th iteration begins.

In ATP, all ants are put into a start location initially, and then they select their next edges step by step according to the transition probability obtained by (7.28). If an ant has traversed all POIs or no more POIs are permitted to be visited (i.e., the maximal time or budget would be exceeded if one more POI were visited), the ant finishes its travel. The obtained POI sequence is a feasible solution and its trip quality value can be computed by (7.20). When all ants finish their trips the iteration is completed. After this, all the ants return to the start location and pheromone on each edge is updated, and then a new iteration starts. The process repeats until the specified maximal iteration-count is reached. Algorithm 7.3 shows the main steps of ATP algorithm, including the parameter and ant initialization process, iterative process and pheromone update process.

Algorithm 7.3 ATP Algorithm

Input: G, P, p_0, t_0, T_{max}, B_{max}, α , β, λ

Output: Γ

1. Parameter and ant initialization process, see algorithm 7.3.1

2. Iteration, see algorithm 7.3.2

3. Update the pheromone on edges, see algorithm 7.3.3

4. Re-initialization after all the ants' travels finish

5. **if** $(r < R)$ **then**

6.   Go to Step 2

7. **else**

8.   Output the optimal trip Γ

9. **end if**

10. **return**

In the following, Algorithm 7.3.1–7.3.3 will give detailed steps of the parameter and ant initialization process, iterative process and pheromone update process, respectively.

Algorithm 7.3.1 Initialization

Input: G, p_0, ω

Output: $\Gamma_k(t), U_k(t), V_k(t)$

Step 1 Parameter Initialization

1. Set $t := 0$ // time-counter

2. Set $r := 0$ // iteration-counter

3. **for** each edge e_{ij} **do**

4.   Set $\delta_{ij}(t) := \omega$ // ω is the initial pheromone-count

5.   Set $\Delta_{ij}(t) := 0$

6. **end for**

Step 2 Ant Initialization

7. **for** $k = 1 \; To \; N$ **do**

8. k is placed in p_0 // p_0 is the start location

9. $\Gamma_k(t) = \langle p_0 \rangle$ // the trip that has been visited by ant k

10. $U_k(t) = \{p_0\}$ // it contains the POIs visited by ant k

11. $V_k(t) = P - \{p_0\}$ //it contains the POIs not visited by ant k

12. **end for**

13. **return**

Algorithm 7.3.1 shows the initialization process of parameters and ants. For the parameters, the initialization values of the time-counter and iteration-counter are set to 0, the number of pheromone-count on the side is set to the initial value ω, and the pheromone-increment is initialized to 0. For ants, in the initial state, they are placed in the initial POI p_0. Meanwhile, put p_0 in the "POI set that has been visited" and "sequence of the accessed location", and delete p_0 from the "POI set that not accessed by ants".

Algorithm 7.3.2 Iteration

    Input: $P, t_0, T_{max}, B_{max}, \alpha, \beta, \lambda$

    Output: Γ_k

1. **repeat**

2.   **for** $k = 1 \, To \, N$ **do** // one-step transition of ant colony

3.   // assume that ant k is located in p_i at t

4.   **for** $p_j \in V_k(t)$ **do**

5.   Compute the transition probability $\mathbb{P}_{ij}^k(t)$ by (7-29)

6.   **end for**

7.   Select p_j as the next POI of ant k by using Roulette Wheel Selection

8. $\Gamma_k(t) = \langle \Gamma_k(t), p_j \rangle$

9. $U_k(t) = U_k(t) \cup p_j$

10. $V_k(t) = V_k(t) - p_j$

11.   **end for**

12. **until** $C_{\Gamma_k(t)} > B_{max} \| T_{\Gamma_k(t)} > T_{max}$

Algorithm 7.3.2 shows the specific steps of the iteration. In one iteration, the ant should start from the initial POI and use the Roulette Wheel Selection method step by step to select the location to be accessed next. The ant's current access process is terminated until the time or amount spent on the POI sequence exceeds the maximum value of the budget. Then this iteration ends until all the ants have completed their access process.

Algorithm 7.3.3 shows the specific steps of the pheromone update process. After an iteration, the pheromone update on each side can be completed by (7.30)–(7.32) for the sequence of locations that have been accessed during the iteration.

For the example shown in Fig. 7.7, the ATP algorithm is used to complete the trip planning process. The specific steps are shown in Fig. 7.9: "0.383 (0.268)" on e_{01} denotes the transition probability from p_0 to p_1 for an ant $u_1(u_2)$ is 0.383 (0.268). Here we suppose that $\alpha = 1.0$, $\beta = 1.0$, $\rho = 0.5$, and $\omega = \Omega = 0.1$. For the first iteration, pheromones on all edges are equal to the initial value 0.1. We can calculate the transition probabilities from p0 to other POIs with (7.28).

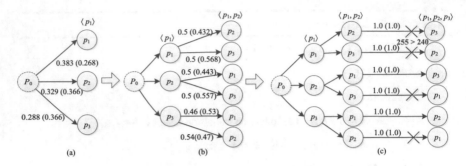

Fig. 7.9 Example for ATP algorithm

Algorithm 7.3.3 Update The Pheromone on Edges

Input: G , p_0, t_0, Γ_k

Output: $\delta_{ij}(t)$

1.   **for** $k = 1\ To\ N$ **do** // t_0 is the start time

2.   Compute the quality value of each ant's trip that is traveled in this

       iteration   according to equation (7.21)

3.   Update the current optimal trip

4.   **end for**

5.   **for** each edge e_{ij} **do**

6.   **for** $k = 1\ To\ N$ **do**

7.   Compute the pheromone increment by equations (7.30)-(7.31)

8.   **end for**

9.   Update its whole pheromone according to equation(7.32)

        $t = t + \tau^r$

10. $r = r + 1$

11.   Set $\Delta_{ij}(t) := 0$

12. **end for**

13. **return**

Table 7.6 Time complexity of three methods

	Computation time	Time complexity
BFA	$C_n^1 + C_n^2 \times 2! + C_n^3 \times 3! + \cdots + C_n^n \times n!$	$O(n!)$
Trip-Mine$^+$	$C_n^1 + C_n^2 \times 2! + C_n^3 \times 3! + \cdots + C_n^K \times K!$	$O(n^K)$
ATP	$N \times R \times [n + (n-1) + \cdots + (n-K+1)]$	$O(nNRK)$

Here we take u_1 as an example, and the transition probability from p_0 to p_1 can be calculated as follows.

$$P_{01}^k(0) = \frac{[\delta_{01}(0)]^\alpha \times [Q_{p_1}^k(8:00)]^\beta}{\sum_{i \in [1,2,3]} [\delta_{0i}(t)]^\alpha \times [Q_{p_i}^k(8:00)\eta_{is}(t)]^\beta}$$

$$= \frac{(0.1)^{1.0} \times (0.7)^{1.0}}{(0.1)^{1.0} \times (0.7)^{1.0} + (0.1)^{1.0} \times (0.6)^{1.0} + (0.1)^{0.1} \times (0.525)^{1.0}} \approx 0.383$$

Similarly, we can obtain transition probabilities from p_0 to other POIs for $u_1(u_2)$, as shown in Fig. 7.9a. According to them, each ant can select its next POI by using the Roulette Wheel Selection method. Then the ant may visit p_1, p_2 or p_3 as its next POI. After that we continue to calculate the transition probabilities for the next steps. The results are shown in Fig. 7.9b, c. If an edge is traversed by an ant, a unit of pheromone (i.e., 0.1) is added to it. After the first iteration, pheromone on each edge is updated by using (7.30)–(7.32). Note that there are some uncertainty in an ant's choice for the next POI. We only show a part of the procedure.

② Complexity Analysis

ATP is more efficient than the up-to-date two trip recommendation ones: Brute Force Approach (BFA) and Trip-Mine. Since trip planning is an online procedure, their time complexity is not related to the offline procedure. Though the computation of POI similarity is related to the number of levels in the category taxonomy, it is not a part of our ATP algorithm. Thus increasing the number of levels in the category taxonomy will not increase the computation complexity of our planning algorithm.

Given n POIs in total, BFA needs to compute all permutation of POIs while Trip-Mine + can skip unnecessary computing via pruning. Assume that K is the number of POIs in the trip that contains the most POIs among those satisfying the time and budget constraints, the numbers of ants and iterations respectively are N and R in ATP. Its computation time is $N \times R \times [n + (n-1) + \cdots + (n-K+1)]$, where N and R are usually much less than n. Thus we have $O(NRKn) > O(Kn^3)$. Computation time and complexities of the three methods are shown in Table 7.6. The time complexities of BFA and Trip-Mine + are factorial and exponential with the problem size, respectively. That of ATP is polynomial. Though ATP cannot give an optimal solution while both its two peers can, when the POI count in a trip is above 15, it becomes intractable for its peers.

References

1. H. Wu, *Smart Tourism Practice* (Posts & Telecom Press, Beijing, 2018)
2. C. Jiang, C. Yan, J. Cheng, et al. *Collaborative filtering recommendation method based on multi similarity among users*: 201910058902.3, 2019-06-14
3. C. Jiang, C. Yan, H. Chen, et al. Personalized *service platform based on large-scale real-time traffic index system* 201410078686.6, 2016-10-12
4. J. Li, G. Liu, C. Yan et al., Research advance and prospects of learning to rank. Acta Automat. Sinica **44**(8), 1345–1369 (2018)
5. W. Luan, G. Liu, C. Jiang, *Collaborative tensor factorization and its application in POI recommendation* (Mexico, Proc. IEEE ICNSC, 2016), pp. 1–6
6. W. Luan, G. Liu, C. Jiang, et al., Partition-based collaborative tensor factorization for POI recommendation. IEEE/CAA J Automat Sinica 4(3), 437–446
7. W. Luan, G. Liu, C. Jiang et al., Mptr: a Maximal-Marginal-Relevance-Based Personalized Trip Recommendation Method. IEEE Trans. Intell. Transp. Syst. **19**(11), 3461–3474 (2018)
8. J. Li, G. Liu, C. Yan et al., LORI: A Learning-to-rank Based Integration Method of Location Recommendation. IEEE Transactions on Computational Social Systems 6(3), 430–440 (2019)
9. Y. Zheng, X. Xie.Learning travel recommendations from user-generated GPS traces.ACM Transactions on Intelligent Systems and Technology, 2011, 2(1):2
10. T.T. Horozov, N. Narasimhan, V. Vasudevan, *Using location for personalized POI recommendations in mobile environments* (Phoenix, AZ, USA, Proc. IEEE SAINT, 2006), pp. 124–129
11. J. Bao, Y. Zheng, M.F. Mokbel, *Location-based and preference-aware recommendation using sparse geo-social networking data* (Redondo Beach, California, Proc.ACM SIGSPATIAL, 2012), pp. 199–208
12. M. Ye, P.F. Yin, W. Lee et al., *Exploiting geographical influence for collaborative point-of-interest recommendation* (Beijing, China, Proc.ACM SIGIR, 2011), pp. 325–334
13. M. Ye, P. Yin, W. Lee.Location recommendation for location-based social networks. Proc.ACM SIGSPATIAL, 2010:458–461
14. Z. Chen, H.T. Shen, X. Zhou et al., *Searching trajectories by locations: an efficiency study* (Indianapolis, Indiana, USA, Proc.ACM SIGMOD, 2010), pp. 255–266
15. L. Wei, Y. Zheng, W. Peng, *Constructing popular routes from uncertain trajectories* (Beijing, China, Proc.ACM SIGKDD, 2012), pp. 195–203
16. Y. Zheng, L. Zhang, X. Xie et al., *Mining interesting locations and travel sequences from GPS trajectories* (Madrid, Spain, Proc.WWW, 2009), pp. 791–800
17. Y. Zheng, Q. Li, Y. Chen et al., *Understanding mobility based on GPS data* (Seoul, Korea, Proc.ACM UbiComp, 2008), pp. 312–321
18. J. Yuan, Y. Zheng, C. Zhang et al., *T-drive: driving directions based on taxi trajectories* (New York, NY, USA, Proc.ACM SIGSPATIAL, 2010), pp. 99–108
19. J.C. Ying, H.C. Lu, B.N. Shi et al., *TripCloud : an intelligent cloud-based trip recommendation system* (Munich, Germany, Proc.SSTD, 2013), pp. 472–477
20. H. P. Hsieh, C. T. Li, S. Lin.Measuring and Recommending Time-Sensitive Routes from Location-Based Data.ACM Transactions on Intelligent Systems and Technology, 2014, 5(3):45
21. T. Kurashima, T. Iwata, G. Irie et al., *Travel route recommendation using geotags in photo sharing sites* (Toronto, ON, Canada, Proc.ACM CIKM, 2010), pp. 579–588
22. C. Zhou, X. Meng, *OrientSTS: spatio-temporal sequence searching in flickr* (Beijing, China, Proc.ACM SIGIR, 2011), pp. 1265–1266
23. Z. Yin, L. Cao, J. Han et al., *Diversified trajectory pattern ranking in geo-tagged social media* (Mesa, Arizona, USA, Proc.SDM, 2011), pp. 980–991
24. S. Chen, F. Zhu, J. Cao, Growing Spatially Embedded Social Networks for Activity-Travel Analysis Based on Artificial Transportation Systems. IEEE Trans. Intell. Transp. Syst. **15**(5), 2111–2120 (2014)
25. C. Lee, Y. Chang, M. Wang.Ontological recommendation multi-agent for Tainan City travel.Expert Systems With Applications, 2009, 36(3):6740–6753

26. H.C. Lu, C.Y. Lin, V.S. Tseng, *Trip-Mine: An Efficient Trip Planning Approach with Travel Time Constraints* (Lulea, Sweden, Proc. IEEE MDM, 2011), pp. 152–161

27. H.C. Lu, C.Y. Chen, V.S. Tseng, *Personalized trip recommendation with multiple constraints by mining user check-in behaviors* (Redondo Beach, California, Proc.ACM SIGSPATIAL, 2012), pp. 209–218

28. C. Chen, D. Zhang, B. Guo et al., TripPlanner: Personalized Trip Planning Leveraging Heterogeneous Crowdsourced Digital Footprints. IEEE Trans. Intell. Transp. Syst. **16**(3), 1259–1273 (2014)

29. F. Alhasoun, M. Alhazzani, M. C.Gonza'lez.City scale next place prediction from sparse data through similar strangers. Proc.UrbComp, Halifax, NS, Canada, 2017:1–8

30. J. Feng, Y. Li, C. Zhang et al., *DeepMove: Predicting Human Mobility with Attentional Recurrent Networks* (Lyon, France, Proc.WWW, 2018), pp. 1459–1468

31. D. Feillet, P. Dejax, M. Gendreau, Traveling Salesman Problems with Profits. Transportation Science **39**(2), 188–205 (2005)

32. Y. Zheng, X. Xie, W. Ma.GeoLife: A Collaborative Social Networking Service among User, location and trajectory.IEEE Data(base) Engineering Bulletin, 2010, 33(2):32–39

33. L. Lü, M. Medo, H. Y. Chi, et al.Recommender systems.Physics Reports, 2012, 519(1):1–49

34. X. Luo, M. Zhou, Y. Xia et al., An Efficient Non-Negative Matrix-Factorization-Based Approach to Collaborative Filtering for Recommender Systems. IEEE Trans. Industr. Inf. **10**(2), 1273–1284 (2014)

35. D.D. Lee, H.S. Seung, *Unsupervised Learning by Convex and Conic Coding* (Denver, CO, USA, Proc.NIPS, 1996), pp. 515–521

36. N. Guan, D. Tao, Z. Luo et al., Online Nonnegative Matrix Factorization With Robust Stochastic Approximation. IEEE Trans. Neural Networks **23**(7), 1087–1099 (2012)

37. J. Li, G. Liu, C. Jiang et al., *A hybrid method of recommending POIs based on context and personal preference confidence* (Washington DC, USA, Proc. IEEE BigData, 2016), pp. 287–292

38. W. Luan. Research on Service Recommendation Model and Method Based on Object Space-time Trajectory. Tongji University PhD thesis, 2018

39. Y. Zheng, Introduction to Urban Computing. Geomatics and Information Science of Wuhan University **40**(1), 1–13 (2015)

40. V.W. Zheng, B. Cao, Y. Zheng et al., *Collaborative filtering meets mobile recommendation: a user-centered approach* (Atlanta, Proc.AAAI, 2010), pp. 236–241

41. Y. Wang, Y. Zheng, Y. Xue, *Travel time estimation of a path using sparse trajectories* (New York, NY, USA, Proc.ACM SIGKDD, 2014), pp. 25–34

42. V. W. Zheng, Y. Zheng, X. Xie, et al.Towards mobile intelligence: Learning from GPS history data for collaborative recommendation.Artificial Intelligence, 2012, 184–185:17-37

43. F. Zhang, D. Wilkie, Y. Zheng et al., *Sensing the pulse of urban refueling behavior* (Zurich, Switzerland, Proc.ACM UbiComp, 2013), pp. 13–22

44. J. Shang, Y. Zheng, W. Tong et al., *Inferring gas consumption and pollution emission of vehicles throughout a city* (New York, NY, USA, Proc.ACM SIGKDD, 2014), pp. 1027–1036

45. Y. Zheng, T. Liu, Y. Wang et al., *Diagnosing New York city's noises with ubiquitous data* (Seattle, Washington, Proc.ACM UbiComp, 2014), pp. 715–725

46. V.W. Zheng, Y. Zheng, X. Xie et al., *Collaborative location and activity recommendations with GPS history data* (Raleigh, North Carolina, USA, Proc.WWW, 2010), pp. 1029–1038

47. C. Cheng, H. Yang, I. King et al., *Fused matrix factorization with geographical and social influence in location-based social networks* (Toronto, Ontario, Canada, Proc.AAAI, 2012), pp. 17–23

48. X. Li, G. Cong, X. Li et al., *Rank-GeoFM: A Ranking based Geographical Factorization Method for Point of Interest Recommendation* (Northampton, Massachusetts, USA, Proc.ACM SIGIR, 2015), pp. 433–442

49. N. Srebro, J.D.M. Rennie, T.S. Jaakkola, *Maximum-Margin Matrix Factorization* (Vancouver, British Columbia, Canada, Proc.NIPS, 2004), pp. 1329–1336

50. M. Weimer, A. Karatzoglou, A. J. Smola.Improving maximum margin matrix factorization.Machine Learning, 2008, 72(3):14–14
51. P.J. Huber, E.M. Ronchetti, *Robust Statistics*, 2nd edn. (Wiley, New Jersey, USA, 2009)
52. M. Weimer, A. Karatzoglou, M. Bruch, *Maximum Margin Code Recommendation* (New York, NY, USA, Proc.ACM RecSys, 2009), pp. 309–312
53. O.L. Mangasarian, Linear and Nonlinear Separation of Patterns by Linear Programming. Oper. Res. **13**(3), 444–452 (1965)
54. G. Fung, O. L. Mangasarian, A. J. Smola.Minimal kernel classifiers.Journal of Machine Learning Research, 2003, 3(2):303–321
55. A.P. Singh, G.J. Gordon, *Relational learning via collective matrix factorization* (Las Vegas, Nevada, USA, Proc.ACM SIGKDD, 2008), pp. 650–658
56. L. R. Tucker, C. W. Harris.Implications of factor analysis of three way matrices for measurements of change.USA:University of Wisconsin Press,1963
57. L. R. Tucker.Some mathematical notes on three-mode factor analysis.Psychometrika, 1966, 31(3):279–311
58. T. G. Kolda, B. W. Bader.Tensor Decompositions and Applications.SIAM Review, 2009, 51(3):455–500
59. A. Karatzoglou, X. Amatriain, L. Baltrunas et al., *Multiverse recommendation: n-dimensional tensor factorization for context-aware collaborative filtering* (Barcelona, Spain, Proc.ACM RecSys, 2010), pp. 79–86
60. Y. Koren, R.M. Bell, C. Volinsky, Matrix Factorization Techniques for Recommender Systems. IEEE Comput. **42**(8), 30–37 (2009)
61. C. A. Andersson, R. Bro.The N-way Toolbox for MATLAB.Chemometrics and Intelligent Laboratory Systems, 2000, 52(1):1–4
62. U. Kang, E.E. Papalexakis, A. Harpale et al., *GigaTensor: scaling tensor analysis up by 100 times - algorithms and discoveries* (Beijing, China, Proc.ACM SIGKDD, 2012), pp. 316–324
63. E.E. Papalexakis, C. Faloutsos, N.D. Sidiropoulos, *Parcube: Sparse parallelizable tensor decompositions* (Bristol, UK, Proc.ECML PKDD, 2012), pp. 521–536
64. A.H. Phan, A. Cichocki, *Block decomposition for very large-scale nonnegative tensor factorization* (Aruba, Dutch Antilles, Netherlands, Proc. IEEE CAMSAP, 2009), pp. 316–319
65. X. Li, S. Huang, K. Candan et al., *Focusing Decomposition Accuracy by Personalizing Tensor Decomposition (PTD)* (Shanghai, China, Proc.ACM CIKM, 2014), pp. 689–698
66. J.B. Macqueen, *Some methods for classification and analysis of multivariate observations* (Berkeley, California, USA, Proc.BSMSP, 1967), pp. 281–297
67. X.S. Lu, M. Zhou, *Analyzing the evolution of rare events via social media data and k-means clustering algorithm* (Mexico, Proc. IEEE ICNSC, 2016), pp. 1–6
68. R. P. Ebstein, O. Novick, R. Umansky, et al.Dopamine D4 receptor (D4DR) exon III polymorphism associated with the human personality trait of Novelty Seeking.Nature Genetics, 1996, 12(1):78–80
69. E. Cho, S.A. Myers, J. Leskovec, *Friendship and mobility: user movement in location-based social networks* (San Diego, California, USA, Proc.ACM SIGKDD, 2011), pp. 1082–1090
70. F. Zhang, K. Zheng, N.J. Yuan et al., *A Novelty-Seeking based Dining Recommender System* (Florence, Italy, Proc.WWW, 2015), pp. 1362–1372
71. A. Colorni, M. Dorigo, V. Maniezzo et al., *Distributed Optimization by Ant Colonies* (Paris, France, Proc.ECAL, 1992), pp. 134–142
72. M. Dorigo, V. Maniezzo, A. Colorni, *Positive feedback as a search strategy* (Report, Politecnico di Milano, 1991)
73. M. Dorigo, L. M. Gambardella.Ant colony system: a cooperative learning approach to the traveling salesman problem.IEEE Transactions on Evolutionary Computation, 1997, 1(1):53–66
74. M. Dorigo, V. Maniezzo, A. Colorni.Ant system: optimization by a colony of cooperating agents. IEEE Transactions on Systems Man & Cybernetics Part B, 1996, 26(1):29–41
75. J. Carbinell, J. Goldstein, *The use of MMR, diversity-based reranking for reordering documents and producing summaries* (Pisa, Italy, Proc.ACM SIGIR, 2016), pp. 335–336

Chapter 8
Mobile Payment Authentication

Abstract The user's behavior features are unique and hardly to be imitated, identity authentication based on user behaviors has become a research hotspot. However, none of the existing research has considered the influence of user posture on users' gesture behavior authentication. In order to make the identity authentication method adapt to the use of the application in different postures, this chapter presents a touch screen behavior authentication system based on user gestures. We collect the user's gesture behavior data through the touch screen of the mobile phone, collect the user's posture behavior data through the mobile phone's orientation sensor and acceleration sensor, and finally extract the user's posture behavior features and gesture behavior features. In addition, based on this authentication system architecture, we respectively provide two forms of authentication model construction methods: login authentication and continuous authentication. It is possible to monitor from user login to the entire usage process for improving the payment security of mobile devices by using login authentication and continuous authentication comprehensively.

8.1 Related Applications and Technologies

With the rapid popularity of mobile electronic devices (e.g., smart phones and tablet PCs), mobile phone shopping, mobile payment, O2O services and other services are developing rapidly. Mobile payment is a typical application of network mobile information services. The most popular mobile payment APPs in China are Alipay, Wing Payment, Cloud Flash Pay, WeChat Pay, Fast Money and mobile phone clients of major domestic banks. The most widely used of the above APPs are Alipay and WeChat Pay. These mobile client APPs not only support online consumption, but also expand offline payment services in the form of scan code payment, which can be used as a digital wallet and further support mobile e-commerce, financial transactions, insurance credit, and cryptographic currency. Many similar mobile payment APPs have been launched abroad, such as Paypal, Google Pay, Apple Pay, Cash Pay, and social-based Venmo, blockchain-based cryptocurrency transactions Jaxx [1].

Mobile payment greatly facilitates people's daily life, it also brings opportunities to criminals. Various types of mobile phone security incidents such as fraud, privacy

© Springer Nature Singapore Pte Ltd. & Science Press 2020

C. Jiang and Z. Li, *Mobile Information Service for Networks*,

https://doi.org/10.1007/978-981-15-4569-6_8

theft, and malicious harassment emerged in an endless stream. They not only caused the user's private information to be leaked, but also caused direct or indirect economic losses to many users. According to statistics, in the whole year of 2018, 360 Internet Security Center has intercepted 4.342 million malicious programs, 36.93 billion phishing websites attack, 44.93 billion harassing calls, and 8.4 billion spam messages. Compared with 2017, these data have a significant decline, but the security of mobile phones is still not optimistic, especially in terms of fraud. According to the report, in the 2018 year, 360 mobile phones received a total of 7716 tip-offs, including 3,380 fraudulent compensations, involving a total amount of 19.279 million yuan. Among all fraudulent compensations, malicious programs accounted for the highest percentage, at 19.3%; followed by financial management (14.9%), false part-time (13.0%), identity impersonation (8.4%) and gambling betting (8.2%). In recent years, criminals have "upgraded" the way of capital transfer. In addition to the common online banking/third-party platform transfer and scanning of QR code payment orders/transfers, they also use new technologies such as cloud flash payment and free-secret payment to dispel user doubts and achieve the purpose of defrauding money.

The frequent occurrence of various mobile security events indicates that traditional mobile authentication methods are difficult to meet the increasingly complex mobile security environment. Currently, user authentication systems for mobile phones are mainly based on three kinds of techniques [2]. The first authentication technique is based on passwords, such as PINs and password patterns. Though it's traditional and most commonly used, this technique exists two drawbacks. (1) The passwords can easily be stolen by malicious programs such as Trojans and phishing websites. (2) On the one hand, setting a complex password is difficult to memory and use for user. On the other hand, setting a simple one can easily be cracked. That is to say, between security and convenience, users can only choose either-or. In order to facilitate the memory and use, many users use one password for multiple different APPs. Once an account is leaked, other accounts also have the risk of leaking, and the security risks are large. The second one is based on physiological biometrics of users, such as fingerprint [3–8] or face [9–17]. This kind of technique has good authentication effects. And the fingerprint and face identification functions have been added into part of newly produced high-end mobiles. However, it often needs extra or high-demanding hardware and not suitable for many low-end and old phones. The third one is based on behavioral biometrics, such as user's behavior on soft keyboard inputting [18–20], gait [21–23], and gesture behavior [24–29]. The soft keyboard inputting collects finger behavior data when the user inputs using the soft keyboard authentication through the touch screen of the mobile phone, and extracts features such as finger pressing time, finger pressing interval time, finger pressure, contact area. Finally, the authentication model is trained for the user's soft keyboard inputting to achieve identity authentication. The gait behavior realizes identity authentication by collecting the user's walking direction and acceleration to characterize the user's gait information. Gesture behavior is authenticated by user gesture behavior information collected by the touch screen. The user's behavioral features refer to the habitual behavior characteristics unique to the user. This kind of authentication technique has a good application prospect due to its difficult imitativeness and copy, and without the need of additional hardware support.

For the above-mentioned authentication method, the book *Risk Control Theory of Online Transactions* published by us has given some innovations in the aspect of user authentication based authentication technology, including user keyboard knocking behavior authentication and user mouse sliding behavior analysis technology. These techniques give the confidence coefficient of the current user identity by comparing the current user's behavior sequence with the behavior model to achieve the purpose of identity authentication and early warning. Recently, we have made some new research progress in the identity authentication of network mobile information services based on gesture behavior [30–34].

A robust gesture behavior authentication method needs to consider the influence of various factors (such as user posture, device size, screen orientation) on user gesture behavior. The user posture here refers to the combination of the user's body action (station, sitting, lying, walking, etc.), the direction of the screen (inclination angle), and the position of the device (held on the hand, placed on the table). At present, the research on identity authentication based on user gestures does not consider the influence of user posture on user's gesture behavior habits. Therefore, in order to solve this problem, this chapter flistly gives a user-postures based touch screen behavior mobile terminal authentication system architecture. Subsequently, this chapter introduces the model construction and authentication methods for "login authentication" and "continuous authentication" in detail. Login authentication is achieved by adding behavior authentication to the gesture password. Only the correct gesture password is input and the user behaviors can be logged in through the authentication model, thereby improving the security of the gesture password. Continuous authentication is realized by collecting gestures and gesture behavior data when the user uses the application, thereby achieving continuous monitoring of the user's identity.

8.2 Touch Screen Behavior Authentication System Based on User Postures

Since the posture of the user has a great influence on the gesture behavior habit of the user, the authentication effect based on the user gesture for identity authentication will be directly affected. In order to solve this problem, this section gives the touch screen behavior authentication system architecture based on the user gesture, which is designed to adapt to the user's use of the application in different conditions. Compared with the traditional authentication methods based on user gesture behavior, the system uses the direction sensor and the acceleration sensor of the mobile phone to gather more user's posture data, and then extracts the posture feature from data for posture clustering. Finally, it trains a gesture authentication sub-model for each posture by clustering different postures of the user [35].

8.2.1   Overall Architecture

The overall architecture of the authentication system is shown in Fig. 8.1. Since the training calculations of the model are relatively large, the training and authentication of the model are all placed on the server. Therefore, the authentication system architecture includes two parts: the mobile client and the server. The mobile phone client mainly includes a data collection module, which is used to collect user behavior information and upload it to the server. The server mainly includes feature extraction module, posture clustering module, gesture sub-model training module, model storage module, and authentication module. The server is responsible for receiving user behavior information, performs the training and storing of the user authentication model, and authenticates the user identity.

The modules of this system architecture are briefly introduced as follows.

(1) Data collection module. When the user inputs a gesture password to log in (login authentication) or performs a sliding gesture operation (continuous authentication), the user's gesture behavior data is collected by using the touch screen of the mobile phone. And the posture behavior data of the user is collected by using the direction sensor and the acceleration sensor (The specific data collected is detailed in Sect. 8.2.2) and uploaded to the server.

(2) Feature extraction module. The feature extraction module receives the user posture behavior data and the gesture behavior data uploaded by the user end, respectively calculates the posture feature (Sect. 8.2.3) and the gesture feature

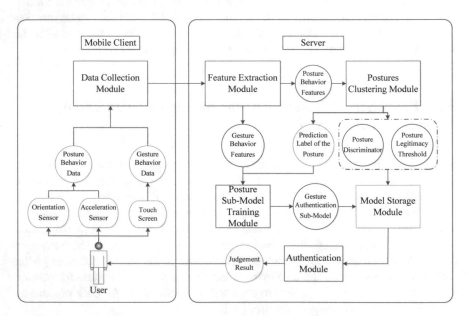

Fig. 8.1 System architecture

according to the behavior data, and performs feature transformation and feature reduction. Due to the difference of login and continuous authentication, the gesture behavior features are different (see Sect. 8.3.1 for the login authentication gesture features and Sect. 8.4.1 for the continuous authentication gesture features). The extracted posture features are passed to the posture clustering module, and the gesture features are passed to the gesture sub-model training module.

(3) Postures clustering module. The postures clustering module receives the posture features of the user and clusters different postures of the user according to the postures clustering algorithm. Thereby it obtains prediction labels of the posture feature (for separately training the gesture authentication sub-model for each posture), posture discriminator (i.e. K pose cluster centers for judging which posture the posture feature vector belongs to) and posture legitimacy threshold (for judging whether a posture feature belongs to the user). The postures clustering algorithm is shown in Sect. 8.2.4.

(4) Posture sub-model training module. The posture sub-model training module is used to train a posture authentication sub-model for each posture of the user. The posture sub-model training module receives the user's posture behavior features and predicted posture labels, and selects different algorithms for training the posture sub-model according to different authentication types (login authentication and continuous authentication) (see Sects. 8.3.2 and 8.4.2 in detail). These posture authentication sub-models are used to judge whether the posture behavior of the user in a certain posture is legal.

(5) Model storage module. The model storage module is mainly used for storing the posture discriminator and the posture legality threshold trained by the postures clustering module, and the posture authentication sub-model separately trained by the posture sub-model training module for each posture of the user. When the user identity is authenticated, the authentication module reads the required model from it.

(6) Authentication module. The authentication module is used to authenticate the user identity. The authentication module can be applied to both login and continuous authentication. In fact, these two methods require the legality authentication of posture and gesture. But the two authentication methods have different authentication procedures, see Sects. 8.3.3 and 8.4.3 in detail. When the legality authentication of posture and gesture is performed (i.e. the user performs a login operation by inputting a gesture password or performs a sliding gesture operation), the user's posture behavior features and the gesture behavior features can be obtained through the data collection module and the feature extraction module. The authentication module requires the posture discriminator and the posture legality threshold trained by the posture clustering module from the model storage module. Meanwhile, it also extracts the posture authentication sub-model separately trained by the posture sub-model training module for each posture of the user. When the posture and gesture legality authentication is performed, authentication module firstly judges whether the user's posture is legal through the posture legality threshold. If the posture is illegal, it is directly

judge to be illegal; if the posture is legal, then the posture discriminator is used to judge the current user's posture type. After that, authentication module takes out the gesture authentication sub-model corresponding to the user's posture, and uses the gesture authentication sub-model to judge the legitimacy of the user's gesture behavior, for obtaining the final judgment result. The flow chart of the legality authentication of posture and gesture is shown in Fig. 8.2.

Based on the architecture of the authentication system. This chapter presents two authentication methods for implementing full-course security monitoring from login to using-the login authentication and continuous authentication. Since the login authentication and continuous authentication have their own features, they have great differences in posture feature extraction, posture authentication sub-model training and specific authentication methods. Therefore, the remaining sections of this chapter mainly describe the common parts of the two authentication methods in the authentication system architecture (i.e. data collection, posture features extraction and postures clustering algorithm). The unique parts of the login authentication and continuous authentication (i.e. gesture features extraction, training method for the

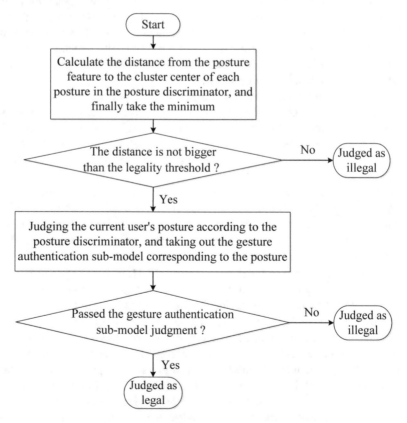

Fig. 8.2 The flow chart of the legality authentication of posture and gesture

gesture authentication sub-model under each posture, and authentication method) are introduced in Sects. 8.3 and 8.4, respectively.

8.2.2 Data Collection

The authentication system is designed to solve the impact of user postures on the gesture authentication effect, so the user's posture behavior data needs to be collected. Considering that most mobile phones equiped with directional sensors and acceleration sensors, the direction and acceleration of the mobile phone can describe the user's posture behavior to a certain extent. Therefore, besides using the user's gesture behavior data collected from the touch screen of the mobile phone, the authentication system uses the direction sensor and accceleration sensor to collect more behavior data.

When inputting the gesture password (login authentication) or performing a sliding gesture behavior (continuous authentication), the application we developed can collect two kinds of user behavioral data. The first kind of data is collected by touch screen which includes the X, Y coordinate of finger position (finger_x, finger_y), the pressure (pressure), the size of contact area (size) and the timestamp (timestamp). The example data of it is shown in Table 8.1. Because these data reflect user's gesture behavior, we call them gesture behavioral data. The other kind of data includes the X, Y, Z coordinate of screen orientation (orient_x, orient_y, orient_z) which are collected by mobile's orientation sensor, and mobile's acceleration [36] (acc_x, acc_y, acc_z) by acceleration sensor. We call them posture behavioral data. The meanings of coordinates of screen orientation and acceleration are shown in Figs. 8.3 and 8.4. And the example data collected by orientation sensor and acceleration sensor is presented in Tables 8.2 and 8.3, respectively.

Because each kind of data (such as pressure, contact area) can be viewed as a time series [37]. For a certain kind of data S, we use $[S]$ to represent the time series, denoted as $[S] = \left[s_{t_0}, s_{t_1}, \ldots, s_{t_{n-1}} \right]$, where t_i represents a certain timestamp and $t_0 < t_1 < \cdots < t_{n-1}$, s_{t_i} is the data point in t_i, and n is the length of the time series.

By Eq. (8.1), the time series of average velocity $\left[\text{velocity} \right] = \left[v_{t_0}, v_{t_1}, \ldots, v_{t_{n-2}} \right]$ can be calculated from finger_x, finger_y and timestamp.

Table 8.1 The example data collected by touch screen

timestamp	finger_x	finger_y	pressure	size
16,047,921	90	278	0.22352943	0.23333335
16,047,930	91	278	0.36862746	0.33333334
16,047,944	91	278	0.37254903	0.36666667

Fig. 8.3 The sketch-map of X, Y, Z coordinate of mobile orientation

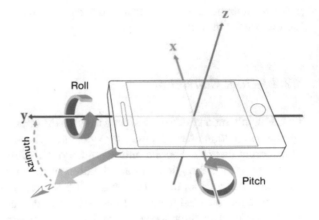

Fig. 8.4 The sketch-map of X, Y, Z coordinate of mobile acceleration

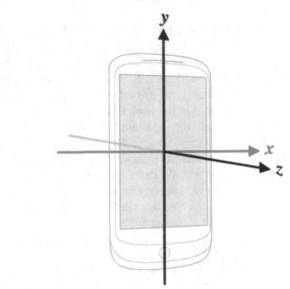

Table 8.2 The example data collected by orientation sensor

orient$_x$	orient$_y$	orient$_z$
−41.112537	8.184002	−131.44785
−1.112537	8.184002	−132.0875
−40.30289	5.2750325	−132.09087

Table 8.3 The example data collected by acceleration

acc$_x$	acc$_y$	acc$_z$
−1.0247183	6.2823853	7.1251445
−0.58418524	6.167464	7.0485296
−0.6799533	6.2728086	7.3645644

$$v_{t_i} = \frac{\sqrt{\left(x_{t_{i+1}} - x_{t_i}\right)^2 + \left(y_{t_{i+1}} - y_{t_i}\right)^2}}{t_{i+1} - t_i} \tag{8.1}$$

Therefore, the posture behavioral data produced by inputting a gesture password or performing a gesture sliding operation can be represented as $\langle[\mathrm{orient}_x], [\mathrm{orient}_y], [\mathrm{orient}_z], [\mathrm{acc}_x][\mathrm{acc}_y], [\mathrm{acc}_z]\rangle$. And the corresponding gesture behavioral data can be represented as $\langle[\mathrm{finger}_x], [\mathrm{finger}_y], [\mathrm{pressure}], [\mathrm{size}], [\mathrm{velocity}]\rangle$.

8.2.3 Posture Feature Extraction

1. **Calculation of Posture Features**

As Sect. 8.2.2 shown, the posture behavioral data $\langle[\mathrm{orient}_x], [\mathrm{orient}_y], [\mathrm{orient}_z], [\mathrm{acc}_x][\mathrm{acc}_y], [\mathrm{acc}_z]\rangle$ can be viewed as the collection of time series. So features can be extracted from the time series' point of view for describing the postures of user. For each time series, the following features can be extracted:

(1) Features that reflect the overall characteristics of time sequences, such as mean, variance, maximum value, minimum value and duration.
(2) Features that reflect the differences between time sequences. In most cases, the lengths of time series n are different due to different durations of user's gestures. To evaluate the differences between time series, DTW [38] algorithm is used. The algorithm uses the idea of dynamic programming, and the smaller the distance obtained is, the more similar the two time series are. So the acquisition frequency of the application for collecting data is high, the length of the time sequence is long, and the feature changes little between adjacent timestamps. To reduce the computation time, we extract sample data points from original time series. For a certain time sequence $[S] = [s_{t_0}, s_{t_1}, \ldots, s_{t_{n-1}}]$, we use sample time series $[S'] = [s_{t_0}, s_{t_3}, \ldots s_{t_{3i}} \ldots, s_{t_{3k}}]$, where $k = \lfloor \frac{n-1}{3} \rfloor$. Since we only consider the relative distance of time series, we use the first sample time series in user's training set as reference time series. Therefore, for a certain kind of data S, set the size of the training set to m, i.e. the training set has m time series of S, which denotes as $([S]_0, [S]_1, \ldots, [S]_{m-1})$. Here takes $[S]_{ref} = [S']_0$, the distance relationship between the i-th time series and the reference time series is $d_{s_i} = \mathrm{DTW}([S']_i, [S]_{ref})$.

The features extracted from the posture behavior data are referred to as posture features, and the specific posture features used are shown in Table 8.4.

Table 8.4 Posture features

Overall features	Mean, variance and range of the X, Y coordinate of screen orientation
	Mean, variance and range of the X, Y, Z coordinate of mobile acceleration
Difference features	The distance between the time series consisting of the X and Y coordinate of the screen orientation and its corresponding reference time series

2. Feature Transformation and Reduction

After the feature calculation, the feature vectors obtained are directly submitted to the classification or clustering algorithm. If the effect is poor, further processing is needed.

Since the calculated features' meanings are different, the range of values varies, and even varies greatly. For example, the touch screen pressure and contact area of the mobile phone range between [0, 1], so the mean value is also between [0, 1]. The X coordinate of the screen orientation has a value range of $[-180, 180]$, and the mean value is also between $[-180, 180]$. Different values of various features cause interferences to the classification and clustering algorithms below. Therefore, feature transformation is needed to change the range of values of each feature to be the same. For each feature x, we use $(x_i - x_{min})/(x_{max} - x_{min})$ [39] to transform it. After feature transformation for improving the certification effect, all features are in range [0, 1].

When actually using machine learning algorithms to solve classification or clustering problems, the amount of calculated features will be relatively large. These features may be unrelated or may be dependent on each other. Moreover, when the volume of features is too large, the training time of the model is correspondingly increased. And there may be some redundant information, which may lead to a decrease in the effect of the machine learning algorithm, which is called "dimensional disaster". In order to solve this problem, feature reduction is required. At present, the common feature dimension reduction methods are divided into two categories, one is feature selection and the other is feature reduction. Feature selection is to remove extra and unrelated features from existing features. Feature reduction is to transform existing feature vectors into feature vectors with lower dimensions by mathematical methods. This section adopts principal component analysis (PCA) algorithm [40] to handle posture feature vectors for reducing the dimension of feature vector. PCA algorithm maps original features to low-dimensional space by coordinate transformation. The new feature is a linear combination of the original features that maximizes the sample variance to make the new features as irrelevant as possible. By the PCA algorithm, the interference of redundant information to the algorithm can be reduced, and the training speed of subsequent models can be accelerated.

After feature extraction, the feature vector set of a user can be represented as $V_{user} = \left(\vec{v^1}, \vec{v^2}, \ldots, \vec{v^i}, \ldots \vec{v^n}\right)$, where n is the number of feature vector. Each feature vector $\vec{v^i}$ represents an inputting operation of the password pattern or a sliding operation, and consists of posture feature vector $\vec{v^i_{pos}}$ and gesture feature vector $\vec{v^i_{ges}}$, written as $\overrightarrow{v^i} = \left(\overrightarrow{v^i_{pos}}, \overrightarrow{v^i_{ges}}\right)$. Due to the different gesture features extracted during login authentication and continuous authentication, the specific gesture features are shown in Sects. 8.3.1 and 8.4.1 in detail.

8.2.4 Postures Clustering

The idea of the authentication system architecture is to construct a gesture authentication sub-model for each gesture of the user. Since it is impossible to directly obtain the user's current posture in practical application, it is necessary to analyze according to the collected posture behavior data (i.e. orientation and acceleration of the mobile phone). In the model training, in order to mark the posture of each feature vector, and then train the gesture authentication sub-model separately for different postures, this section clusters different postures based on the idea of clustering according to its behavioral characteristics.

Here use K-means algorithm [41] on posture feature vector $\overrightarrow{v_{pos}}$. The K-means clustering algorithm firstly selects K nodes from all nodes as the cluster center, and then repeats the following two steps until the cluster no longer changes or reaches the maximum number of iterations. The first step is to calculate the distance from all nodes to the center of the cluster and assign the node to the cluster center closest to it. The second step is to recalculate the cluster center of each cluster. We use the Euclidean distance in clustering distance calculations.

The K-means clustering algorithm can be used to cluster different postures of the user. Then we obtain a posture discriminator for judging which the user posture belong to, and a pose prediction label for training the gesture authentication sub-model separately for each gesture. However, there are two problems to be solved. One is to determine the number of postures, and the other is to find a way to judge the legality of the user's posture.

(1) **Determination of the Number of Postures**

K-means algorithm needs to preset the number of clusters (K). However, it's impossible to know the number of user's postures in practical application, so we use silhouette coefficient [42] to determine K's value. The method to calculate the silhouette coefficient is as follows: for the i-th feature vector, we calculate the distances to the other vectors that are in the same cluster with the i-th feature vector, and then calculate the average of them, denote as $a(i)$. Also, we calculate the distances to the vectors that aren't in the same cluster with the i-th feature vector, and then calculate the average of them, denote as $b(i)$. The silhouette coefficient of the feature vector is calculated by $s(i) = \frac{b(i)-a(i)}{\max\{a(i),b(i)\}}$. The bigger silhouette coefficient is, the better K is.

Regarding the determination of the upper bound of the K, considering that the user may be in a different state such as sitting, standing, walking, lying, when using the mobile phone, and the phone may be held in the hand or placed on a table. So there is a possibility of multiple postures. However, for a certain user, the number of his postures is not large. Also, similar postures can be clustered as one posture. Therefore, the upper bound of the K in this Chapter is set as 6. We increase K's value from 2 to 6, and calculate silhouette coefficients for each K. And we adopt the K which makes silhouette coefficient biggest as the final K.

(2) Legality Judgment of Postures

The posture discriminator (i.e., K cluster centers) obtained by the K-means clustering algorithm can be used to judge which posture a feature belongs to. However, illegal users may use different postures. Therefore, it is necessary to find a way to distinguish between the gesture of the illegal user and the legal user, i.e., to judge whether the posture represented by a certain feature vector belongs to a legal user. Consequently, this section presents a threshold-based method for judging the legality of a gesture.

K cluster centers are considered as K postures of legal user, and can be calculated by K-means algorithm. The feature vector has the smallest Euclidean distance from one cluster center, and the eigenvector belongs to the cluster. What's more, a feature vector that represents illegal postures (i.e., the posture corresponding to the eigenvector does not belong to the user) should have a bigger distance to the closest cluster center than a legal one to its cluster center. Therefore, our idea is to determine a threshold which reflects the largest possible value of the distances. When the minimum distance is still greater than the threshold, we think the posture of the feature vector doesn't belong to the legal user.

The method to calculate threshold is as follows: The distances of all feature vectors to their cluster center are calculated respectively. And then their average $\bar{d}$ and variance σ^2 are calculated. The threshold is the linear combination of the two values, written as threshold $= a * \bar{d} + b * \sigma^2$. We make a increase from 1 to 5, b increase from 1 to 10. After experiments, we find that the authentication effect is best if $a = 3$ and $b = 7$.

(3) Procedures of Postures Clustering

The procedure of postures clustering is as follows: we use silhouette coefficient to determine the number of postures K, and K-means algorithm to get posture estimator (K cluster centers) and the predicted labels of posture. After that, we calculate the threshold that is used to determine whether posture of a feature vector belongs to the legal user. The specific process is shown in Algorithm 8.1.

Algorithm 8.1 Postures Clustering Algorithm

Input: User's set of feature vector, V_{user}

Output: Posture estimator, Predicted labels of posture, Threshold of postures legality

1. Extracting the posture feature sub-vector $V_{user-pos}$ from the feature vector V_{user} of the user,

$$V_{user-pos} = \left(\overrightarrow{v^1_{pos}}, \overrightarrow{v^2_{pos}}, \ldots, \overrightarrow{v^i_{pos}}, \ldots \overrightarrow{v^n_{pos}} \right)$$

2. The K value increases from 2 to 6. Clustering postures using K-means algorithm respectively. Calculate silhouette coefficients for each K. Adopt the K which makes silhouette coefficient biggest as the final K. Finally, the posture estimator is trained and the predicted labels of posture are obtained.

3. Calculate the distance of each feature vector to the center of the cluster to which it belongs.

4. Calculate the mean and variance of the distance from the feature vector to the center of the cluster to which it belongs, and thereby obtain the threshold by calculation,

threshold = 3 * the mean of the distance from the feature vector to the cluster center which it belongs + 7 * the variance of the distance from the feature vector to the cluster center which it belongs

---

8.2.5   Experiments and Analysis

This section aims to design an authentication model that can adapt to the change of posture. In order to evaluate the quality of the model, it is necessary to collect the behavior data of the slipping gesture when the user inputs the gesture password in different postures to log in and uses the application. The main four different postures are as follows:

a. The user is standing and holding the mobile in hand.
b. The user is sitting on chair and holding the mobile in hand.

c.   The user is sitting on chair and putting the mobile on table.

d.   The user is lying on bed or sofa and holding the mobile in hand.

(1)   Analysis of the Clustering Effect

In order to evaluate the quality of the posture clustering, it is necessary to record the real postures of the user each time during data collection when the gesture password is input. The predicted labels of posture can be obtained by Algorithm 8.1 and the real labels are recorded when we collect data. We can evaluate the effect of posture clustering algorithm by comparing the predicted labels with real labels.

The Adjusted Rand index (ARI) [43] is used to evaluate the effect of clustering. The index ranges from –1 to 1. It shows that the closer it is to 1, the better the result is. The ARIs of users who are randomly selected result are shown in Fig. 8.5. As Fig. 8.5 shown, most ARIs are bigger than 0.8, which means that the effect of clustering algorithm is good.

(2)   Analysis of the Predicted Posture Number

We randomly picked the behavioral data of four users from the total users' data to further analyze the effect of the posture clustering algorithm. And according to Algorithm 8.1, this section uses the biggest value K of the silhouette coefficient as the number of predicted postures. Through experimental observation, it is found that the number of postures predicted by the silhouette coefficient in the postures clustering algorithm may not be the same as the number of real postures of the user. There are three cases about the comparison between the number of predicted postures and that of real postures. The first is that the number of predicted postures is less than that of real postures. The reason is that some real postures of the user are similar. They

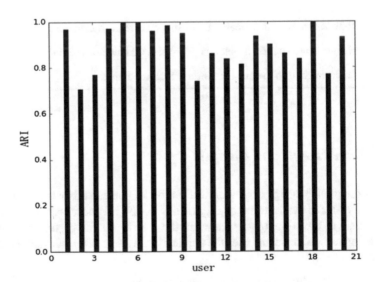

Fig. 8.5   Adjusted rand index of clustering

are relatively close in the feature vector space and clustered into the same posture when performing postures clustering algorithm. The second is that the number of predicted postures is larger than that of real postures. The reason is that the distances between the behavior data of some user postures are too large in the space of the feature vector when it is projected onto the feature vector space, and is divided into different clusters by the clustering algorithm. Thus, the user's certain real postures are divided into two or more postures, resulting in more predicted postures than real postures. The third is that the number of predicted postures is exactly the same as the number of real postures. Above all, although that of predicted postures may be different from that of real postures, the data of the same posture may be divided into finer postures, and similar postures may be merged into one posture, the final clustering result will be reasonable.

8.3 Construction and Certification of Login Authentication Model

Gesture password has become a common login authentication method on the mobile side, but it is easily stolen by malware, and there are certain security risks. Adding behavior mode authentication to gesture passwords has become an important research for improving the security of gesture passwords. When the user performs the login operation through the gesture password, besides requiring the user to input the preset gesture password normally, it is also required to record and analyze the user's gesture and posture behavior information in the background of the program, extract the behavior features and use the behavior authentication model to judge. In order to improve the security of gesture password, the user can log in normally only when the correct gesture password is inputted and his gesture and posture behavior is verified by the behavior authentication model. This chapter presents a method for constructing and authenticating a login authentication model, which uses the user gesture-based touch screen behavior authentication system given in Sect. 8.2 to accommodate changes in user posture. This section firstly introduces the extraction method of gesture behavior features used in login authentication, and then introduces how to separately train the gesture authentication sub-model for each gesture of the user, and gives the login authentication method. Finally, we analyze the experimental effect of login authentication.

8.3.1 Gesture Features Extraction of Login Authentication

As can be seen from Sect. 8.2, when the user inputs a gesture password to perform a login operation, the gesture behavior data can be collected through the touch screen of the mobile phone. The gestures data collected by touch screen can be denoted as

$\langle [\text{finger}_x], [\text{finger}_y], [\text{pressure}], [\text{size}], [\text{velocity}] \rangle$, which represents the X, Y coordinates, pressure, contact area, and finger movement speed on the touch screen. It can be seen as a set of time series of several indicators. Similar to the extracted posture features, we can extract the gesture behavior from the perspective of time series. For the case of gesture passwords and each time series, the following features can be extracted:

(1) Features that reflect the overall characteristics of time series, such as mean, variance, maximum value, minimum value, and duration.
(2) Features that reflect the local characteristics of time series, such as the initial position value (S_{init}, see Eq. (8.2)), the middle position value (S_{mid} see Eq. (8.3)), the ending position value (S_{end}, see Eq. (8.4)), the relative location of maximum value (S_{max_loc}, see Eq. (8.5)) and the relative location of minimum value (S_{min_loc}, see Eq. (8.6)).

$$S_{init} = \frac{S_{t_0} + S_{t_1} + S_{t_2}}{3} \tag{8.2}$$

$$S_{mid} = \frac{S_{t_{\lfloor \frac{n}{2} \rfloor - 1}} + S_{t_{\lfloor \frac{n}{2} \rfloor}} + S_{t_{\lfloor \frac{n}{2} \rfloor + 1}}}{3} \tag{8.3}$$

$$S_{end} = \frac{S_{t_{n-3}} + S_{t_{n-2}} + S_{t_{n-1}}}{3} \tag{8.4}$$

$$S_{max\_loc} = \frac{i}{n}, \ s_i \ is \ maximum \ of \ [s] \tag{8.5}$$

$$S_{min\_loc} = \frac{j}{n}, \ s_j \ is \ minimum \ of \ [s] \tag{8.6}$$

(3) Features that reflect the differences between time series. See Sect. 8.2.3 for details.

Here, the feature extracted from the gesture behavior data generated when the user logs in using the gesture password is defined as the login gesture feature.

The login gesture features used in login authentication are shown in Table 8.5.

Similar to the posture feature, the login gesture feature is processed using the formula $(x_i - x_{min})/(x_{max} - x_{min})$ so that all login gesture features are in range [0, 1]. Similarly, we adopt the principal component analysis algorithm (PCA) to process the login gesture features for reducing the dimension of the feature vector.

Table 8.5 The gesture characteristics of login authentication

Overall features	Finger pressure, mean of contact area, variance, maximum and minimum
	Total duration of gesture passwords
	Mean, variance, maximum and minimum speeds between adjacent timestamps
Local features	X, Y coordinates of finger, pressure, contact area at the initial position, middle position, and ending position
	The position at which the pressure and contact area take the maximum and minimum values in the total time
Difference features	The distance between the time series containing the X, Y coordinates of the finger, pressure, and contact area and its corresponding reference time series
	The distance between the time series of the average speed between the adjacent timestamps of the finger and the corresponding reference time series

8.3.2 Training the Gesture Authentication Sub-model Under Each Posture

After postures clustering, we can get the predicted labels of posture for feature vectors, and divide feature vectors into K groups (i.e. K postures) according to them. Then we need to train a gesture authentication sub-model for each posture to judge whether the gesture behavior is legal.

The gesture feature vector $\overrightarrow{v_{ges}}$ is used when training gesture authentication sub-models. Most users have only their own behavior information on their mobile phones, and few even no illegal users' information can be found on a mobile in reality. And password patterns set by different users are diverse. Even on the server side, there is no guarantee that the gesture behavior data of the users who have set the same password pattern can be found. Let the user's gesture behavior data as a positive sample for training the user gesture authentication sub-model. However in the vast majority of cases, the negative samples can't be found. Therefore, we treat it as a novelty detection question and use one-class SVM [44] to train the model.

The procedure of training gesture authentication sub-models is as follows: first of all, we group the feature vectors of same posture together according to the predicted labels of posture obtained by the Algorithm 8.1. Then we use one-class SVM algorithm to train a gesture authentication sub-model for each posture. The specific process is shown in Algorithm 8.2.

Algorithm 8.2 The Training Algorithm of Gesture Authentication Sub-models

---

Input: User's set of feature vector V_{user}, Predicted labels of posture

Output: Gesture authentication sub-model for each posture

1. Extracting the gesture feature sub-vector $V_{user-ges}$ from the feature vector V_{user} of the user,

$$V_{user-ges} = \left(\vec{v^1_{ges}}, \vec{v^2_{ges}}, \ldots, \vec{v^i_{ges}}, \ldots \vec{v^n_{ges}} \right)$$

2. Gather feature vectors belonging to the same posture according to the predicted posture labels and gesture feature sub-vector $V_{user-ges}$, i.e., generate feature vectors for cluster postures.

3. For each posture, the user gesture feature sub-vector of the posture is used to train the model by the one-class SVM algorithm, and then obtain the gesture authentication sub-model under the gesture.

8.3.3 Login Authentication

The threshold that is used to judge whether a gesture belongs to the user and the posture estimator (i.e. K cluster centers) can be generated by Algorithm 8.1. K gesture authentication sub-models which corresponding to the user's K postures can be generated by Algorithm 8.2.

These authentication models can be used to add behavioral authentication to gesture passwords. When a user is inputting a password pattern, in addition to verifying that the password pattern is same with the default one, the above behavioral models can be used to further authenticate the user's posture and gesture legality, thereby improving the security of the gesture password.

As is shown in Fig. 8.6, the authentication procedure is as follows: when a user logs in, the interface of inputting the password pattern is shown. And user's posture and gesture behavior data (i.e. data about user postures and gesture behavior listed in Sect. 8.2.2) are collected by orientation sensor, acceleration sensor and touch screen. Firstly, we verify that the password pattern inputted is same as the default one. Secondly, we determine whether current posture belongs to the legal user. If the posture is legal, then we judge which posture does it belong to and use the gesture authentication sub-model of the posture to determine whether the user's gesture behavior is legal.

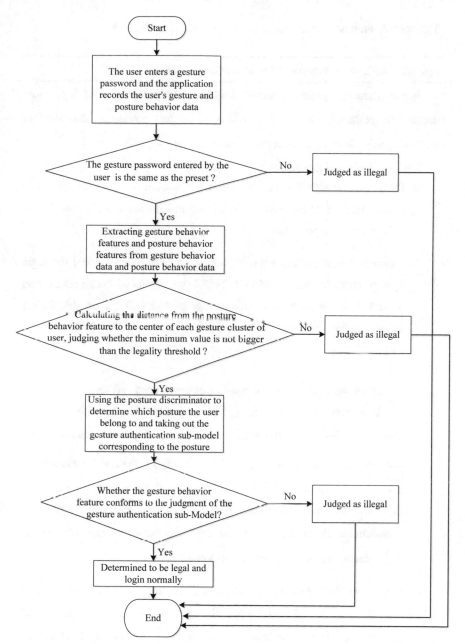

Fig. 8.6 The flow chart of login authentication

The specific authentication process is shown in Algorithm 8.3.

Algorithm 8.3 The Procedure of Login Authentication

Input: Password pattern inputted, Default password pattern of legal user, Posture data collected, Gesture data collected, Posture estimator, Threshold of postures legality, Gesture authentication sub-model for each posture

Output: Authentication result (legal or illegal)

1. Determine whether the gesture password is correct. Compare password pattern inputted by user with default password pattern of legal user. If it is different, it is judged illegal.

2. Features extraction. The posture features listed in Table 8.4 and the login gesture characteristics listed in Table 8.5 are calculated from posture data collected and gesture data collected, respectively. Then do the feature transformation and dimension reduction to obtain the feature vector $\vec{v} = \left(\overrightarrow{v_{pos}}, \overrightarrow{v_{ges}} \right)$.

3. Determine whether the current user's posture is legal and further determine which posture it belongs to (if it is legal). Calculate the distance $d_1, d_2, \ldots, d_K$ from $\overrightarrow{v_{pos}}$ to the center of K clusters of posture estimator, and take the minimum value d_{min}. If d_{min} is bigger than the threshold of postures legality, the current user's posture is considered to be not a legitimate user, and it is illegal. Otherwise, the current user's posture is considered legal, and the number i of the cluster center corresponding to d_{min} is defined as the current user's posture number.

4. Determine whether the gesture is legal. According to the posture number i obtained in the previous step, the gesture authentication sub-model corresponding to the gesture is taken out. Input $\overrightarrow{v_{ges}}$ to judge the final result.

8.3.4 Results and Analysis of Experiments

The experiments' data is collected by an Android application we developed. The application shows an interface for user to input the password pattern. And when user is inputting, the application records the posture and gesture behavioral data of user.

We collect 30 users' data including 14 postgraduate students and 16 programmers who have worked for 1–5 years. Among them, 15 users are asked to input the password pattern shown in Fig. 8.7, and the others are asked to input the one shown Fig. 8.8.

This section aims to present a method for constructing a gesture authentication model that can adapt to posture changes. In order to verify the effectiveness of the method, it is necessary to collect data from users in different postures. Each user is asked to choose 3 or 4 different postures from the postures listed in Sect. 8.2.5, and input the password pattern in each posture. And 16 users chose 3 different postures

Fig. 8.7 Password pattern 1

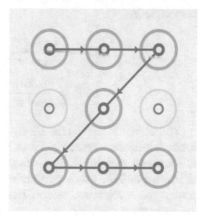

Fig. 8.8 Password pattern 2

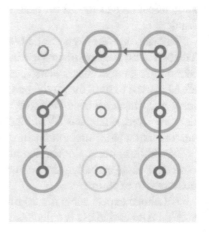

and others chose 4. For each user, we collect 30 inputting operations (i.e. 30 valid data) for each posture. Finally, we get totally the valid data of 3120 inputting operations.

The data are collected by the HUAWEI Ascend P6 mobile. The mobile's CPU is Hisilicon K3V2E and its touch screen size is 4.7 in. The capacity of RAM and ROM is 2 GB and 8 GB respectively. And its system is Android 4.2.

We use the numpy and scikit-learn libraries in the Python language to achieve data processing, model training and authentication.

The data are divided into training set and testing set by 6:4 proportion randomly. The behavior authentication pattern is trained on the data of the training set. And we evaluate the effect of pattern on the data of testing set. Data of current user is regarded as legal user's login data. And the same amount of data with legal user's which is randomly picked from other users, is viewed as illegal user's login data.

False Acceptance Rate (FAR) and False Rejection Rate (FRR) [45] is used to evaluate the effect of authentication. FAR indicates the probability that an illegal user is judged to be legal, and FRR indicates the probability that a legal user is judged to be illegal. Their specific definitions are shown in Eqs. (8.7) and (8.8), respectively.

$$FAR = \frac{\text{number of allowing access to illegal user}}{\text{number of illegal user's login sttempts}} \tag{8.7}$$

$$FRR = \frac{\text{number of legal user is denied access}}{\text{number of legal user's login sttempts}} \tag{8.8}$$

The authentication method designed in this section adopts the touch screen behavior authentication system given in Sect. 8.2. Compared with the existing methods, this method mainly has two changes to adapt to the user's posture change. One is that we add the user's posture behavioral data collected by mobile's orientation sensor and acceleration sensor. The other is that we propose the different behavior authentication methods. We use posture behavioral data to cluster user's postures and get a threshold to judge the legality of posture firstly. Then we train a gesture authentication sub-model for each posture to judge whether the gesture behavior is legal.

To evaluate the effects of the two changes, we design two contrast experiments. The two contrast experiments use the data including different postures of user. In the first contrast experiment, users' posture behavioral data aren't used. And one-class SVM is used to train the model on the feature vectors extracted from gesture behavioral data. In the second contrast experiment, both posture and gesture behavioral data are used. One-class SVM algorithm is used to train the model on the feature vectors extracted from both posture and gesture behavioral data.

In addition, we implement the methods of paper [27] and paper [28], and use the collected data (including the behavior data generated when the user is in different postures) to experiment.

All above experiments run 20 times on the data we collected. The average of all user's FARs and FRRs is calculated in each time, as shown in Table 8.6.

Table 8.6 The contrast effects of login authentication

Experiment	FAR (%)	FRR (%)
Paper [27]	23.87	25.22
Paper [28]	9.93	10.06
1st contrast Exp	9.98	10.14
2nd contrast Exp	7.55	7.73
Our method	4.50	4.85

Comparing the experimental results of the 1st contrast Exp with the 2nd contrast Exp, we can find that the use of posture behavior data can improve the effect of identity authentication. Comparing the experimental results of the 2nd contrast Exp with the method given in this section, we can find that the method proposed (i.e. we cluster according to the posture behavior data firstly, and then train a gesture authentication sub-model for each posture separately) has a good effect than directly using the posture behavior data authentication. Meanwhile, the method given in this section has a certain improvement over the certification effect of the existing literature.

8.4 Construction and Certification of Continuous Authentication Model

Most of the existing applications only contain login authentication, i.e., users are required to authenticate by inputting a password only when the user enters the application. Moreover, in order to enhance the user experience, many applications provide the option to remember the password or not have to log in again for a certain period of time after logged in. This brings convenience to the user, but also leaves a certain security risk. This section presents a construction and certification method for continuous authentication model. In the process of the using the application, the method analyzes and processes the gesture behavior data and the posture behavior data collected by the users' sliding gesture operation in the background, and uses the behavior authentication model to judge the user identity. It provides continuous protection for user information security. Therefore, even if an illegal user logs in the application due to the theft of the password or the loss of the mobile phone, the authentication method will verify the identity by monitoring the behavior characteristics of the user, thereby achieving the purpose of improving the security of the application. The method adopts the user gesture-based touch screen behavior authentication system designed in Sect. 8.2 to adapt to the user's posture changes. This section firstly introduces the calculation and processing methods of gesture features used in continuous authentication, and then introduces the method of training the user's gesture authentication sub-model in each posture and gives the continuous authentication method. Finally, this section analyzes the experimental results of the continuous authentication method.

8.4.1   Gesture Features Extraction of Continuous Authentication

Common gestures of users include click, slide, two-finger zoom, etc. Although the simple click operation occurs most frequently, it reflects less user behavior habits. In contrast, complex operations such as two-finger scaling reflect relatively more user behavior habits, but they occur relatively less frequently. Therefore, these operations are not suitable for continuous identity authentication. Since the sliding gesture operation reflects more user behavior habits and the frequency of occurrence is higher, this section will select it for the user's continuous identity authentication.

A schematic diagram of a user's sliding gesture operation is shown in Fig. 8.9. Seven points—A, B, C, D, E, F and G represent the position of the finger on the touch screen at each acquisition time. Point A represents the starting point of the sliding gesture (i.e. the user's finger first touches the phone screen), and G point represents the end point of the sliding gesture (i.e. the user gesture leaves the phone screen).

As shown in Sect. 8.2.2, during continuous authentication, the X, Y coordinates, pressure, contact area, and timestamp data of the finger position can be collected through the touch screen of the mobile phone when the user performs a sliding gesture operation. The posture behavioral data generated by a user's sliding gesture operation can be represented as $\langle[\text{finger}_x], [\text{finger}_y], [\text{pressure}], [\text{size}], [\text{velocity}]\rangle$. Similar to login authentication, it can be thought of as a set of several indicators' time series. In order to better describe the user's sliding gesture behavior, besides the overall and local features which reflect the time series' situation used by login authentication, we also extract the following features in the user's sliding gesture operation:

Fig. 8.9 Schematic diagram of user sliding gesture

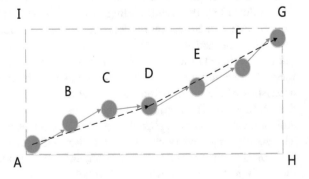

(1) Distance Feature. It is defined as the absolute distance between the start point and end point of the sliding gesture, i.e., $dis_x = finger_{x_{n-1}} - finger_{x_0}$ (i.e., the length of the AH line in Fig. 8.9), $dis_y = finger_{y_{n-1}} - finger_{y_0}$ (i.e., the length of the HG line in Fig. 8.9), $dis_{total} = \sqrt{dis_x^2 + dis_y^2}$ (i.e., the length of the AG line in Fig. 8.9).

(2) Length Feature. It is defined as the sum of the distances between any two adjacent points from the start point to the end point of the sliding gesture (i.e. The sum of the lengths of the lines AB, BC, CD, DE, EF, FG in Fig. 8.9).

(3) Orientation Feature. It mainly includes the offset direction between the starting point and the neutral point of the sliding gesture (i.e., point D in Fig. 8.9), the offset direction between the middle point and the end point, and the offset direction between the starting point and the ending point (i.e., the offset direction of AD line, DG line and the AG line in Fig. 8.9).

The features of continuous authentication gestures are shown in Table 8.7.

Similar to the posture feature, the continuous authentication gesture feature is processed using the formula $(x_i - x_{min})/(x_{max} - x_{min})$ so that all features are in range [0, 1]. Similarly, we adopt the principal component analysis algorithm (PCA) to process the continuous authentication gesture features for reducing the dimension of the feature vector.

Table 8.7 The features of specific continuous authentication gestures

Overall features	Average, variance, maximum, and minimum values of finger pressure and contact area
	Average, variance, maximum, and minimum values of the finger moving speed between adjacent timestamps
	Duration of the gesture
Local features	X, Y coordinates of finger, pressure, contact area, speed at the initial position, middle position, and ending position
	The position of the finger's pressure, contact area, and speed at the maximum and minimum times in the total time
Distance features	Horizontal, vertical and linear distance between the starting point and the ending point
Length features	Total length from start to end
Orientation features	The offset direction between the starting point and the neutral point, the offset direction between the middle point and the end point and the offset direction between the starting point and the ending point

8.4.2 Training the Gesture Authentication Sub-model Under Each Posture

As shown in Sect. 8.2, in the case of continuous authentication, we firstly cluster the postures to obtain the predicted posture label for each feature vector, and then classify the feature vectors into K groups (i.e., K different postures) based on these labels. A gesture authentication sub-model is separately trained for each posture to judge whether the gesture behavior of the user in the posture is legal.

The gesture feature vector $\overrightarrow{v_{ges}}$ is used when training gesture authentication sub-models. We take the user's posture feature vectors as a positive sample, and randomly extract the same number of feature vectors from the other users as the negative samples. We use the binary classification algorithms such as SVM [46], Logistic Regression [47], K Nearest Neighbor [48], Random Forest [49] to train the user's gesture authentication sub-model under this posture. And we use the cross validation method to adjust the parameters of the algorithm model. This section uses 3-fold cross validation, which divides the training set into three parts and loops three times. Two parts are taken for training model and one part is taken for validating effect of the model each time. We calculate the average of three FAR and FRR as the final result.

Table 8.8 lists the authentication effects of four different classification algorithms. It can be concluded that the SVM, Logistic Regression and Random Forest have similar authentication effects, and the K Nearest Neighbor has relatively poor effect. Since SVM has the best authentication effect, this section uses it.

The training process of the gesture authentication sub-model of each posture is as follows: firstly, the feature vectors belonging to the same posture are gathered according to the predicted posture label obtained by the Algorithm 8.1; secondly, in order to obtain the gesture authentication sub-model under the posture, the SVM is used to train the model for each posture according to the gesture features of the user. The specific process is shown in Algorithm 8.4.

Table 8.8 The comparison of two-class classification algorithms

Two-class classification algorithm	FAR (%)	FRR (%)
SVM	3.88	3.67
Logistic regression	4.13	3.89
K nearest neighbor	8.22	7.63
Random forest	4.37	4.52

Algorithm 8.4 The Training Algorithm of Gesture Authentication Sub-Models in Continuous Authentication

---

Input: User's set of feature vector V_{user} , Predicted labels of posture

Output: Gesture authentication sub-model for each posture

1. Extracting the gesture feature sub-vector $V_{user-ges}$ from the feature vector V_{user} of the user,

$$V_{user-ges} = \left(\overrightarrow{v_{ges}^1}, \overrightarrow{v_{ges}^2}, \ldots, \overrightarrow{v_{ges}^i}, \ldots \overrightarrow{v_{ges}^n} \right)$$

2. Gather feature vectors belonging to the same posture according to the predicted posture labels and gesture feature sub-vector $V_{user-ges}$, i.e., generate feature vectors for cluster postures.

3. According to clustering postures feature vectors, treat the feature vectors of each posture as a positive sample, randomly select the same number of feature vectors from the other users as negative samples. The user gesture feature sub-vector of the posture is used to train the model by the one-class SVM algorithm, and then obtain the gesture authentication sub-model under the gesture.

8.4.3   Continuous Authentication

This section gives a continuous authentication method according to touch screen behavior-based authentication system designed in Sect. 8.2. During the using process of user, the applications gather the data of user's sliding gesture operation in the background, and collect the user's gesture behavior and posture behavior information to authenticate the user identity.

Login authentication requires the user to input the gesture password only once, so the authentication can only be performed based on the behavior data. Unlike continuous authentication, users are likely to generate multiple sliding gestures during the process of application operation. Therefore, in order to improve the accuracy of the authentication, the final result can be determined by comprehensively analyzing the judgment results of multiple sliding gestures. This section uses the principle of majority rule to determine the final result. Suppose that we continuously collect m times user's sliding gestures and get the corresponding judgment result. There are two cases for judgment result of each sliding gesture operation (1 is legal and 0 is illegal). We add these m results to get the final result. If the final result is greater than or equal to $\lfloor m/2 \rfloor + 1$, the judgment result is legal; otherwise, it is illegal.

Note that m should be odd. The larger the m is, the higher the accuracy is. But the more user gestures need to be collected, the lower the judgment frequency is, and the longer the decision time is. In order to prevent the number of the user sliding gestures times is not enough, the value of m cannot be too large. It has been tested that the value range of m set from 1 to 9, the changes of FAR and FRR are shown in Fig. 8.10. Although the FAR and FRR are smaller when m is 7 or 9, the degree of improvement is not large. Considering the actual application, the user may exit the application with only a small amount of sliding gestures, so the value of m is set to 5.

As shown in Fig. 8.11, the authentication process is as follows:

The user's posture and gesture behavior data (i.e. data about user postures and gesture behavior listed in Sect. 8.2.2) will be collected by orientation sensor, acceleration sensor and touch screen when the user performs a sliding gesture operation on the phone. We extract posture and gesture features from these behavioral data. We judge whether the user's posture is legal according to the threshold. If it is legal, we will judge the current user's posture according to the user's posture discriminator and find the gesture authentication sub-model corresponding to the posture . According

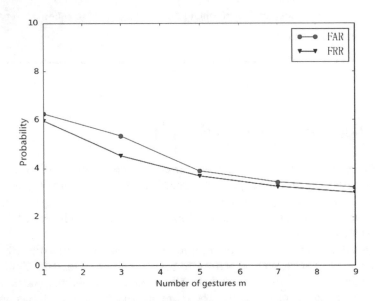

Fig. 8.10 The probability changing of FAR and FRR with the number of gestures m

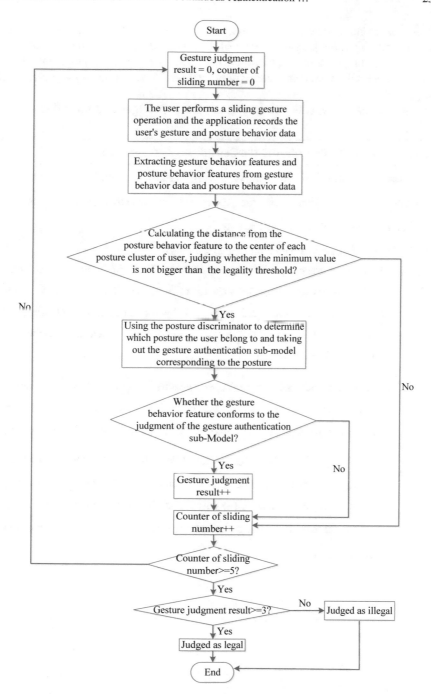

Fig. 8.11 The flow chart of continuous authentication

to the gesture authentication sub-model, we judge whether the user gesture behavior is legal and obtain the judgment result of the sliding gesture. We continuously collect m user sliding gesture operations and obtain the corresponding judgment results, and then obtain the final user identity judgment results according to the principle of majority rule.

The continuous authentication process is shown in Algorithm 8.5 in detail.

Algorithm 8.5 The Procedure of the Continuous Authentication

Input: Posture behavior data of sliding gesture, Gesture behavior data of sliding gesture, Posture estimator, Threshold of postures legality, Gesture authentication sub-model for each posture

Output: Authentication Result (legal or illegal)

1. Features extraction. The posture features listed in Table 8.4 and the continuous gesture characteristics listed in Table 8.7 are calculated from posture behavior data and gesture behavior data of sliding gesture, respectively. Then do the feature transformation and dimension reduction to obtain the feature vector $\vec{v} = \left(\overrightarrow{v_{pos}}, \overrightarrow{v_{ges}} \right)$.

2. Determine whether the current user's posture is legal and further determine which posture it belongs to (if it is legal). Calculate the distance $d_1, d_2, \ldots, d_K$ from $\overrightarrow{v_{pos}}$ to the center of K clusters of posture estimator, and take the minimum value d_{min}. If d_{min} larger than the threshold of postures legality, the current user's posture is considered to be not a legitimate user, and it is illegal. Otherwise, the current user's posture is considered legal, and the number i of the cluster center corresponding to d_{min} is defined as the current user's posture number.

3. Determine whether the gesture is legal. According to the posture number i obtained in the previous step, the gesture authentication sub-model corresponding to the posture is taken out. Input $\overline{v_{ges}}$ to judge the final result (i.e. legal is 1, illegal is 0).

4. Loop the above process 5 times to get the judgment results of the user's 5 sliding gestures.

5. Adding the judgment results of the 5 sliding gestures, if it is greater than or equal to 3, it is determined that the user is legal. Otherwise, the judgment of user is illegal.

8.4.4 Experiments and Analysis

In the study of continuous authentication, the experimental data is collected by an Android application we developed (as shown in Fig. 8.12), which displays an interface for the user to input the sliding gestures. The direction of the swipe gesture (turn up, turn down, turn left, turn right) is randomly generated by the application program. The user is required to perform a sliding gesture operation according to the specified direction and habits. Each time the user inputs a sliding gesture, the gesture direction is updated once. The application program will record the user's gesture behavior data and posture behavior data in the background.

The experiment collects 30 users' data. Each user is asked to choose 3 or 4 different postures from the postures listed in Sect. 8.2.5, and input the sliding gesture under each posture. And 16 users chose 3 different postures and others chose 4. For each user, we collect 50 sliding gestures inputted for each posture. Finally, we get totally the data of 5200 inputting valid data.

The data are collected by the HUAWEI Ascend P6 mobile. The mobile's CPU is Hisilicon K3V2E and its touch screen size is 4.7 in. The capacity of RAM and ROM is 2 GB and 8 GB respectively. And its system is Android 4.2.

We use the numpy and scikit-learn libraries in the Python language to achieve data processing, model training and authentication.

The data are divided into training set and testing set by 6:4 proportion randomly. The behavior authentication pattern is trained on the data of the training set. And we evaluate the effect of pattern on the data of testing set.

Data of current user is regarded as legal user's login data. And the same amount of data with legal user's which is randomly picked from other users, is viewed as illegal user's login data.

Fig. 8.12 Data collector of
continuous authentication
gesture

Same as login authentication, False Acceptance Rate (FAR) and False Rejection
Rate (FRR) is used to evaluate the effect of authentication.

This section aims to propose a continuous authentication method which can adapt
the change of user's posture. Therefore, the authentication method designed in this
section adopts the touch screen behavior authentication system given in Sect. 8.2.
Compared with the existing methods, this method mainly has two changes to adapt
to the user's posture change. One is that we add much user's posture data by mobile's
orientation sensor and acceleration sensor when user inputs the sliding gesture. The
other is that we propose the different behavior authentication method. We use posture
behavioral data to cluster user's postures and get a threshold to judge the legality of
posture firstly. Then we train a gesture authentication sub-model for each posture to

Table 8.9 The contrast effects of continuous authentication

Experiment	FAR (%)	FRR (%)
Paper [29]	7.36	7.14
Paper [30]	6.79	7.02
1st contrast Exp	7.13	6.97
2nd contrast Exp	5.09	5.21
Our method	3.88	3.67

judge whether the gesture behavior is legal. The authentication process is as follows: We firstly judge whether the gesture is legal, then judge which posture it belongs to, and finally determine the legality of the gesture behavior according to the gesture authentication sub-model corresponding to the posture.

To evaluate the effects of the two changes, we design two contrast experiments similar to the login authentication. The two contrast experiments use the data including different postures of user. In the first contrast experiment, users' posture behavioral data aren't used. And we only use gesture behavior data and SVM algorithm training behavior authentication model for authentication. In the second contrast experiment, both posture and gesture behavioral data are used. We do not perform postures clustering and directly use the SVM algorithm to train the authentication model.

Meanwhile, we implement the methods of paper [29] and paper [30], and use the collected data (including the behavior data generated when the user is in different postures) to experiment.

All above experiments run 20 times on the collected data. The averages of all users' FARs and FRRs are calculated in each time. And Table 8.9 shows the averages of FARs and FRRs.

From the experimental results, the 1st contrast Exp does not use the user's posture behavior data, and its FAR and FRR are 7.13% and 6.97%, respectively; the 2nd contrast Exp use posture behavior data, but does not cluster postures, and its FAR and FRR are 5.09% and 5.21%, respectively. It can be concluded that the use of posture behavior data can improve the authentication effect. Our approach is to cluster the poses firstly, and then train a gesture authentication sub-model for each posture. Its authentication averages are 3.88% and 3.67%. Compared with the 2nd contrast Exp, our method has improved the effect, i.e., the method given in this section is better than the authentication using only the posture features and has a promising application prospect.

References

1. J. Changjun, Y. Wangyang, *Risk Control Theory of Online Transactions* (Science Press, Beijing, 2018)
2. Y. Meng, D.S. Wong, R. Schlegel et al., Touch gestures based biometric authentication scheme for touchscreen mobile phones, in *Proceedings of ICISC*, Seoul, Korea (2012), pp. 331–350
3. Y. Ding, A. Rattani, A. Ross, Bayesian belief models for integrating match scores with liveness and quality measures in a fingerprint verification system, in *Proceedings of ICB*, Halmstad, Sweden (2016), pp. 1–8
4. A. Rattani, N. Poh, A. Ross, A Bayesian approach for modeling sensor influence on quality, liveness and match score values in fingerprint verification, in *Proceedings of WIFS*, Guangzhou, China (2013), pp. 37–42
5. D. Peralta, M. Galar, I. Triguero et al., A survey on fingerprint minutiae-based local matching for verification and identification. Inf. Sci. **315**, 67–87 (2015)
6. S. Yadav, Fingerprint recognition based on minutiae information. Int. J. Comput. Appl. **120**(10), 39–42 (2015)
7. S. Yang, I. Verbauwhede, Automatic secure fingerprint verification system based on fuzzy vault scheme, in *Proceedings of ICASSP*, Philadelphia, PA, USA (2005), pp. 609–612
8. C. Pintavirooj, F.S. Cohen, W. Iampa, Fingerprint verification and identification based on local geometric invariants constructed from minutiae points and augmented with global directional filterbank features. IEICE Trans. Inf. Syst. **97**(6), 1599–1613 (2014)
9. Y. Taigman, M. Yang, M. Ranzato et al., DeepFace: closing the gap to human-level performance in face verification, in *Proceedings of CVPR*, Columbus, Ohio, USA (2014), pp. 1701–1708
10. O.M. Parkhi, A. Vedaldi, A. Zisserman, Deep face recognition, in *Proceeding of BMVC*, Swansea, UK (2015), pp. 1–12
11. F. Schroff, D. Kalenichenko, J. Philbin, FaceNet: a unified embedding for face recognition and clustering, in *Proceedings of CVPR*, Boston, Massachusetts, USA (2015), pp. 815–823
12. A. Tefas, C. Kotropoulos, I. Pitas, Using support vector machines to enhance the performance of elastic graph matching for frontal face authentication. IEEE Trans. Pattern Anal. Mach. Intell. **23**(7), 735–746 (2001)
13. D. Li, H. Zhou, K. Lam, High-resolution face verification using pore-scale facial features. IEEE Trans. Image Process. **24**(8), 2317–2327 (2015)
14. Y. Sun, X. Wang, X. Tang, Hybrid deep learning for face verification. IEEE Trans. Pattern Anal. Mach. Intell. **38**(10), 1997–2009 (2016)
15. J. Chen, V.M. Patel, R. Chellappa, Unconstrained face verification using deep CNN features, in *Proceedings of WACV*, Lake Placid, NY, USA (2016), pp. 1–9
16. H. Li, L. Zhang, B. Huang et al., Sequential three-way decision and granulation for cost-sensitive face recognition. Knowl. Based Syst. **91**, 241–251 (2016)
17. W. Deng, J. Hu, N. Zhang et al., Fine-grained face verification: FGLFW database, baselines, and human-DCMN partnership. Pattern Recognit. **66**, 63–73 (2017)
18. D. Buschek, A. De Luca, F. Alt, Improving accuracy, applicability and usability of keystroke biometrics on mobile touchscreen device, in. *Proceedings of CHI*, Seoul, Republic of Korea (2015), pp. 1393–1402
19. N. Zheng, K. Bai, H. Huang et al., You are how you touch: user verification on smartphones via tapping behaviors, in *Proceedings of ICNP*, Raleigh, NC, USA (2014), pp. 221–232
20. B. Draffin, J. Zhu, J. Zhang, KeySens: passive user authentication through micro-behavior modeling of soft keyboard interaction, in *Proceedings of MobiCASE*, Paris, France (2013), pp. 184–201
21. T.T. Ngo, Y. Makihara, H. Nagahara et al., The largest inertial sensor-based gait database and performance evaluation of gait-based personal authentication. Pattern Recognit. **47**(1):228–237 (2014)
22. I. Youn, S. Choi, R. L. May et al., New gait metrics for biometric authentication using a 3-axis acceleration, in *Proceedings of CCNC*, Las Vegas, NV, USA (2014), pp. 596–601

23. M. Muaaz, R. Mayrhofer, Orientation independent cell phone based gait authentication, in *Proceedings of MOMM*, Kaohsiung, Taiwan (2014), pp. 161–164
24. M. Frank, R. Biedert, E. Ma et al., Touchalytics: on the applicability of touchscreen input as a behavioral biometric for continuous authentication. IEEE Trans. Inf. Forensics Secur. **8**(1), 136–148 (2013)
25. C. Shen, Y. Zhang, Z. Cai et al., Touch-interaction behavior for continuous user authentication on smartphones, in *Proceedings of ICB*, Phuket, Thailand (2015), pp. 157–162
26. A. De Luca, A. Hang, F. Brudy et al., Touch me once and i know it's you!: implicit authentication based on touch screen patterns, in *Proceedings of CHI*, Austin, Texas, USA (2012), pp. 987–996
27. Z. Ding, Y. Wu, A mobile authentication method based on touch screen behavior for password pattern. J. Comput. Inf. Syst. **2015**(1):1–8 (2015)
28. Z. Syed, J. Helmick, S. Banerjee et al., Effect of user posture and device size on the performance of touch-based authentication systems, in *Proceedings of HASE*, Daytona Beach Shores, FL, USA (2015), pp. 10–17
29. N. Palaskar, Z. Syed, S. Banerjee et al., Empirical techniques to detect and mitigate the effects of irrevocably evolving user profiles in touch-based authentication systems, in *Proceedings of HASE*, Orlando, FL, USA (2016), pp. 9–16
30. Q. Liu, M. Wang, P. Zhao et al., A behavioral authentication method for mobile gesture against resilient user posture, in *Proceedings of IEEE International Conference on Systems and Informatics*, Shanghai, China (2016), pp. 324–331
31. W. Yu, C. Yan, Z. Ding et al., Modeling and verification of online shopping business processes by considering malicious behavior patterns. IEEE Trans. Autom. Sci. Eng. **13**(2), 647–662 (2016)
32. J. Changjun, Y. Chungang, C. Hongzhong et al., Pattern construction and analysis system and its identification method for touch-screen user click behavior. 201510713975.3, 28 October 2015
33. J. Changjun, Y. Chungang, D. Zhijun et al., Browsing behavior authentication method and system for handheld devices by integrating multiple factors. 201711033546.7, 30 October 2017
34. J. Changjun, Y. Chungang, D. Zhijun et al., A construction method and system based on changes of postures for gesture behavior authentication, 201611106000.5, 5 December 2016
35. L. Qiang, Research of touch screen behavior authentication method based on user posture. Tongji University Master thesis (2017)
36. R. Meier, Professional Android 4 Application Development. Wiley, Hoboken (2012)
37. G.E.P. Box, G.M. Jenkins, *Time Series Analysis: Forecasting and Control* (Wiley, Hoboken, 2015)
38. P. Senin, Dynamic time warping algorithm review. Report, Information and Computer Science Department University of Hawaii at Manoa Honolulu (2008)
39. P.-N. Tan, M. Steinbach, V. Kumar, Introduction to Data Mining. Pearson Addison-Wesley, Hoboken (2006)
40. I.T. Jolliffe, *Principal Component Analysis* (Wiley, Hoboken, 2002)
41. J.B. Macqueen, Some methods for classification and analysis of multivariate observations, in *Proceedings of BSMSP*, Berkeley, USA (1967), pp. 281–297
42. P.J. Rousseeuw, Silhouettes: a graphical aid to the interpretation and validation of cluster analysis. J. Comput. Appl. Math. **20**(1), 53–65 (1987)
43. L. Hubert, P. Arabie, Comparing partitions. J. Classif. **2**(1):193–218 (1985)
44. B. Schölkopf, R.C. Williamson, A.J. Smola et al., Support vector method for novelty detection, in *Proceedings of NIPS*, Denver, Colorado, USA (1999), pp. 582–588
45. F. Tao, Z. Liu, K.A. Kwon et al., Continuous mobile authentication using touchscreen gestures, in *Proceedings of HST*, Waltham, MA, USA (2013), pp. 451–456
46. C. Cortes, V. Vapnik, Support-vector networks. Mach. Learn. **20**(3), 273–297 (1995)
47. D.R. Cox, The regression analysis of binary sequences. J. R. Stat. Soc. Ser. B-Methodol. **20**(1), 215–232 (1958)

48. T.M. Cover, P.E. Hart, Nearest neighbor pattern classification. IEEE Trans. Inf. Theory **13**(1), 21–27 (1967)
49. L. Breiman, Random forests. Mach. Learn. **45**(1), 5–32 (2001)

Printed in the United States
by Baker & Taylor Publisher Services